"We all hit ceilings in our careers that we need to break through if we want to achieve greater effectiveness and satisfaction as leaders. Gustavo Rabin's *Becoming a Great Leader* offers a brilliantly conceived, story-based approach to learning high-level leadership behaviors. An invaluable read for any executive, business owner, or entrepreneur." —**Michelle Gale, Human Resources Director, Twitter**

"Too often, leaders fail to identify the real problems they face before they embark on executing a solution. *Becoming a Great Leader* is an elegantly simple playbook that provides techniques and strategies to find the real problem, and then equips readers with solutions … A must read for anyone wanting to be a better leader or in a position to make better leaders of others." —**Steve Cadigan, VP of HR, Linkedin**

"What a refreshing way to focus on leadership—Rather than introduce yet another theoretical model, Dr. Rabin tells us stories about real leaders, grappling with real problems that leaders face, and uncovering real solutions they found to these problems. These case studies offer terrific insight into what leadership is all about in a very accessible way. The stories are inspiring, too; We should all be so fortunate as to have Gustavo Rabin coach us through our rough spots!" —**Jay Moldenhauer-Salazar, Ph.D., Vice President of Talent Management, Gap**

"If you have decided either for yourself or someone on your team that leadership growth ends early in someone's career, you are wrong. Gustavo documents proof through very human, relatable stories that with a customized coaching approach growth can happen at any age, at any position, in any situation." —**Marianne Jackson, Senior VP of HR, Blue Shield**

"Gustavo has woven together personal and inspiring examples on what is required to becoming a great leader. I appreciate his thoughtful and practical examples that can be immediately applied in our fast paced environments—thank you Gustavo for sharing your wonderful experiences for the next generation of great leaders … well done!" —**Steven Rice, EVP of Human Resources, Juniper**

"Stories determine how we think, feel, and see. Stories explain how things work. Stories determine how we create meaning in our lives. In a very lucid, playful way, through story telling (and thankfully free from the usual management jargon), Gustavo explains the workings of organizations, the people in them, and how to help them change for the better. Anyone who wants to really understand what makes for high performance companies would do well to carefully study this book." —**Manfred F. R. Kets de Vries, Clinical Professor of Leadership and Organizational Change, The Raoul de Vitry d'Avaucourt Chaired Professor of Leadership Development**

Writers of the Round Table Press
1670 Valencia Way
Mundelein, IL 60060

Writers of the Round Table Press and logo are trademarks of
Round Table Companies and Writers of the Round Table Inc.

Front cover design by Tamiko Rast and Nathan Brown
Interior design/layout and back cover by Sunny DiMartino

Printed in Canada

First Edition: March 2012
10 9 8 7 6 5 4 3 2 1

Library of Congress Cataloging-in-Publication Data

Rabin, Gustavo
Becoming a Great Leader / Gustavo Rabin.—1st ed. p. cm.
ISBN 9781610660266
Library of Congress Control Number: 2012931906
1. Leadership. 2. Success in business. I. Title.

Becoming A
GREAT
LEADER

[Lessons from Silicon Valley]

GUSTAVO RABIN Ph.D.

TABLE OF CONTENTS

ACKNOWLEDGMENTS

I often ask my clients if they consider themselves lucky. There are so many blessings we enjoy every day and my hope is that they will consider gratefulness as the key to a profound sense of fulfillment.

I am lucky. I have a loving and supportive family circle. Thank you to my wife, Stacy, best friend, lover, partner, and rock of many years. You sacrificed time together to create the space for this book to take shape. I am grateful to my daughters—Patricia, Natalia, and Gabriela—for providing continuous encouragement, and to my grandchildren—Magali, Alex, Valerie, and Tommy—for bringing renewed joy and hope to the world.

I am also indebted to my friends and colleagues for the many ways in which they extended their friendship and support. Thank you Michael and Nani Powers for sharing your beautiful studio—it was inspiring to write this book while overlooking the Pacific Ocean. I also want to thank Pablo Piekar, Thuy Sindell, George Pfeffer, Steve Cadigan, Michelle Gale, David Karnstedt, Stu Winby, Marianne Jackson, Ash Lilani, John Hamm, Ken Schroeder, Dan Stickel, Mauro Di Nucci, Annie Hart, Jose E. Abadi, Cari Williams, and many other colleagues and friends that at one point or another provided feedback and encouragement. Thank you Tamiko Rast for your inspired contribution to the book cover.

I want to acknowledge and express my deep gratitude to my clients with whom I worked on breaking the barriers and ceilings that—almost always inadvertently—we create for ourselves. Their work brings leadership and passion to some of the most remarkable companies in Silicon Valley and we have all seen the fruits of their creativity everywhere around the world. Though you remain anonymous to protect confidentiality, you made this book come alive.

To Corey Michael Blake and his wonderful team at Writers of the Round Table Press, thank you for your warm and professional attention to every single detail related to the publishing of this book.

PREFACE

"I NEVER did a day's work in my life. It was all fun."

When I read those words by Thomas Alva Edison I felt a lighting bolt hitting me full force. That phrase did not describe my life. At the time, I'd been working for about 12 years as an attorney. I had moved from one field of law to another, trying to find my place in the world and pursuing the feeling that Edison called "fun." I was definitely not having fun.

I had finally settled into corporate law but felt bored, uninterested, and that I wasn't contributing much to the world. Intellectually, I knew this was a good path, but it didn't feel like my path. How could I find what Edison found? By this time, I had already learned that it wasn't about financial reward, prestige, or the glamour of traveling to the cosmopolitan centers of the world. I was looking for meaning and for a sense of fulfillment.

In trying to understand myself better I started reading about psychology, sociology, and anthropology. The more I read the more interested I became. Eventually, my interest became all consuming. I felt passionate about learning and understanding—myself, others, the world—and how to help others in a way that was aligned with who I was. I was starting to have some "fun"!

After a few years of experiencing this new aliveness about learning, I decided to change careers and went back to school. By then, I was in my late 30s. (My schoolmates "confessed" sometime later, that when I entered the classroom the first day of class, they thought I was the professor!)

Later, as a psychologist, I realized that I wasn't going to "find" meaning, but was going to create it by helping others. Almost 30 years have passed, and the magic hasn't faded.

I had been working in the clinical field for about 10 years when I was asked if I could help an executive in a high post become more effective. Wow! I "discovered" the world of executive coaching. My level of interest and passionate focus hit a new high. I felt deeply challenged and excited. Could I really help brilliant people achieve new highs of inspiration and leadership?

For the last 20 years, I've had the privilege of working with amazing people at some of the largest and most cutting edge companies in the world. As an executive coach I get to interact with bright, intelligent people that work at creative organizations that are changing the world as we know it. These amazing people are interested in becoming even better! I assist my clients in gaining the awareness of what's detracting them from greatness and how to overcome it. Now, this is fun!

At the beginning of a coaching engagement, I am a detective looking for clues. My client is already very good; what would it take to get closer to greatness? Does something in how s/he thinks, behaves, or relates to others preclude further success? The process I initiate with clients begins with raising the level of awareness of the participants about themselves.

Usually, the first step in the investigation is to review my client's SELF Leadership Profile. I created this profile based on many years of research on best practices, traits, and tendencies that drive successful leadership. The profile displays two sets of scores: raw and standard (or normative).

The raw scores present an overview of the client's personality that is driving her/his leadership style. Usually, these results yield valuable learning but no major surprises to the participant. After all, it's a self-assessment.

On the other hand, the standard scores are where most of the insights lie, and where the participant finds highest value. On the standard scores, the subject's results are compared and contrasted with the normative data (the standards) collected from more than 2,000 executives who have completed this assessment. Often, individuals discover—much to their surprise!—that how they view themselves differs greatly from how others would probably perceive them.

That gap is powerful! It is here that my clients start realizing that they may have developed some blind spots.

We are built in such a way that we inevitably develop blind spots. If I had a big black smudge on my forehead, you might be able to see it from a block away. But me? I wouldn't have any idea the black smudge existed. It's my blind spot.

The same inability to see the "black smudge" applies to certain behaviors and attitudes. You may not consciously know these areas exist, but others can perceive them easily—or, worse, suffer from them! That's what makes it necessary to regularly uncover and gain awareness of our developing blind spots, allowing us to periodically realign our behaviors with our intentions. No matter what you're evaluating in your professional or personal life, this is a crucial first step.

How do we uncover our blind spots? We do so by receiving feedback, by allowing others to act as a mirror for us.

The clues yielded by the SELF Leadership Profile build momentum toward the 360° Feedback Process, the next step in a client's process of discovery. The 360° feedback survey includes data from a client's direct reports, boss(es), and peers, as well as ratings and comments (quantitative and qualitative data) from various other people in the organization with whom the individual regularly interacts. Through this anonymous feedback process, the participant gains keen awareness of his/her blind spots and the impact he/she is having on people around him/her. Sometimes, this process is applied to an intact team, allowing the team members to learn to work better together, improve team dynamics and create alignment towards common goals.

It's an unfortunate and deeply embedded part of our culture that people shy away from providing feedback to each other in a direct, on-the-spot, real-time constructive way. Fear of damaging the relationship or alienating the other person (or myriad other reasons) creates strong motivation for co-workers to keep their opinions to themselves. That's why the online 360° feedback process works so well. It gives people a chance to *anonymously* provide their reaction to others' ways of interacting with them. Sometimes, people crave this opportunity so much that giving it to them not only increases their leader's awareness and enhances the way the leader interacts with them, but also elevates their own motivation and job performance—because they finally feel heard.

When combined, the knowledge about our own personality, our traits and tendencies driving our leadership style and the feedback we receive from colleagues at work can be extremely powerful. Something usually "clicks" in my clients' minds when they see their own profile, and then understand how those characteristics and traits impact others. This realization provides the first step towards a personal and professional transformation that positively changes my clients' lives—which is spelled out, time and again, through the different journeys I've taken with the subjects in this book.

It's important to note here that *feedback is not enough to effect change.* Telling someone: "You need to be more strategic," or "You need to delegate more," is usually equivalent to telling the person: "You need to be happier." The person may wholeheartedly agree but might not have a garden path, the "stepping stones" to follow through the personal transformation needed. That's where the coaching begins.

I present in this book, *Becoming a Great Leader,* eight distinct stories of transformation I have witnessed in Silicon Valley, and I also share two sets of information that I break out in each chapter: the challenges facing each client; and the client solutions, summarized as takeaway points that you can quickly integrate into your business and operations.

As you read these stories, picture yourself in the shoes of the subject, receiving feedback about yourself, identifying areas to improve, and most importantly, the solution, how to gain the new skill, master a new competency. In so doing, you will help fulfill the purpose of this book. And I trust that you will significantly enhance your overall performance, the quality of your leadership, and the performance of your organization.

In the conclusion of this book, you'll find that I have set up an online 360° feedback assessment you can take to begin your own journey. If you want to obtain your personal 360° feedback report, please contact us at *info@SkylineG.com*.

—Gustavo Rabin, Author
 Summer, 2011

CHAPTER 1

Randy: A Tight Ship With No Course

Good Execution of a Flawed Strategy

WHAT KEEPS THE CEO UP AT NIGHT?

Randy woke up before his alarm went off. His bedroom was cloaked in darkness, and his wife, Sarah, slept silently beside him. The bed-side clock read 5:37 a.m.

Sighing, Randy turned off his alarm, which was scheduled to wake him at 6 a.m. There was no point trying to reclaim sleep for a few minutes, or even relax in bed. He'd been through this routine for 10 days in a row. His neck and shoulders felt stiff, and he had the vague memory of strange, confusing dreams. The day hadn't yet started and already he felt tired, weary.

He quietly slid from beneath the sheets, careful not to wake his wife Sarah, and glanced at his image as he passed the big hallway mirror. In his home office, Randy turned on a lamp and sat at his desk, looking without actually *seeing* the company reports on which he'd worked half the night. Yesterday's meeting with his management team had been difficult. It was never easy to examine diminishing sales, and nobody brought new ideas to the table.

Randy was the CEO of a 1.2 billion dollar public software com-pany. The last three quarters had been challenging. Sales numbers had continued sliding from one quarter to the next, and every day he felt pressure from shareholders, the board, the media, Wall Street, and even the employees' rumor mill. Everybody was expressing discouragement at the loss of market share and the increasing success of the competition. Randy's high-tech company slid from number three in the market to number five, and was on the verge of becoming irrelevant—or a target for an unfulfilling acquisition.

Sarah had mentioned to Randy a few times that he looked tired and worried, but he never fully confided his anxiety about work. In his eyes, her own high stress job gave her enough to handle. Furthermore, their younger child was fighting a stubborn, slow-burning flu, which demanded attention and concern from both of them. Randy hadn't even shared his growing worries about the company's predicament with his best friend, Jerry. What could Jerry say? He was a doctor specializing in reconstructive surgery, not a businessperson.

Randy knew he needed help and that it could not come from inside his company. Over the years, he'd learned that it wasn't useful to brainstorm ideas and share concerns with his team without bringing at least a half-baked plan to the table. When he'd approached them with different ideas, some members felt confused, and others reacted as if he were rapidly shifting plans without a clear process.

He reflected for a moment on his management team. Quite simply, as a team, they were not producing the results the company needed. Before the economy slipped, the company had experienced moderate but steady growth. Instinctively, Randy understood that the good market conditions—not his company's competitive edge—contributed to that success. *Rising tides lift all boats,* he thought. Now that the altered business environment had sharpened their competitors' teeth, his team was not responding adequately. But where was he to turn?

With a deep sigh, Randy decided it was time to take the emphatic advice of a colleague, a CEO of another large company: hire a business coach.

MEETING THE COACH

Randy and I met later that week at his office, an area on the top floor
of the main company building that housed the executive suites.
Randy's office was at the end of an ample waiting area. His efficient-
looking assistant—seated in front of two computer monitors—answered phone calls from her desk in front of his frosted glass double
doors.

I didn't have to wait long before an athletic looking Randy in his
mid-fifties came out to greet me. I thought there was a "disconnect"
between his smile and the deep frown lines between his eyebrows.
I wondered if he knew how worried he looked.

Randy guided me to the conference table in his office after asking
his assistant to hold his calls. On the other side of the room, piles of
paper covered a commanding desk. Acronyms and numbers fought
for position and solutions on a whiteboard on wheels.

I decided to take the next few minutes to introduce myself and
discuss my work. It was always good, I thought, to build some extra
credibility; it's reassuring to someone worried and calling for assistance.

"I'm a business psychologist," I said. "The focus of my work is to
increase the level of effectiveness of individuals and teams. It may
sound obscure, but when you look at the organizational process from
thirty thousand feet high, it's rather simple. You can frame the whole
picture in three steps: As the CEO, you first enroll the right people;
secondly, you put them in a room together to create and strategize
a common vision; and thirdly, together you focus on the execution
of that strategy. Usually, when a company is struggling, one of these
steps is failing. That's where I come in."

Randy nodded thoughtfully. "I like the simplicity of that," he finally said.

"I've learned that there's something fundamentally wrong if I can't
describe what I do in a way that my grandmother would understand
it," I said, smiling. "I used to work as a corporate law attorney, and

I saw how much my clients were annoyed by *legalese*. I don't care much for *consultese*."

Randy laughed. "Consultant-speak can get old fast. Well, to keep things simple, then—things are not going great at our company, and I don't understand why."

During the next twenty minutes, Randy explained the difficult market his company faced. He also expressed conflicting thoughts of confidence and bafflement about his management group. "My team is good," he said. "I carefully hand-picked and recruited every person on the team. They're reliable, energetic people who know how to get things done. I trust them, and I know they're dedicated. So I don't know why we're stuck."

"How's the team working with each other?"

"Oh, excellent," he said. "There's a deep sense of trust, and everyone works well together. Yet here we are, in this predicament. Why are we stuck? Why are we unable to come up with a strategy that improves our position in the market? What's missing?"

"Situations like the one you're describing are rarely caused by one single element," I said. "What, in your mind, are the top two or three reasons for the company's current situation?"

Randy shook his head. "I've been waking up before my alarm goes off for the last few weeks, thinking about this question. Obviously, if I had an answer, I would have already taken action. What is clear to me, though, is that we haven't developed the right *strategy* to regain market share, and it's not that we haven't dedicated enough time to the issue. I feel responsible, but at the same time, I will not dictate strategy from an ivory tower. It has to come from our common thinking. It has to be a team effort."

"You seem to be clear that the issue with your company is one of strategy and not of execution. What leads you to this conclusion?"

"My team and I have spent a lot of time and energy focused on attaining operational excellence. We've developed metrics for all our core processes, we obsessively track execution, and our operations group runs a tight ship. Our issue is how to steer the ship in the right direction."

Randy stopped speaking and gazed through the window, his eyes were unfocused. It seemed to me that he was trying to plumb deeper within himself to find answers to his quandary.

"What I'm saying doesn't explain anything," Randy said quietly. "If we're losing to our competition, it's because we don't have the right strategy. The question is: why? Why are we failing to set the right path? I know we can execute well, but we need a better game plan. In a company our size, there are a lot of moving parts. What should we change to transform the situation?"

I appreciated Randy's use of the word "we." It implied recognition that he couldn't turn around the situation by himself; that this was going to be a team effort. From everything I heard from Randy, it was clear that the company needed a new direction, an injection of energy, and a new way of looking at itself in order to get out of the doldrums. Would Randy be willing to step outside of his "comfort zone" to achieve these results?

"To help answer your question," I said, "I'd need to perform a rapid assessment of the leadership team—including you—and interview some key people in the organization. After that, I will come back to you with my report and suggestions on how to improve the organization's ability to set a winning course."

"That sounds great—but how long would it take?" Randy asked.

"About three weeks."

"Fast enough."

"Let me ask you, though—what prompted you to seek help at this point, and not earlier or at some point in the future?"

After a moment, Randy said, "Until recently, I used to think that if only my team would apply more effort, think harder, we would find a way out of our situation. But we've had plenty of meetings focused on what to do differently, and I don't see the team gaining any more clarity. After three negative quarters, we have to turn this situation around real soon." He sighed heavily. "If we don't, it'd only be ethical for me to acknowledge my poor leadership and present my resignation to the board of directors."

"How is your relationship with the board?"

"So far, they have been very supportive. But lately I have a growing feeling that if I don't turn the situation around quickly, the board will look to replace me. And that's not a scenario I like to think about."

Over the next half hour, we agreed that I'd assess Randy's management team in multiple dimensions, survey middle management using my company's execution diagnostic tool, and meet with him to report on my findings and suggest a course of action. We also decided that to create the right stage for this initiative we would frame it as an organizational effectiveness effort. By the time we ended the meeting, Randy's smile seemed a little more genuine and his forehead a little less furrowed. I sensed that he was glad to have taken the first step.

SELLING THE IDEA TO THE TEAM

My own first step in this engagement was a rapid but thorough assessment of Randy's management team. Since Randy was intent on acting quickly, I met with him and the nine members of his team just a few days later.

We met in a conference room that, like the rest of Randy's office setting, was fairly traditional: gleaming wood, big whiteboards, and refreshments readily available. Randy remained seated as he introduced me.

"I want you all to meet Gustavo," he said. "As I mentioned in my email, he is my executive coach. He will be assessing the organization and offering some suggestions as to how the team can function better as a whole."

Though Randy looked pleased with his concise introduction, I caught several team members exchanging wary glances. The introduction seemed awkward; it didn't offer enough explanation of why I was there or what the team could expect.

"With all due respect, Randy—and Gustavo," said Doug, the vice president of engineering, "we have so many urgent things on our plate. Why do we need to do this right now?"

Randy looked at me. "Would you like to respond to that question?"

"Sure." I glanced around the room. I thought the group felt threatened and defensive about an outsider meddling with their affairs. Would I be able to overcome their concerns?

"I understand that, right now, your organization is suffering some level of stress from trying to figure out how to improve its position in the marketplace," I said. "From what Randy has told me, this has been going on for a while. Maybe it's time for this team to take a look at itself, and determine what part of the process could work better, and how to make that happen."

I paused for a moment. As I thought I had their attention, I continued. "As human beings, we are built in such a way that we periodically develop blind areas. I could have a black spot on my forehead about five inches wide, and you would be able to see it from a block away, maybe wonder why I have it. Meanwhile, I may not have the slightest idea that the big black spot exists. It's a blind spot. The same happens with organizations. At times, it's useful to have someone from outside come in, look at us, and say, 'Hey, you have a black spot on your forehead,' or, 'That organizational process is broken,' and suggest an intervention that could take care of the problem. It's like presenting a mirror for the organization to see itself."

Some of the people nodded. I decided to take a risk and further explore the openness of the group. I added, "On the other hand, if you don't think that the process I'm suggesting will add value, it's better to drop the whole idea and not waste any time."

A long silence ensued.

Randy did not push for resolution. He acted cautiously and allowed the team to resolve the situation on its own. Eventually, someone else in the group said, "It would be a stretch to say that we don't need to look at ourselves in the mirror. If it doesn't take a lot of time and we could keep it simple, I support it."

Randy looked around the table at the group of people he knew so well. "What about the rest of you?" he asked.

Everybody but Doug nodded. Then, a moment later, Doug said, "I was just thinking about my latest visit to our engineers in Ireland. The main team there was perplexed by a code problem. I came out as a genius—which I'm certainly not—when I suggested a simple fix that took care of the problem. It took only a few minutes to re-solve something that they'd been fussing with for a week because they were too involved in the problem: everybody was too focused on the same wrong issue. It'd be refreshing to have someone with fresh eyes to look at how we work."

"Okay, then," Randy said, nodding at me. "How are we going to do this?"

I took a few minutes to describe the next steps. First, I said, each member of the team would complete SELF1 leadership profiles, which would indicate their individual leadership styles and how their differences might be impacting the group's internal dynamics and how the team made decisions.

After that, I would conduct structured interviews with everyone on the management team, as well as other executives in charge of the company's critical areas. The purpose of these interviews would be to gather opinions on the strengths and weaknesses of the indi-vidual management team members and the organization. Then we would launch an online 360° feedback process for each team mem-ber; about 25 to 30 individuals would provide feedback on the 36 competencies our feedback survey measures, broken into four dis-tinct domains: Leading Self (the intrapersonal), Leading Others (the

---

[1] SELF: refers to our company's leadership profile Skyline Executive Leadership Factors

interpersonal), Leading the Organization (the system), and Managing Implementation (focused on execution).

To complete the data gathering process and see the team in action, I'd also attend a couple of the meetings that Randy conducted regularly with the management team. I would evaluate the team dynamics and the quality of the group's strategic thinking first-hand. From there, we could move forward to analyze the data, complete an assessment process and eventually suggest the needed interventions.

EVALUATING THE DATA AND THE TEAM

Three weeks later, a mountain of data sat in front of me. It was time to sift through it and reflect. It was vital to be accurate about what *not* to fix. Too many times, I'd seen organizations correct poor execution by changing their strategy, which they had misdiagnosed as the problem. But with Randy's company, an interesting picture started to emerge.

Our company's execution diagnostic tool largely confirmed Randy's assertions. The organization's portfolio of projects and programs was well managed, and its business processes provided "good enough" support to achieve the goals and objectives set by the company's strategy. Although there was room for improvement, the execution was clearly not broken. This was important to determine, as many good strategies fail due to poor execution. However, the organization was like a well-driven vehicle—headed in the wrong direction. We had to turn that car around, and focus on the capacity of the organization's leadership to process all the market intelligence and devise a successful plan.

Randy and I met again shortly after I processed the results of the 360° feedback to review conclusions and discuss possible courses of action. I started by identifying the three key positions in the team that needed to be sources of creative thinking and functional focus in support of the CEO leading the organization's strategy formation:

9

1. The Chief Marketing Officer (CMO) in charge of interpreting the market intelligence and creating competitive advantage for the organization;

2. The Chief Technology Officer (CTO) that oversees the Research and Development department where the innovative products would be conceived, designed and moved to production; and

3. The Chief Financial Officer (CFO), providing the financial modeling and the understanding of financial constraints.

This list was by no means exhaustive—you can't discount the keen perspective of Sales and its understanding of the market place. Everybody on the team needed to contribute to the effort of defining a winning strategy; but for this engagement, based on the challenges the company was facing, I saw these three as the crucial roles for defining strategy.

I proceeded to review the three people in Randy's team holding those positions.

Curt, the company's CFO, had a great reputation for accountability, effectiveness, and accuracy on how he "crunched the numbers." The feedback he received stressed his deep level of financial and accounting knowledge. He could manage complex financial information and present an enormous amount of data but didn't extract from it and share the insights needed to influence strategy. The numbers were accurate, but what do they mean? How should our current financial situation influence how we define our strategy moving forward?

There was no doubt that Curt was great with numbers, cash-flow projections, and spreadsheets. Curt was thorough, organized, and methodical, with a strong tendency to focus on details—all positive qualities that one would like to see in a Chief Financial Officer. What was lacking in Curt's DNA was the brilliant strategic thinking, measured risk taking, and the capacity to inspire others. He didn't seem able to contribute to a meaningful group vision. Curt was a solid player with good technical knowledge, a reliable member of the team, but he was not someone who would contribute to an innovative approach to improving the company's future.

Bob, the Chief Marketing Officer, received similar feedback. Comments emphasized his consistent delivery of good work, and people saw him as reliable, a hard worker, and very devoted to his job. He also seemed able to effectively manage his people. The emphatic word on everything about Bob, however, was *solid,* not *creative.* Bob and his team were able to gather good market intelligence and develop excellent relationships with customers and vendors. But they would not hit the ball out of the park. While Bob had the capacity to look at market data and suggest tactical operational changes, he just didn't generate the kind of disruptive creative thinking that would help generate new momentum against the competition.

The biggest pressure to gain competitive advantage fell squarely on Doug's shoulders. Doug was the head of engineering and although he didn't have the official title of CTO, that was certainly part of his role; the research and development department was part of his organization. Thus, Doug and his group needed to lead the effort to move the company to a more competitive market position.

As the CEO of the company, Randy had decided to hire Doug three years ago, based on Doug's significant experience in their industry, managing the complex relationship between engineering and manufacturing. There was no sense in advancing the company's technology if the organization was not able to deliver consistent manufacturing processes and reliable delivery to its customers. With many customers requiring customization of the company's products to strict specifications standards, Doug's experience proved extremely valuable when times were good and orders rolled in. At that time, operational excellence was the Holy Grail for the organization.

11

But now, something quite different was needed: thought leadership and radical innovation.

Doug's profile did not show him as a likely candidate to deliver those qualities. His profile highlighted his pragmatism, a strong tendency to stick to the familiar, and a practical approach to problem solving. He was highly analytical, inclined to be fascinated while solving technical problems, and good at coordinating people's efforts towards the execution of set goals. Doug was an excellent person to have on the team for providing an efficient interface with the manufacturing plants and reliable support to customers. He could lead reliable execution of a technology roadmap. However, he was not the person to envision and draw that roadmap.

Between Curt, Bob, and Doug, a theme emerged: Randy had put together a solid team that, given a plan, could execute well and deliver consistent and reliable results. They had *operational savvy,* but the urgent need was for *innovation focus.* When it came to vision and strategy, the "team had an okay batting average but nothing to include them in the Hall of Fame," one member said in his feedback.

This team was definitely not able to generate new ideas, spawn innovation, and turn around the company's situation.

HOW DID THIS COME TO BE?

My next question was crucial: how had Randy contributed to creating this situation? For our next meeting, I asked him to reflect deeply on this.

Randy had a lot of information to digest. The company was facing fierce competition, it was losing the race in the marketplace, and his team was not capable of assisting him in turning it around. Randy also mentioned that he'd never had a true "thinking partner" within the team. Instead, he oversaw dependable folks who executed reliably. How had he contributed to creating this situation? I believed it was important to deconstruct the issue and truly understand the answer in order to create an authentic paradigm shift.

We met again about a week after going over the results of the 360° feedback. As soon as we sat at the conference table in his office, Randy said, "I kept thinking about your provocative question: how have I contributed to the current situation in our company? After all, I was the one who hired these guys. But it's hard to look under the hood of my own mind." Randy stared down at the leadership profiles of his team. "I'd like to come up with an intelligent response but … honestly? I have no idea."

I had some preliminary ideas, but I needed to provide Randy the opportunity to form insights independent of my thoughts.

"Take your time," I said. "Do you have an inkling, a half-baked thought about this?"

"Not really. I wasn't able to come up with anything."

"Randy, would you be willing to try a little experiment?"

"What do you have in mind?"

"It's a guided imagination exercise that may help us better understand the current situation."

"Guided imagination?" Randy didn't try to conceal his skepticism. "I'm sorry, but it sounds like hocus pocus to me."

"You've spent a lot of time thinking about your company's predicament."

"That's true."

"My understanding is that all that thinking, all that *analyzing,* has not worked—at least not yet. So it's time to use a different part of your brain: your imagination."

Randy emitted a bemused smile. "All right. What do I have to do?"

"Well, when we use our imagination, a different part of our brain is activated than when we think and reason. I want you to sit back for a moment. Relax and let all thoughts go. This is not your usual way of interacting in the office," I added with a laugh, "but I'm a quirky psychologist, and you need a creative solution."

"Agreed," Randy smiled.

"Just relax for a moment." I kept my voice low, soothing. Randy took a deep breath and closed his eyes, leaning back in his chair.

"Good ... yes, you can keep your eyes closed. There's nothing you need to see right now that's not in your mind's eye. Now, I want you to imagine that you are here in your office sometime in the future; say it's two years down the road. It's the end of the day, almost dark outside. Everybody has left the building, and you're taking advantage of this quiet time to review your situation. Are you able, in your mind's eye, to picture yourself in your office about two years from now?"

"Yes," Randy responded very softly, nodding.

"Good. Things are going well, the company is thriving, you've regained the market share you lost some time ago—and then some—and you are actually beating the competition. The situation has changed for the better, and it looks stable. Please spend a moment considering all this. The company's shares have gone up steadily, and your shareholders are happy. Imagine giving big bonuses to your employees and receiving kudos from your investors. Finally, the good times have arrived. Tell me, how do you feel realizing how successful you and your company have been?"

Randy smiled, and I felt pleased by his willingness to engage in this exercise. After a moment, he said, "I feel very content. I knew that if we worked hard enough, we would turn the situation around."

"What else comes up for you?"

"I feel happy for my employees. Whatever we accomplished is because of them."

"You clearly remember the process used to achieve this," I said. "About two years ago, you decided to bring in a new team. The old members of your team did not need to leave the company; most of them were repositioned inside the organization and are doing well. Today, your team includes one or two folks from your old group, but everybody else joined the company about two years ago. You find yourself surrounded by a group of bright individuals. They are creative and sharp, real thinkers and innovators. They create value. I want you to imagine yourself in that situation … What's the feeling that comes up for you?"

Randy's brow furrowed. He seemed to be more in touch with his thoughts than with his feelings. *This was not going to be easy.* But I sensed that he'd find value in exploring this alternative scenario.

A long silence followed. Finally, Randy said, "I don't know. I'm glad that things are going well."

"How do you feel about your new team? Can you see them in your mind's eye?"

Another thirty seconds passed before Randy said, in a voice so low I had trouble hearing, "No. I can't see them."

"Our minds always present us with some image," I pressed gently. "What do you see?"

"I see a wall."

"Can you describe it?

"It's a brick wall. It's tall. It looks like the wall in my church's garden."

"Good. Can you find a place to sit in this garden?"

"There's a stone bench."

"Would it be okay to sit there for a moment?"

"Yes."

"Please sit on that bench, and spend some quiet time in the garden next to this brick wall." After a while, I asked, "What's your feeling as you sit there?"

"Calm," Randy said, his eyes still closed. "Peaceful." His face looked relaxed, serene.

Though I was tempted to go further, my intuition was telling me that pushing forward would not do any good for Randy. It was the right time to wrap up our meeting and build into Randy's growing comfort to continue the exercise some time later.

"It's okay to sit there for a moment," I said. "Enjoy the peaceful time; we all need those moments every now and then. When you are ready, I want you to come back to your office today, sitting in your chair. As you start to move your fingers, your hands, you can let your eyes open."

Randy opened his eyes and rubbed them, reorienting himself in the room. He sat straight in his chair. In a very soft voice he said, "That was something! That place felt very real."

"For your mind, it was real."

"I could feel the breeze and the leaves on the trees rustling …"

"This was a good start, and it sounds like a good time to stop," I said. "Next time we meet, I'd like to continue this exercise, if you're agreeable."

"I don't know if it's useful," Randy said, doubt creeping back into his voice, "but I trust that you know what you're doing."

"I do." We both laughed.

I reflected on the meeting while driving back to my office. No amount of *thinking* would allow Randy to develop an insight into his unconscious participation in the current situation. After all, if it was unconscious, how could he *know* about it?

In crime stories, the motto is *cherchez la femme,* or "look for the woman."

In business dealings, what works is to *follow the money.*

But in psychological matters, when you are trying to make sense of unconscious behavior, you look for the emotion. *Thinking about it* would not allow Randy to access the driving emotion. Only by using his imagination to create a situation in which the avoided emotion emerged could he access insights about what was driving his actions. I was committed to continue approaching Randy's internal process with patience and respect, hoping that eventually powerful insights would surface.

OUR SECOND ATTEMPT

When Randy and I met a few days later, his dark eyes were alert and focused. I followed the lead I sensed in his expression and asked, "Ready to get started again?"

"Absolutely," Randy said. "What are we doing today?"

"Did you have a chance to reflect on what we discussed about your team?"

Randy fidgeted slightly in his chair. "Can you be more clear?"

"We broached the subject of you having assembled a solid team," I said. "One that seems ideal for excellent execution but is not necessarily geared to innovate and generate creative market strategies."

"Yes, but I'm puzzled by that. Thinking about my team members one by one, I still think they're ideal for the job. Yet, when you talk about execution versus innovation," Randy paused, grabbing a pen and rapping it against his desk, "I can see the disconnect. I'm not sure where to go from here."

Randy's frustration was obvious. "Well," I said, "I suggest we finish the guided imagination exercise from a few days ago."

"Is it the best use of our time?"

"Every time you're puzzled by your own decision or behavior, it means that a different part of yourself is at work. In your case, it sounds as if a part of you is saying 'If I had to hire a team again, I would hire the same people.'"

"Right. I do feel that way."

"Meanwhile, another part of you doesn't know why you'd hire these guys if they weren't the right ones to help craft strategy for the company."

"That's also true."

"I believe that just 'thinking' about it will not give us an answer to that question. There may be something to be learned from exploring your imagination, and on our last meeting, we only went halfway. I don't think you are a halfway kind of person," I said, smiling.

Randy grinned. "You really know how to cajole a person, eh? Okay, let's do it."

I guided Randy to the same inner place he'd found on our previous meeting. After several minutes, I said, "Randy, I want you to nod if you are sitting on that bench near the brick wall."

Randy nodded.

"This seems to be such a quiet place. Last time you mentioned that it was calm, peaceful. Do you still feel that way?"

Randy nodded again, smiling. I imagined that he rarely experiences this sense of stillness and inner harmony.

"Quiet places like this allow us to reflect and get clear about things."

I asked Randy to again project himself about two years into the future, imagining his company as a successful, dominant force in the market. I also suggested, again, that this was accomplished with a new team, where—except for one or two people—everybody had joined the company about two years earlier. This time, Randy was able to move more quickly into this imagined future world. He listened thoughtfully to the picture I was painting for him.

"This new team is great, Randy. You find yourself surrounded by a group of really smart people. They are creative, sharp, have great ideas, and are top thinkers and innovators. These are 'A' players. They create value. As you think about this, what's the feeling that comes up for you?"

A long silence.

"I'd feel proud in that situation, and maybe also worried," he said finally.

"Follow that trail, Randy. Let yourself feel worried for a moment. Where's the worry coming from?"

"I don't know."

"What worries you?"

"It's hard to put in words."

"It's okay, Randy. You know, worry is a milder and more acceptable version of fear. Ponder for a moment about this: Exploring our fears of tomorrow lets us act courageously today. I want you to be as honest as you can. Not just honest with me, but honest with yourself. Let yourself fully experience what you feel when you imagine yourself surrounded by this great team of smart, creative folks."

Randy's eyes were closed. He clenched his teeth as I could see his jaw muscle tightening.

"You know," I continued, "sometimes, when we feel strongly about something, we can almost hear a voice inside ourselves. What are you telling yourself about all this? What is the self talk surrounding the worry and the fear?"

In a rush, as if Randy needed to get the words out before he silenced them internally, he said, "I'm not as smart as these people. How could I lead a group of people who are smarter than me? I'm obsolete. The team is leaving me behind. Everybody will see this—the board, my team, their reports—everybody."

I encouraged Randy to continue this exploration. "What else comes up for you?"

"Well, the worst is facing the board," he said. "They're really smart people; they would quickly realize that everyone on my team is sharper and more creative than me. Very soon they'd say, 'Randy's had his run. Maybe it's time to start looking for a new CEO. Maybe one of the new team members would be a great candidate to replace him!'"

"Stay with that for a moment, Randy," I said, leaning forward. "There's nothing that you have to do about it. Just stay with the feeling and with those thoughts for a moment. See if there's anything else to learn from what you are experiencing."

"I feel inadequate. It reminds me of when I hear some of our young guys in the engineering department. They are so ahead of my game; the technology has advanced enormously since I graduated twenty-five years ago, and I haven't been able to keep up with the technical nuances. Understanding our financials, dealing with Wall Street, our biggest investors, employees' issues … When would I focus on deep technology? That makes me feel inadequate."

"It comes with the job," I said. "Being CEO leaves no time to catch up with technology. What could you contribute to the group instead?"

After a long while, Randy said, "I'm good with people, and I'm good at bringing a team together. I provide the glue that binds the group. I bring leadership to make the different parts work well together. I believe I'm also a good ambassador for the company, facing Wall Street, our suppliers, and the industry as a whole."

"When you think about these assets you bring to the company, how do you feel?"

"Motivated." Randy's voice drew out, as if he was surprising himself. "Energized. Proud." I could see his face changing expression and relaxing as he was transitioning to a different emotion.

"As you feel all that, do you still feel worried?"

"No. I don't."

"Randy, there seems to be so much to learn from this experience. Let's come back to here and now and reflect on this," I said.

HARVESTING THE INSIGHT

He opened his eyes and reoriented himself. He looked around his office as if seeing it for the first time, and then his dark eyes came to rest on me. "Wow! I didn't imagine all of that would come up. What's it all about?"

"You're the only expert on Randy. Let's approach it as a detective would—looking at clues, hints. What do you think is happening here?"

Randy looked pensive. Eventually he said, "This is very humbling and not easy for me to admit: I believe I've surrounded myself with 'solid' managers because I've been afraid of the alternative. Without thinking, I hired people who would let me shine." He took a deep breath and met my gaze straight on, not easy with this kind of self-recognition.

20

"That's a very humbling insight," I said quietly. "It takes courage and uncompromising honesty to see it. What else do you see here?"

"I've never seen things under this light. I believe I 'dumb down' my team in a very subtle way to be able to make myself look great—to myself and to everybody around me. I lower the average to a point where I can stand way above. This is appalling," Randy said, shaking his head. "I shot myself in the foot."

"First of all," I cautioned him, "don't jump to judgment; that will cut you off from accessing your insights. The best approach here is to better understand your self in order to correct course. Judgment will make you burn up a lot of energy without moving forward. It's as if you're applying the brakes while what you want is to accelerate towards change. Also, what you are doing requires integrity and courage, and you are displaying both: integrity to acknowledge a difficult insight and courage to face your fears and move ahead in the way that your integrity dictates."

Randy nodded, but his grim expression spoke to the anger he was feeling toward himself. "Looking at what I realized today, it feels as if I've fed my own ego and sense of importance instead of acting in the best interest of our company."

"Self indulgence," I continued, "is realizing that and not doing anything about it. You just had an insight. Now you will turn around and use that insight to guide your future behavior. I believe that's a very healthy, functional way of operating in the world. Looking at your insight today, how would you like that to inform your next steps?"

Again, Randy looked pensive. I appreciated that he was taking time to reflect and act intentionally. "What do you think?" he asked.

"I firmly believe that the main role of a CEO is not to spearhead innovation all by himself. It's not his responsibility to be the creative genius that comes up with the next technological advancement to propel a company forward. That could be okay for a small start-up working out of a garage, but not for a public company with 4,500 employees."

Randy nodded when I paused. "Go on."

"I believe that the main role of a CEO is to create the conditions for success. That means bringing the best possible team to the table, creating the environment where creativity and innovation can thrive and flourish, and then harnessing that creativity into excellent execution. Think of an orchestra conductor. It is not the role of the conductor to play any of the instruments, but to have the whole perform to delight an audience and themselves with great music."

After listening attentively, Randy spoke up. "I want to respect the group of people who surround me today. These are dedicated, loyal folks. They've supported the company's strategy—and me—through thick and thin. I feel loyalty toward them. At the same time, I now understand that this is not the group of people who will generate the ideas and creativity we need today."

"What does that mean to you?"

"I will not let my own fears of not being smart enough harm all the good people who work for this company." Randy's voice was steady, his eyes filled with new determination. But his next words were still uncertain: "So, it looks like I'm in a tough spot. I owe loyalty to my current team, and I also owe loyalty to the shareholders—and to our employees, who want to be part of a winning organization."

"Randy, you may be looking at this in black and white, as an either/or situation," I suggested. "How about a both/and approach to integrate all the different elements? You have a great team that can execute well, but you are also missing the innovation ingredient. Yet, great innovation without excellent execution wouldn't work, either. How can you have both?"

"I'd like to hear your ideas about that."

"Well, great companies stand on two feet. One foot is in the world of ideas and visionary dreams. Here," I said, holding out my left hand, "we are looking at innovation and creativity, the capacity to generate cutting-edge thinking and revolutionary products and services."

I extended my right hand. "The other side looks at execution, making the ideas and dreams a reality."

I smiled. "By the way that's why I called our company Skyline. One definition of *skyline* is 'where heaven meets earth.' We need our minds in heaven and our feet on the ground."

"I hear you." Randy looked reflective, concentrating on my words.

"So, don't let go of your 'unrelenting focus on execution,' quoting a comment from the execution assessment we performed. I've witnessed a couple of your team meetings, and it's obvious that implementation is at the top of the group's priorities. That's great! Don't let it go, rather make it one side of a two-prong approach. The other side is to reinforce the team and its capacity to strategize creatively."

Randy grabbed a pen and legal pad from the central drawer of his desk. "I can see a model that would work," he said. "I need to bring the research and development group to a whole new level. I could bring in a whole new R&D team that would excel, and I could elevate them to be a new department, independent and not bound by the daily constraints of delivering to clients." His pen raced over the paper. "The head of R&D would be an integral part of the management team, and that person would have a deep reputation in the field and act as a magnet to attract great talent. I can see us developing the next generation of products and becoming a thinking engine for our industry. I can see all this innovation *supported* by the team I have today, which could bring all these ideas to reality. With the right game plan, my guys could deliver. This is really exciting," he said, grinning. "I'm burning to find the right people and put these ideas to work!"

I nodded enthusiastically. Randy had reached an insight that was out of reach to him before. I was proud of him. "I see your vision as realistic and possible, the kind of vision that would make you the CEO I mentioned earlier—the one who doesn't try to create success by himself but creates the conditions for success. If you accomplish what you have in mind now, how would you feel? What about the fear?"

Randy laughed. "Oh, don't worry. The fear would still be there. I'll probably always have my tough moments comparing myself against other smart people. I'll probably always believe that I should be more steeped in the technology instead of participating in meeting after meeting. I miss being in front of my computer with a design software program open. But I'm clear that my work today is to bring leadership and inspiration to let *other* people reach new solutions."

Randy's words were powerful, but the passion behind them was even more moving. He had reached a good place; best to end the meeting on this positive note. "I can't wait to keep working these ideas," he said as I left.

ENROLLING THE TEAM AND THE BOARD IN THE NEW PLAN

During the next few weeks, Randy worked feverishly to refine his plan. He asked me to facilitate a seminal team meeting during which he would present a compelling vision of all the insights he had learned about himself, the team, and the company.

A few days later, the team reconvened in the conference room. Curt, Bob, Doug, and about a dozen other men and women gathered around the conference table with laptops or legal pads before them, their expressions both curious and wary.

The first thing Randy did was acknowledge the value of having such a dedicated and capable team that, like himself, was keenly focused on execution of the company's plans. Then he compared the team to a man hopping on one leg.

"From now on," he said at one point, "we are going to use both our legs. To that purpose, we are going to start a number of initiatives. We will create a new and expanded Research and Development department and find an extraordinary individual to lead it. The person in that role will have the title of Senior Vice President of R&D and will be a member of our team. Then we'll keep the momentum and continue the recruiting effort by—under the guidance of our new R&D leader—building a powerful team with deep knowledge and experience in our field. R&D will no longer be simply a means to support execution. We will conduct expert panel meetings in which we'll bring in industry researchers, technology journalists, and creative people from non-competing companies to enrich our thinking. But, most of all, we are going to have periodic strategy meetings to keep creating and refining ideas that create competitive advantage for our organization."

Randy looked around the table. "I do not expect any slacking on execution, but we will add more of the ingredients we're currently missing—namely, creativity and innovation."

Doug, initially the most skeptical about this endeavor, didn't look very excited about Randy's ideas. "This is not about being territorial," he said, "but what's the rationale for removing R&D from my department? Couldn't we achieve the same goal keeping the existing organizational structure?"

Randy looked at me for a fleeting moment. We were prepared for some resistance and had discussed specifically how to approach it. Randy was ready. "Doug," he said, "would you rather have a larger department of a sinking company or a smaller one of a thriving enterprise? Please choose wisely."

Doug nodded quietly. "By having the head of R&D be a Vice President," continued Randy, "an integral part of this team and a peer of yours, we are acknowledging that the function is a keystone to how we are going to operate from now on. We are literally moving R&D from a subordinate position to a leading one. What do you think, team?"

A long silence followed. I signaled to Randy to wait. Suddenly, Doug stood up and extended his right hand towards Randy while smiling, "I was being territorial. Mea culpa. I do want a thriving enterprise. I like your idea, let's act on it." Doug and Randy shook hands effusively.

Without any prompting, the other members of the team stood up and shook hands with Randy and each other. They were warming to Randy's ideas, though it was possible that some—such as Bob, who didn't look very enthusiastic—viewed this as a temporary fix or fascination. I knew that Randy's commitment and determination would eventually win their hearts and minds, at least of the majority of the team, even if Bob didn't decide to throw away his skepticism and join the group in the transformational work needed by the organization.

The next step for Randy was to share his plan—and revelations—with the board. "Gustavo," he told me during one of our subsequent sessions, "it will take all the courage I have and then some to share with the board my insight about my team and hiring in such a way that I'd feel comfortable instead of challenged. I'm not proud of that. But I'm committed to being honest. I also have a new vision for what's possible. I just need the board to hear it and, I hope, support it."

In preparation for Randy's meeting with the board, he and I spent significant time role-playing and refining his presentation. Eventually, speaking the plan out loud, he was coming across self-assured and convincing.

On a Monday, about three months after we started working together, Randy stood before the eight members of the board and clearly and concisely summarized the results of our coaching engagement. He explained to the directors—he would later tell me that they were all watching him with remarkable poker faces—that the company's current situation resulted from the team excelling in execution but not in setting a winning strategy. And, in a humbling moment, he admitted his private motivations for hiring such a team.

"It was my own version of creating a false security for myself," Randy explained, smiling dryly. "Learning these things has not been easy. But I believe it will only benefit the company as we move forward with assembling a new team, one that—in collaboration with the individuals already working here—will not shy away from innovation."

The day after Randy's presentation, I met with a couple of the board members to debrief. The first told me that if Randy hadn't already been the CEO, she would have offered him that position on the spot. The second was cautiously optimistic. Overall, the board endorsed the CEO's new vision and focus.

A BI-FOCAL APPROACH

Over the next few weeks, Randy placed numerous calls to colleagues, recruiters, and friends in the industry to locate people with the caliber of creative thinking and experience needed to jumpstart the new R&D group. Randy told me that he was determined to hire above—way above—his own level of expertise, IQ, and creativity.

"I want to bring in people whom I can learn from," he told me during one of our meetings. "Clearly, I was confused about roles. I thought I needed to be the most brilliant person in the room, as if I were still in college. Now I don't want to impress people, I want them to impress me. I want to be inspired and reassured by my team's smarts, not the other way around. I'm content being the glue that holds everything together."

Randy felt impatient about moving the change process forward. Step by step, however, the different parts fell into place.

Six months after we started working together, Randy believed that his company possessed the ideal conditions to create success. By then, he'd welcomed a bright head of R&D, Joanne, to the management team, as well as a new group of intensely creative people under her leadership. That group was excited about the possibilities ahead, and Joanne was proving to be an impeccable leader. Randy also brought in a new Chief Marketing Officer, as Bob—presented with an attractive severance package—decided to take early retirement to focus on his family. The new CMO, Gordon, was an injection of energy and dynamism, someone with a great track record of matching creativity and innovation in the marketplace.

Six months after we began our engagement, the newly configured management team took a fresh look at the organization's identity (who are we?) and aspirations (who do we want to be?), and completed a comprehensive analysis of the company's intellectual property, the market trends, and the most likely scenarios for technology evolution in the field. A new vision was crafted and a new technology strategy shaped. This process was not completely smooth, hitting a significant level of resistance from some of the older members of the team. I was not surprised when Doug, the VP of Engineering, repeatedly expressed concerns about (in his words) "taking eyes off the current business of the company that was bringing in the revenue and paying the bills."

I met with Randy shortly after his most recent team meeting, which had focused on setting the new direction for the company. It was time to switch the focus of our work for this last leg of the journey. We would gear our final effort toward implementing the organization's new strategy.

"We've spent a lot of time discovering why the company was stuck in the market," Randy said, "and then putting together a team that would help propel us forward. But at this juncture, how can we embark on a new strategy when all of our efforts are going toward maintaining the company's existing business?"

"That's the million-dollar question. And here's the answer: you can't."

"So …?" Randy's eyebrows drew together.

"You can't embark on a new strategy," I said bluntly. "At least, that is, without implementing a radical new approach. In chess, I'd call it a bi-focal maneuver. This approach will call for two different but parallel areas of focus sustained at the same time."

"I play occasionally," Randy said. "Go on."

"For the first move, the vast majority of your team and your people will keep exclusive focus on executing the current strategy and maintaining revenue. For the second move, you will create a 'virtual company' inside your company. This new virtual company, unencumbered by the current business, will focus exclusively on jump-starting the implementation of the new strategy. Eventually— as expected—the old business will bring diminishing returns while the new one will be on a growth path. All the effort should be geared toward ensuring as smooth a transition as possible. You will know when the time is right to let the old business go."

Randy nodded. "What's the expected downside to this approach? What problems should I anticipate?"

"There are two main obstacles, and they are both related to human factors," I said. "First, people working toward executing the current strategy will see this as a huge distraction for the organization. They will want you to have the whole company single-mindedly working on the current business. They won't understand or support dedicating resources and people on a pipe dream with no immediate benefit in sight. But you'd rather see innovation coming from inside the company than from a garage in Palo Alto."

"I already see people resisting the new direction. Doug is a good example of that," Randy said.

"And he's right. For him, all conversations about the new direction of the company are a distraction and he should not have to spend any time on that, other than being informed of progress."

"So, he will not be part of what the company will become some time from now?" Randy seemed perturbed at the thought of his number-two man being expelled from the new vision.

"Not at the beginning," I said. "Once the virtual company is ready to launch marketing and production of its products, you will involve Doug in a big way, but not until then."

"I see. And what's the second hurdle to having this virtual company?"

"It's the virtual company not receiving the support it'll need. The team involved in its growth will call human resources asking for recruiting help, for example, or call your legal department asking someone to review a contract, and they will hear something like this: 'We are busy taking care of our mobile division; they have twelve hundred employees. You're a team of twenty-five. We want to help you, but we have to have our priorities clear.'"

"I can see that happening. What the best way of preventing it?"

"Dedicated resources," I said without hesitation. "There must be at least one person in all support functions—IT, HR, legal, etc.—that knows to drop everything if the virtual company calls. The head of each support function will arrange for this to happen and monitor compliance."

Randy's phone rang; he ignored it. "What can I do to support this?"

"If you do only one thing, express time and again that this is not a passing idea," I said. "You, as the CEO, are personally sponsoring the effort and will see that it succeeds. Everybody in the organization should know that the people in the virtual company are being personally instructed to call you directly, bypassing any concern about hierarchy or organizational chart, when facing difficulty getting the collaboration and support they need."

"That would certainly send a message," Randy said with a laugh.

"Not only that. The first time that you get a call from the virtual company letting you know that they are not getting support from other parts of the organization, you will make a swift intervention that will reverberate through the company."

Randy grinned. "Don't mess with my baby, huh?"

"That's the idea."

Randy was ready to move forward. It took only a couple of weeks to design the new virtual company and create its charter. As expected, there was some initial resistance to this unorthodox approach, but Randy showed his unwavering support and sponsorship of the effort throughout its evolution. He was also instrumental in getting the board's support for the new initiatives.

THE RESULTS

Many of the concerns about the new direction of the company proved unnecessary. About eleven months after it was created, the virtual company launched its first product line, which received great reviews from the media and became an immediate business success. After that, the momentum was unstoppable. The new group kept growing and launching one successful program after another.

Not quite two years after Randy made his first worried call to me, his company moved to number three in the market and was nipping at the heels of number two. The organization had become "a force to contend with," as I read in a well-known industry publication.

During a lunch meeting, Randy shared with me that the dialogue and the quality of the thinking within his team had elevated a few notches. "This is just like playing tennis," he said. "If my opponent is better than me, my game improves exponentially. I believe I'm smarter now that I'm playing within a smarter team."

"As a tennis player," I said, "I can say you're absolutely right!"

"I'm also committed now to always hire above my level. I still remember you telling me at different times that my job was not to have all the answers but to bring in the people who would ask the right questions.'"

I lifted my glass of iced tea in a toast, and Randy instantly followed my lead. "Cheers," he said.

The clink of our glasses will always represent to me Randy's transformation—and the success it brought his company.

Chapter 1 Summary
Randy: *Good Execution of a Flawed Strategy*

Randy is the CEO of a 1.2 billion dollar software company that enjoyed modest growth during economically strong conditions, but experienced a slide from #3 to #5 in industry market share in a three-quarter span during leaner times. He looked at his team, and looked at his own strengths and weaknesses, and couldn't pinpoint the reason for this decline. It came down to a question of strategic thinking and vision—and who (or lack thereof) was doing the visioning.

I. CEO'S ROLE AND CHALLENGE: The main role of a CEO is to create the conditions for success in the marketplace. To be successful a CEO must:

1. Enroll the right people
2. Co-create with them a winning strategy
3. Focus on execution of that strategy

RANDY'S CHALLENGE: to develop the right strategy to allow growth and gain market share. This requires a better game plan, a new direction, and an injection of energy. But where is that energy coming from? Success would require stepping outside the comfort zone, assessing the management team in multiple dimensions, and surveying middle management using an organizational effectiveness framework.

II. IDENTIFYING AND WORKING WITH ORGANIZATIONAL "BLIND AREAS." In order to clearly tackle the problem involving his entire company, Randy needed to look beyond himself and at his management team through these approaches:

1. Complete SELF (Skyline Executive Leadership Factor) Profiles—to understand individual leadership styles and how their differences might be impacting the group's internal dynamics and how the team made decisions.
2. Conduct interviews with management team and key executives to gather points of view on strengths and weaknesses.
3. Complete 360° process, with feedback from 25–30 individuals on key members regarding 4 leadership domains:
   a. Leading self
   b. Leading others
   c. Leading the organization
   d. Managing implementation

It was vital to get clear about what *not* to fix—was it the strategy that needed change or its execution?

III. IDENTIFY KEY POSITIONS THAT NEED HIGHER LEVELS OF CREATIVE THINKING; sometimes, operational savvy is not enough to make a strategy successful. You need innovative focus, thinking partners.

IV. USE OF AN "OUT OF THE BOX" TOOL TO SEE THE PROBLEM FROM A DIFFERENT ANGLE. In this case, we worked with guided imagery and visualization to come up with new ways of thinking, and creative solutions. This enables one to see the company in an ideal light, envisioning how it would function with the team all working innovatively. It includes ways of seeing others' roles and talents from different perspectives, exploring projected fears to act courageously in the moment, facing down fears that are withholding the fullest potential of the company to succeed over its competition.

V. GREAT INNOVATION PLUS EXCELLENT EXECUTION. This combination assures success for virtually any company. For the CEO, it means bringing the best possible team to the table, creating the environment where creativity and innovation can thrive and flourish, and then harnessing that creativity into excellent execution.

VI. CHANGING THE TEAM. The CEO or leader must take steps within the organization to create the two-pronged approach of great innovation plus excellent execution. This includes:

1. Willingness to change high-level management if necessary.
2. Holding periodic strategy meetings to create and refine ideas to establish competitive advantage for the organization.
3. Set the vision: Who are we as a company? Who do we aspire to be?
4. Taking radical approaches, such as setting up a virtual company or department within the organization to drive creative, innovative execution and become the energetic, visionary center of the company.

CHAPTER 2

Susan: Becoming a Strategic Thinker

From the Weeds to the Sky

SUSAN never found life at work easy. As a woman in a male-oriented industry, she always felt she needed to be twice as smart and work twice as hard to be considered an equal. Fortunately, she was accustomed to the challenge. She was the first and only member of her family to graduate from college; no one else had even left the family's Indiana farm. Because she succeeded in moving away, her two brothers were convinced that she thought herself smarter and superior to them. "Remember where you came from," they would say at holidays, gesturing toward the fields as if to say, "You should stay in your place." Susan shrugged off the taunting because she'd always felt drawn to engineering—to finding solutions to complex problems.

Susan graduated at the top of her class as an electrical engineer and completed advanced studies in computer science before joining a Silicon Valley high-tech company. There, as well as in the two other companies that she worked at over time, she found herself surrounded by male engineers that were accustomed to seeing women behind secretaries' desks, not inhabiting the office next door.

Eventually, Susan joined her current employer and rose through the ranks by working hard and proving her capacity to add value time after time. She displayed her excellence with each accomplishment, and knew that she worked harder and longer hours than her colleagues, intent on gaining and sustaining their professional respect. She was also a creative problem solver, the go-to person when technical difficulties stumped the product engineering group or the workers at one of the manufacturing facilities.

One time, she received a last-minute call from the company's manufacturing plant in Suzhou, China. The floor manager had been forced to stop production because the product line was rejecting too many units through the testing process. Susan stayed at the office long after the janitorial staff had turned off the lights and locked the doors behind them. She often focused best in the silence of a darkened building, knowing the pressure was on for her to find a solution.

Her work paid off. Around 2 a.m., she arrived at a brilliant solution. She immediately e-mailed the Chinese floor manager with her findings. It was already the following afternoon overseas, and it took only two hours for the plant to change a key step in the production process. Shortly afterward, the other two fabs adopted the same process and immediately reported an improved yield of nearly 20% in their manufacturing output. Quite a coup!

In Susan's ten years with the company, such examples of her problem-solving abilities were the norm. Her hard work won her the senior director of engineering position inside one of the business units. Seven managers reported directly to her; nine others were indirect, or dotted-line reports. In all, more than 120 engineers and support staff worked in her department. Looking back on her career, she'd done "darn well"—as her father used to say—"for a gal who used to fix tractors while her girlfriends were out shopping."

But Susan knew instinctively that she had hit a ceiling. Her manager, the vice president of engineering, was retiring in nine months, and Susan didn't believe that the CEO or his management team considered her a viable candidate for the position. Proving her point, she had recently learned that the company would be engaging a recruiting firm to help with the search to fill the soon-to-be-open position, and no one—not her boss, not even her peers—mentioned to her that she was expected to be part of that process as a candidate.

Why?

She didn't know.

Susan didn't believe it was merely because she was a woman; the organization was far past gender discrimination. The company's general counsel was a woman and had a firm seat at the management team's table. Susan knew that she was highly regarded by her peers. They often came to her with questions and to brainstorm possible solutions to technical problems, knowing that she would never make them feel less capable because of it. Additionally, the performance review she received three months prior from her boss, Jeff, was stellar. He had expressed great appreciation for her capacity to resolve the endless stream of problems and challenges on the engineering department's docket. Even the comments about her from her direct reports were positive and reassuring.

So what gave?

Susan knew that she was too close to the problem to see it clearly. However, if she openly asked her boss about it, she might seem bitter or dissatisfied with her current situation. She would be approaching the problem from the wrong angle and undermining any chances she might have for the promotion. She would need to get creative about finding a solution.

Tommy, her eldest son, had recently worked with his school's new coach to improve his soccer game. Embarrassed about his poor play and on the verge of quitting the team when the coach came on board, Tommy soon glowed with new confidence and talked often about how his life at school had changed for the better. The evidence of his on-field improvement was there for all to see.

Similarly, Susan's husband had also recently hired a coach to improve his tennis game. She hadn't been able to help smiling at dinnertime the night Jim gleefully told the family that he was now beating Ralph, his archrival of many years. "You should have seen the look on his face when I aced him," Jim said, laughing.

The more Susan thought about it, the more she was convinced that she also needed a coach. She wasn't sure what the process would entail—after all, her goal didn't feel quite as simple as improving her tennis serve—but she wanted to give it a shot. A highly positioned colleague in another company told her that he had successfully worked with an executive coach, so Susan wasted no time in sending that colleague an email. He responded quickly and enthusiastically, giving her the name and contact information of his executive coach.

That was how I met Susan.

COMMITMENT

Susan greeted me in her office with a firm handshake and welcoming smile. The first thing I noticed about the room was that everything around her was neatly placed. Her desk was clear except for the open folder before her, and the desktop shone as though it had just been polished. There weren't many personal items on display—no framed snapshots of family vacations or children's birthdays. The only photo included her and a smiling team in a manufacturing plant somewhere in Asia, according to the sign behind them. A few silver plaques attested to her technical prowess.

After the usual pleasantries, Susan asked, "Gustavo, how do we get started? I'm eager to know more about how we're going to work and how to get things moving forward."

"Well," I asked, "why a coach and why now?"

We sat across from each other in uncomfortable but functional chairs. Her office space was designed for short, expeditious meetings, and I waited patiently for her answer. Before rushing forward into *process,* we needed to get to the heart of what was driving Susan.

She sighed, leaning back in her seat, and then related the upcoming retirement of her boss and her growing sense that she was not being considered a viable candidate to replace him. "I've been working for this company for *fifteen* years, in this role for the last six," she said, exhaustion drawing out her face. "After all this time, I feel I've hit a ceiling. I seem to have a clear path forward, but not upward."

She had obviously been building up energy around the situation, one that, it seemed to me, she kept to herself. She must have read my mind, because her next words were, "I haven't shared my frustration with anyone. Not at work, because I thought that it may be in my detriment to do so. Not at home, although my husband knows about my intentions and has been supportive ... Still, I promised myself a long time ago that I wouldn't bring home my work worries and stress."

"What about your friends?" I asked.

She steepled her hands. "No, I haven't shared my work situation with my friends. I don't want to be perceived by my friends as bitter. Don't get me wrong—I'm grateful for what I've accomplished thus far, but I'm not ready to tell myself that this is as far as I can go in my career."

I nodded, already laying out in my mind the three areas I always explore when dealing with clients experiencing transitional times, like Susan:

1. What personal dreams and desires are driving this person? What is her unique individual definition of success for the coaching process?

2. What skills and competencies does the individual need to develop or refine to achieve success?

3. What kind of support must be gathered to assist the individual on her quest?

One thing was already clear: Susan had completely isolated herself. She didn't have a support group to help her work out her current predicament and evaluate possible pathways to resolution. It was probably her style to be completely self-reliant, to work things out in her mind and in her own way.

I asked, "Susan, how would you define success for our working together?"

She didn't hesitate. "My boss will retire in nine months and I want to be considered a candidate to replace him and acknowledged as the obvious and most qualified person for the position." She sat back in her chair.

I took in her response. "What's driving you? What's the *motivation* behind what you want?"

Again, she was quick to respond. "I've thought a lot about that question. Why do I want to further my career? It may sound obvious, but it's not. I'm good at what I do, and I have influence in my department. I believe that I make life at work easier for people who work for and with me. As the VP of engineering, I'd be able to expand that influence beyond my department. I would also be able to influence big decisions about which I have no say today."

Susan sounded determined. Her voice never wavered, and her still, unblinking blue eyes were focused and intent. Still, I'd heard similar words from plenty of equally ambitious executives. When it came down to the level of availability and commitment to engage in a transformational coaching process, however, sometimes actions and words didn't match up.

In first meetings with potential clients, I often refer to research performed on Olympic athletes. While intensive training and superb physical condition puts these athletes on equally solid footing to win, the athletes who become champions are not necessarily stronger or in better shape; after all, many times they win by only two- or three-hundredths of a second—faster than a rapid blink! The ones who win are the ones who want it most. I see that burning desire as the fuel of champions that creates the conditions for a committed, sustained process of personal transformation.

I turned to Susan. "What you want will not be easy. It will require a focused and intense effort on your part. You'll need to look closely at yourself and how you work, and while you'll find things you like, you may also discover aspects of yourself that are less than flattering and that are challenging to change. You're already a busy person with time constraints. Personal and professional transformation work requires attention, time, and commitment."

"So," I asked, "from one to ten—with ten being the highest—how committed are you to making this happen?"

This time, Susan didn't blurt a response. She sat quietly, one finger tapping her desk, pondering my question. Finally, she looked me square in the eye. "I can't imagine being forever limited by whatever is holding me back. I can't imagine being stuck in my position until I retire. I'm too young to even utter the word *retire* or have reached my top potential. From one to ten, my commitment is a solid ten. When can we get started?"

UNCOVERING BLIND SPOTS

At the beginning of a coaching engagement, I am a detective looking for clues. Susan struck me as such an intelligent, bright person. Was there something in how she thought, behaved, and related to others that precluded her from further success?

In such an investigation, my first step is to ask the client to complete a SELF leadership profile. I created this profile based on ten years of research and hundreds of interviews focused on leading thinking and best practices, as well as on traits and tendencies that drive successful leadership. The raw scores reflect the self-assessment part of the profile and present an overview of the personality driving the leadership style. Usually, this yields no major surprises to the participant.

41

The standard scores, on the other hand, offer the highest value to the participant. Most of the insights lie within them. On the standard scores, the subject's results are compared and contrasted with the normative data (the standards) collected from over 2,000 other executives who completed this assessment. That's when individuals discover that how they see themselves in some aspects sometimes differs greatly from how they are probably perceived by others. That gap is powerful! It is where an individual's blind spots can be found. Which sets the stage for the next step—the 360° feedback—the process by which people around the participant provide feedback about how they actually perceive the individual in question.

THE JOHARI WINDOW

I thought it'd be useful to Susan to review the concept of blind spots and I introduced it by explaining the Johari Window.

THE OPEN AREA

What you and others know about you is the Open Area of the Johari Window *(see Figure 1 below)*; you may also call this the Public Area.

THE HIDDEN AREA

What you know about yourself that others do not know is the Hidden or Private Area. This encompasses everything about you that you choose to keep to yourself.

BLIND SPOTS

The traits and behaviors others observe about you that *you* do not recognize are your Blind Spots. These are areas you may not have any idea exist but that others easily perceive (or suffer from!).

It is inevitable for us to regularly develop blind spots. If I had a big black spot on my forehead, you might be able to see it from a block away. But what about me? I wouldn't have any idea the black spot was there. It's my blind spot. The same inability to see the "black spot" applies to certain behaviors.

THE JOHARI WINDOW

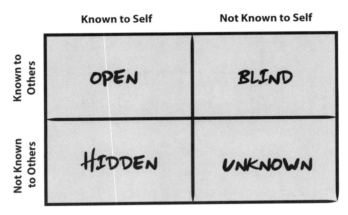

Figure 1

This leads to the question: how do we uncover and reduce our blind spots? We ask for feedback, increasing our awareness of them. Only when others act as a mirror I'm able to become aware of my blind spots. How do we reduce what is hidden or private? Through disclosure, we minimize what's hidden to others—and while it's good to support healthy boundaries it's also good to foster transparency in our working relationships.

The process I initiated with Susan was intended to uncover her blind spots so she could work on those areas where she lacked awareness. The process would also help her gain the confidence to deepen her working relationships by revealing more of herself with her colleagues.

THE JOHARI WINDOW:

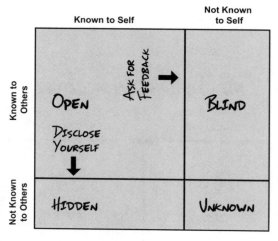

Figure 2

SUSAN'S LEADERSHIP PROFILE

As I sat in my office and reviewed the standard scores of Susan's leadership profile, I noticed what the appearance of her office suggested: she was detail oriented and organized. At the same time, her scores on Strategic Thinking and Future Focus were considerably low.

It's a stereotype, but we know that individuals tend to stand on one end or the other of the continuum between being organized, planful and methodical versus being somewhat messy, creative strategic thinkers. Susan was clearly on the organized and methodical end of the spectrum. Her profile also indicated that she had a low tolerance level for risk; she was practical and pragmatic, but not inclined to be creative and let her imagination roam.

So, in summary, this rock-solid manager held a good capacity to manage her emotional and intellectual self, relate well to others, and deliver reliable execution. However, I was *not* seeing the characteristics of a strategic thinker, someone capable of looking at the big picture and envisioning alternative scenarios while managing risk and creating a bold, daring future for an organization.

These discoveries built our momentum toward the 360° feedback process, which would be our next step. The 360° survey would include data from Susan's direct reports, her boss and peers, and all others who interacted frequently and meaningfully with her.

I found that something usually clicks in people's minds when they get to see their traits and tendencies (their leadership profile) and how those characteristics and habits are impacting others (the 360° feedback). I hoped to flip that switch for Susan!

THE 360° FEEDBACK

I planned to use our firm's 360° online feedback assessment for the wider circle of people around Susan, while I would conduct structured interviews for the key people around her—the inner circle.

That inner circle turned out to be seven key stakeholders in the organization, including the CEO and Susan's boss, the VP of engineering. This group was familiar with her performance and the way she got things done. They provided their point of view on Susan's strengths and weaknesses, though she was so good on so many fronts that many interviewees had to think hard about areas where she could improve. I included some open questions like, "If Susan were to take her game to the next level, what would that look like? What would she do differently than she does today?"

Her boss, Jeff, had an interesting reply. "Sometimes I feel as if Susan is constantly demoting herself," he said. "She goes too deep into the weeds, focusing on details that should be taken care of by someone on her team."

"How could she be more effective?" I asked.

"Susan should stay involved at a higher level of issues and push down decisions," Jeff said. "She has the intellectual capacity and the experience to become a great leader in our organization—but for her to get there, she needs to *do* less and *think* more."

The online 360° feedback report ended up including ratings and comments from more than thirty other people in the organization who interacted regularly with Susan in different capacities. They were asked to fill out a detailed online survey that accurately promised anonymity. It's a deeply embedded part of our culture that people shy away from providing feedback in a direct, face-to face, on-the-spot, real-time constructive way. Fear of damaging the relationship or alienating the other person, among myriad other reasons, creates strong motivation for them to keep their opinions to themselves. That's why the online 360° feedback process works so well. It gives people a chance (which they may have been craving) to anonymously and safely describe how others interact with them and their reaction to that.

The data collected by the 360° feedback is organized into four major domains:

1. **LEADING SELF:** with a focus on intrapersonal areas, such as managing emotions, strategic thinking, coping with stress, and being open to feedback.

2. **LEADING OTHERS:** focused on interpersonal areas, such as displaying competency in listening, resolving conflict, and influencing skills.

3. **LEADING THE ORGANIZATION:** with a focus on big picture, organizational and systemic issues, such as managing change, creating an inspirational vision, organizational awareness, and market and competition focus.

4. **MANAGING IMPLEMENTATION:** with a focus on execution and getting work done; key competencies are delegation, teamwork, and monitoring performance.

Two weeks after discussing her leadership profile, Susan and I met to review her feedback report. Despite the neatness (some might say starkness) of her office, I asked Susan if we could talk in a conference room instead.

"Sure," she said, though she gave me a quizzical look.

"I want us to focus on the feedback, and there are too many distractions in here," I explained. "The beeping of your computer when you get an e-mail, someone coming in to ask a quick question—they seem like little things but can demand your attention."

As if to prove my point, her computer issued a low beep and Susan instinctively turned toward it. Then she turned back to me and smiled sheepishly. "Conference room it is."

The conference room was a long, narrow office at the end of the hall. A table for twelve dominated the middle of the room; blinds framed the glass doors. They could be easily shut for privacy. The room smelled like coffee from a recent meeting, and she poured herself a cup from the still-warm pot.

With a plethora of data in front of us, the picture became clear and compelling: Susan was considered a brilliant and hard-working engineer with good people skills; able to build solid working relationships, she was extremely practical and an eminent problem solver. She had a high level of personal effectiveness; she could get things done and successfully engage other people in doing the same. She could skillfully lead her team through complex execution processes and provide practical solutions to the roadblocks generated on the technology front. She also was adept at navigating through the "white spaces" of the organization, creating a good level of cross-functional coordination with the marketing group, manufacturing team, and key supporting functions (Finance, IT, HR, etc.). All of which are positive traits.

Where Susan fell short, however, involved creating a compelling vision for the organization, sharing the responsibility for setting strategic direction for her department and the company, understanding the forces at work in the market, and anticipating and countering the moves of the competition—in other words, all the areas integral to any success as the VP of engineering.

The composite image of how Susan was perceived clearly emerged from the feedback. She was great at execution ... of a strategy conceived by someone else. Not a flattering impression, considering her aspirations.

Susan's coffee remained untouched. She was nodding, flipping through the paperwork before us. "So," she said thoughtfully, "by focusing on getting going, I forget to reflect on where to go ..." She trailed off briefly but then declared, "I'm not going to be brought down by all this feedback. I'm ready to create an action plan. Let's do it! And let's do it right away!"

I smiled. "Wouldn't that be continuing the same style that you are trying to change?"

I believe that the stronger a trait or a tendency, the more we are "enslaved" or taken hostage by it. I'm asked many times by my students and clients, "What is the ideal leadership profile?" The ideal profile allows the flexibility to react appropriately according to circumstances. Since Susan was strongly action oriented, I wasn't surprised that she reacted by wanting to take action. On the other hand, if an individual is strongly analytical and reflective, she will dive into analysis and reflection. The more one sits in the middle of the continuum between these traits, the more one can flex and respond fittingly to the situation.

Susan stopped in her tracks. After a long silence, she started laughing—at her situation, her impulsiveness, her action-oriented personality, and at the way she tried to correct all of the above through more action. I joined her in the spirited and insightful moment and blurted, "Now you know why angels fly!"

Susan looked at me, puzzled. "Why do angels fly?"

I quoted the humorous G. K. Chesterton, "Angels fly … because they take themselves lightly!"

Humor was the perfect element to alleviate the stress generated by seeing herself in the mirror and realizing that she needed to embark on a personal transformation process.

Susan and I agreed that her action-oriented style, developed and nurtured over many years, was a very strong trait; it made her successful at getting fast results. That leadership style would work brilliantly for operational issues, but she required something else to engage in a personal and professional transformation process. Susan needed deep reflection and a strategic approach to change.

"Take some time," I told her. "Read your feedback report again. Maybe share it with your husband. Bask in all the great comments, and reflect on the areas we'll need to focus on in order to propel your career forward."

She smiled and nodded, but she was already looking pensive, less certain. She shook my hand, and we agreed to meet a week later.

THE DOOR TO CHANGE

An individual's personal and professional development is not an event, but a process. That was Susan's first challenge. After collecting rich data from her profile and 360° feedback, it was time to take stock, establish priorities, and create a development plan and an action plan. The development plan would outline the areas we needed to focus on, and the action plan would spell out the specific steps to take in each area. The action plan would include new *practices* that would help internalize and anchor new behaviors, new ways of responding to challenges; incorporating these new practices is what makes the change sustainable and lasting.

For our next meeting, I again suggested we use the conference room.

Susan showed up for our meeting in a somber mood. After we had settled in, she said, "I read the feedback report a couple more times."

"And ...?"

"And I've become seriously depressed about the whole thing," she said. "I've dedicated so many years to working here, but I feel as though my peers only focused on finding fault in me." She bit her lip. "I feel I've done so much and am still not good enough."

People like Susan—people with a strong, harsh inner critic—often do not focus on the multitude of good ratings and observations. They zero in on the few low scores and negative comments. When emotions get involved, they taint or even obscure the whole feedback.

Quite simply, Susan lost perspective. I needed to bring her back.

Knowing that she was pragmatic, demanded accuracy in data, and had a powerful rational side; I asked for her impression on what percentage of the feedback was negative.

"I can't say *precisely*," she said, glancing at the feedback before her. "But I'd guess at least seventy or eighty percent."

"Susan, this is an important exercise to make sure we get an accurate impression of the feedback provided by your colleagues," I explained. "I'll start reading the Comments section of the report, and I'd like us to determine if each comment is a positive or a negative."

"Okay," she said, almost defiantly. "Let's do it."

As I read the two- or three-line comments written by her colleagues about each competency, we tallied the results in three columns—positive, negative, and mixed—and asked her to tell me where to mark each comment.

Midway through the fourth page of comments, Susan laughed grudgingly and stopped me. "Okay, okay, I get your point!" she said. Of thirty-one comments, twenty-nine were positive and two mixed. Not one was totally negative.

Not relenting, I continued, "Let's look at the quantitative data, the numbers. I know you like numbers." From the twenty-eight different competencies that our 360° feedback assessment measures,

Susan was rated somewhere in the eightieth or ninetieth percentile on more than twenty of them.

On only five items was she below average—all in the domain called Managing the Organization. They included:

1. **STRATEGIC THINKING** – a synthesizing process utilizing intuition and creativity whose outcome is "an integrated perspective."

2. **EXTERNAL AWARENESS** – Identifying and keeping up with trends that affect the organization. Keeping an eye on the competition.

3. **INSPIRATIONAL VISION** – Building a shared and inspirational vision.

4. **INNOVATION** – Applying creative thinking and challenging the status quo.

5. **ORGANIZATIONAL AWARENESS** – Understanding organizational and social dynamics.

"I'm aware now of what I was experiencing," Susan said, a very faint blush gracing her cheeks. "I became emotional. That tainted my impression. Looking over all the feedback, it's easy to see that if I want to be a real contender for the position, I need to work and think differently. But I don't have a clue how to do that or where to start." Then she added, very softly, "And I don't know if I can change who I am."

Susan was expressing her awareness of her limitations, and her doubts about the whole process. It was a point of vulnerability, a turning point, and an opening for transformation. She was saying, "I'm ready but would/could this work? Is it even possible?"

I assured her that at some point, we all wonder whether we are capable of change. Then I drew a triangle and wrote the word *change* inside it. *(See Figure 3)*

Figure 3

"Maybe we want to be better listeners," I continued, "or to delegate more, or, like you, Susan, be more strategic in our thinking—more visionary, more focused on setting direction and coming up with game-changing ideas. To do so, we could try to access change through two doors: The Door of Feelings or the Door of Thoughts." *(See Figure 4)*

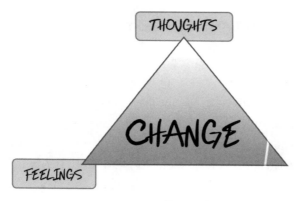

Figure 4

"It stands to reason that if we change our thinking and the feelings that influence and shape how we are in the world, then we would change," I explained. "If you change your *thinking,* Susan—from a tactical, pragmatic, problem-solving mode to a strategic, visionary one—you would be able to change. If you change the *feeling* of being satisfied with immediate results to deriving fulfillment from conceiving new solutions and bringing about innovation, you would also be able to change."

Susan listened intently.

"But changing how we feel and think about the world, ourselves, and the challenges that come our way involves personality change, and that's a long process that takes years," I said. "We don't want to focus on personality change. We want to access change right away through the third door: the Door of Behavior." *(See Figure 5)*

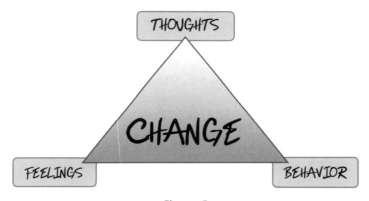

Figure 5

"Luckily, we can open the Door of Behavior any time, and we can literally change aspects of our behavior overnight, just because we say so. We have much more power over our behavior than we do over our deeply ingrained personality."

Susan nodded, seemingly open.

"It's not in my nature to be loud. *But I could raise my voice!*" I said with bravado. "And I could start being louder at meetings where people complained they couldn't hear me well."

I told Susan that I'm naturally shy and introverted, but every now and then, I teach large groups because it fits with my desire to share what I have learned with others, and that's who I want to be. If I had waited for my personality to change to start teaching, I'd still be waiting.

Through the 1980s and 1990s, my work focused on different ways of discovering who we are, so I created personality and leadership profiles and studied archetypes and typology. The adage "Know thyself" ruled my work. Later, I realized that knowing oneself is only the first step of the development process. The second part is discovering who we *want to be* and how to accomplish that. Over the years, I helped people work "against" their traits and tendencies, shaping who they were to live a purposeful, intentional life aligned with who they wanted to be—some wanted to become more creative and innovative, others strategic thinkers or relationship builders, everyone following their heart's desire.

"As we behave in a certain way, again and again, we change who we are in the world," I told Susan. "The old saying from our grandmas is true: 'Fake it till you make it.' If you are always practical and pragmatic, for example, you could—when appropriate—'fake' being creative and innovative until the reward of finding new solutions to old problems became an irresistible force."

Susan looked pensive. After a moment of silence, she asked, "What if this is who I am? How could I be who I'm not? What if this is me—practical, pragmatic, action-oriented Susan, a problem solver?"

Here it was, the fulcrum of this conversation––the fork in the road.

"Susan, you have choices," I said. "You can either focus on who you are or on who you want to be. It's your call."

She still looked undecided. Maybe she needed another little push.

"Practical, pragmatic, action-oriented, and problem solver constitutes a group of muscles that you have developed very well," I told her. "You've become world class at lifting weight using those muscles. Are you interested in developing your strategic thinking muscles?"

Susan let out an audible sigh of relief. "Absolutely," she answered. "Yes. That makes sense. You're talking like my husband. I keep thinking about how he engaged with a coach to improve his serve at tennis and how happy he is about the results!"

I smiled. "You can also achieve what *you* want. It may be difficult, but from what I know about you, you don't shrink away from difficulty."

"No, I don't." Then, with a mischievous smile, she asked, "How are we going to be strategic about creating this change?"

We both laughed as the tension in the room dissipated. Now it was a matter of rolling up our sleeves and getting to work.

During the rest of the meeting, I outlined a possible plan. We started with a time management process in which we looked at her calendar over a four-week period and classified each item into one of four categories. I drew a pyramid with four layers for this exercise *(see Figure 6)*. The top or smallest layer was *Mission Critical,* the core of what Susan needed to address in order to do her job. The second layer was *Very Important* (not critical but still key to her job). The third layer was *Good to Have,* things that would be great to complete but that weren't a high priority. The final layer was *Why the Heck Am I Doing This?* For Susan, this category included meetings where she was neither receiving nor adding value but was nevertheless attending. By looking at one of the most precious assets we have—time—we freed up about fifteen percent of Susan's calendar by focusing on *Mission Critical* and *Very Important* issues. It's a priorities exercise.

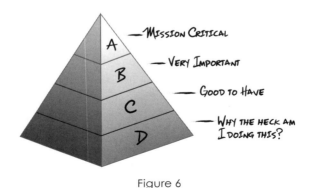

Figure 6

I mentioned to Susan that there would be several phases to the rest of our plan and that, since she was a quick study, we would be able to move decisively.

In the first phase, I told her, we would focus on creating more available time for her to become the creative, strategic thinker that she wanted and needed to be, while keeping an eye on execution. To accomplish the feat of making more time available for herself, she needed to:

1. Coach her team through a learning process that would allow them to work more autonomously, assuming a deeper and wider area of responsibility, and

2. Create a solid plan to delegate more day-to-day decision-making and problem solving to the team.

These two objectives complement each other; indeed, one couldn't work without the other. Paradoxically, increasing delegation to create more time for the leader always requires investing more time at the beginning of the process to make sure that the delegation was made responsibly and effectively.

From what I had learned, too much was going through Susan. She was making too many decisions. The whole team was too dependent on her word every step of the way, a common flaw for many leaders. It is flattering and supportive to our self-esteem to have people come to us for answers and decisions; because of this, leaders fall in the trap of becoming the person with all the answers. This leads to slow and ineffective decision-making, and the leader becomes a choke point that drags down the process. The leader also starts making *flawed* decisions, because most of the time, her team members are the ones who know the details and could make high quality, informed decisions.

In order to escape this cycle, Susan would need to engage her team on a steep learning curve, coach them to become more autonomous, and distribute leadership and responsibilities amongst the whole team. By the same token, her team members would need to learn what was guiding Susan's decision-making processes and become more self-directed. This could not be done without coaching them to perform at a higher level.

Susan stood and started pacing the length of the conference room. She lifted one of the blinds and peeked out at the rest of the office, then let the blind fall back down. "It's overwhelming," she said, turning back to me. "But I'm feeling optimistic."

I needed to confirm that she was indeed ready to do the work. "Checking again, Susan … just in case … from one to ten, what is your level of commitment to this process?"

With a glint of determination in her eyes, Susan sat back down. "Twelve."

A SYSTEM OF SUPPORT

My next step was to interview the seven members of Susan's team. I needed to understand further how they actually worked with her in order to develop a solid plan of action.

As I went through these interviews, I found that all of them were intrigued and interested in supporting my coaching process with Susan. Every individual had provided feedback through the 360° feedback assessment. But that feedback pertained to providing Susan with an impression of how her proficiency and skill was perceived in a number of management and leadership competencies. The interviews with Susan's direct reports were focused on looking in-depth at:

+ The team as a whole, a working system;
+ Each individual's capabilities as perceived by themselves and the other team members, and;
+ The quality of interaction between the team and Susan.

Here is what we found, and what I recommended to address the root causes of the issues uncovered:

A. THE TEAM AS A WHOLE

The team was functioning in a typical spoke-wheel fashion; no real "teamwork" was done *(see Figure 7)*. They were individually reporting to Susan in their different capacities and functions. In a typical meeting, one member would report to Susan and interact with her while the other team members waited their turn.

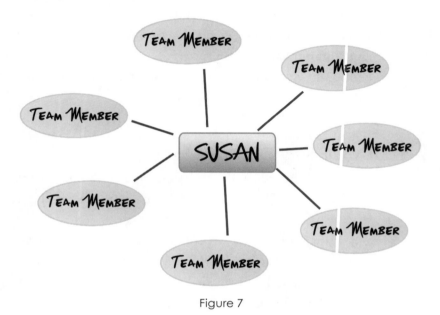

Figure 7

Several team members said that, while waiting for their turns to talk, it wasn't unusual to see some of the others checking email on their smartphones or looking at their laptops.

A couple of problems usually arise from this dynamic. The first is that the team is not engaging in problem solving as a thinking body. I have found time and again that the smartest person in a meeting is never as intelligent as the collective intellectual power present in the room. This team was missing the power of that collective intelligence. Its members were not learning from one another.

The second problem is ingrained in the very nature of the spoke-wheel dynamic. By operating this way, the only person on the team with a systemic view is the one in the center—Susan. She held the answers and, thus, was the only person able to make sound decisions. She was working as the main thinking part of the team instead of creating the conditions for all to contribute their thoughts, the foundation for true distributed leadership.

I needed to suggest to Susan how to change the way the team interacted with her and each other so they could:

1. Start working as a thinking, powerful system; and
2. Push decision-making further down while appropriately distributing leadership.

This graphic illustrates the interactivity of such a team. It is not a coincidence that the graphic looks like a network. *(See Figure 8)*

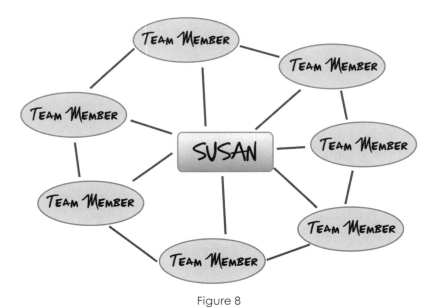

Figure 8

B. ADDRESSING TEAM MEMBERS' CAPABILITIES

As in many fast growing environments, several team members had been recently promoted, sometimes beyond their level of expertise and experience. In their previous positions, five out of the seven members reported to someone with deep experience in his or her field and were accustomed to receiving thorough guidance and direction. Their level of autonomy and inner direction was not developed to the point needed for their new positions on Susan's team. I represented the way the team was performing and delivering on their responsibilities in the following way: *(See Figure 9)*

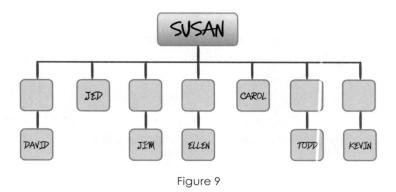

Figure 9

The graphic intends to show that a few members were performing below the level that would allow for distributed leadership and autonomous decision-making. The five team members on the lower tier of the chart would normally consult with an immediate superior (as they did in their previous roles), but the box on that level was vacant. Therefore, all questions were eventually presented to Susan. We would gear our next effort toward bringing those five team members up to the level of competency required for them to operate effectively. *(See Figure 10)*

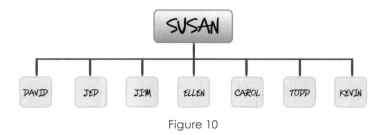

Figure 10

C. TEAM INTERACTIONS WITH SUSAN

From the interviews, it became clear that team members were receiving straightforward directions from Susan but not learning the rationale behind her decisions. When I met with her the following week, I used the old adage, "You're giving them fish but not teaching them how to fish."

Susan nodded. She appeared serious and ready to work.

"One of your team members told me that it's like playing chess and being told where to move each piece on the board without understanding the rules of the game," I continued. "They know that the *quality* of your decision-making processes is good—results speak to it—but they're not learning enough to become self-reliant."

As she nodded in agreement, I could see in Susan's eyes that she was rapidly absorbing this information. "That's the first issue," I continued, "the second one is that you're addressing each of them individually without engaging the whole team in processing the information and making decisions."

In a rare moment of defensiveness, she said, "But it would take so *long* to discuss my thinking and then engage the whole team. Talking with each of them about his or her area of responsibility is so much faster!"

"You're right," I replied. "Raising the performance of your team will take more time at the beginning."

"I'm feeling impatient again. Here's my action-oriented Susan showing up. Please continue."

"Good level of awareness, Susan. I suggest you introduce a distinction between things to discuss one-on-one without wasting the team's time and other issues that need the combined effort of the team. In that way, team meetings would be reserved for team issues, like setting and reviewing team goals, the discussion of interdependencies, coordination between different team members, and brainstorming solutions for problems that affected the team as a whole. I suggest to open things for discussion and to share at some point, not only your point of view but also the reasoning behind it."

Susan looked around the conference room, as if she were envisioning her team members surrounding her. "Yes. That makes sense."

After that, the review of the team members' capabilities went smoothly. Susan knew that there were quite a few "green" people on her team, and we discussed ways of rapidly bringing them up to speed. She committed to co-creating a development plan with each of her reports that would include one-on-one time with her and other resources she'd bring in to support their learning process.

Susan mentioned that "the discussion about how she interacted with her team was enlightening." She viewed her style as one of rapidly taking charge, indicating next steps, and bringing a fast orientation towards execution. We both agreed that her style was suitable and appropriate for crisis or emergency situations when there's no time for explanations and creating learning moments.

On a daily basis, however, she needed to focus on delegation.

Susan and I reviewed the concepts of situational leadership developed by Hersey and Blanchard in the mid-1970s. They categorized leadership styles according to four *behavior* types, which they named S1 through S4:

S1: TELLING – Characterized by one-way communication in which the leader defines the role of the individual and indicates the what, when, and how of the task. Susan needed to reduce her use of this command and control approach to a minimum. The only appropriate situations to use this approach would be urgent or emergency matters that left no time for lengthy explanations.

S2: SELLING – The leader provides the direction but uses two-way communication and provides the support needed for the individual to buy into the process. This is more of an influencing and persuading process. Susan would use this approach for the broad strokes of strategic direction of the group. As the head of her group, she needed to bring leadership into setting the team's focus and defining its course of action to have the necessary alignment within the department.

S3: PARTICIPATING – The leader shares decision-making about how aspects of the task are accomplished and provides less task behaviors while maintaining high relationship behavior. This is a highly participative approach. Susan would adopt this leadership style for those specific issues that constituted the charter of her team, such as the management of interdependencies within the different areas of the department.

S4: DELEGATING – The leader is still involved in decisions; however, the process and responsibility is passed to the individual or group while the leader monitors progress. Susan and each member of her team—her direct reports—would jointly develop a crisp description of each team member's roles and responsibilities. Susan's role would be limited to tracking progress and ensuring alignment with the overall strategic focus of the department.

As I finished, Susan nodded. "I see it now. When the floor is on fire, I make my guys bring a few buckets of water as fast as they can. But I'm treating everything as a fire emergency, and they're not learning." She was focused but smiling, and I knew she was proud of her insight.

We agreed to conduct a couple of meetings with the team to discuss the findings of my interviews and jointly design development and action plans.

Before that week ended, we had the first meeting with the team, no laptops or smartphones allowed.

"I wanted to share with you all the findings and conclusions of the interviews," Susan said. Candidly, she also explained the process of change they would all undertake together to become more autonomous. The team members looked at one another. Then they all looked at Susan. "I'm determined to change how we work together," she said. "Let's look first at how we organize our meetings and how we are going to engage everybody in the room at all times ... I have a few ideas."

She glanced at me, and then she started laughing. "Wait—I'm doing it again! I see everybody looking at me, and I start telling you what we're going to do. Isn't that the dynamic we're trying to change?"

The whole team joined Susan in laughter. It was a light moment, but an insightful one. Susan was bright and a quick study. She did get it. And fast.

We used the ensuing discussion to role model and practice how the team would work as a whole—as an intelligent system where every member was engaged, thinking, and contributing to the conversation. I thought the team turned a corner. Once a team discovers how it can operate as a vibrant, intelligent system, it can't go back to the old ways. It's too painful and frustrating. The team agreed on setting a charter for the group and outlining a clear set of issues that would be discussed using the new approach.

To address the remaining issues uncovered by the interviews, Susan and I worked to design the process for the one-on-one meetings. In these meetings, Susan would be able to co-design a development plan with each team member and the action plan that would allow the individual to move through the process.

She and I agreed to refine this process as we worked together. My role would be mostly to facilitate the meetings with her team members and keep things on track.

We met a few days later with Jed, one of the most senior members of her team. Jed had been with the company seven years, the last three of which he worked as a direct report to Susan. He was in charge of product engineering, and Susan considered him her right hand. She was very supportive of helping him develop his career within the company.

Jed showed up to our meeting with a big coffee mug in his hand and a serious expression on his face. A tall, lanky engineer—probably in his mid-thirties but still looking like a teenager—he was dressed in typical Silicon Valley attire: button-down shirt, chinos, and a pair of loafers. There was something tentative about his demeanor and I had the impression that he was experiencing a little hesitation about our meeting. He mentioned that he didn't know what to expect but was looking forward to our conversation.

Susan started following the process we'd reviewed in advance of this meeting. These were the steps that were covered.

1. Develop a clear description of career ambitions and aspirations as a backdrop to each team member's professional development effort. Jed was very clear about this line of inquiry.

2. Identify the competencies and knowledge needed to perform the member's current job with excellence. Jed's role required mastery in the multiple complex interdependencies between engineering, research and development (R&D), product marketing, and manufacturing.

3. Fill the gap between the existing level of competency and knowledge and the one required for excellence. Jed needed to deepen his knowledge of R&D and manufacturing processes,

65

improve existing relationships with some key individuals in the plants, and initiate an accelerated learning process of the company's mobile technology.

4. For every competency gap, create a list of actions to close that gap. Typical actions included completing a course or training, reading a book and holding conversations with knowledgeable folks. A list of actionable items was jointly designed with Jed to address his learning needs.

5. Identify the organizational resource to consult as a first recourse when at a loss in the process. One person in the R&D department and one in the main manufacturing plant were identified as "mentors" to Jed in their areas of expertise. Susan committed to identifying a resource for Jed in the mobile technology division.

6. Plot a timeline for completion of each stage of the process, and specify key milestones along the way. Jed had twelve weeks to complete this process and would identify the key milestones with his new mentors.

7. Maintain a method of tracking and recording progress. Jed would keep a log of activities. At mid-point and at the end of the process, the mentors would report on his progress and recommend further next steps to keep the learning on track.

We repeated this professional development process with each team member. As with Jed, ambitious twelve-week programs were designed for all team members, with each program uniquely tailored to their strengths and weaknesses. Some team members, for example, needed more technical training, while others needed to learn to manage underperforming employees.

The process was presented to the team as strictly voluntary, but it was clear that if anyone did not see this as an opportunity to enhance and embrace his or her professional future, Susan would find another suitable position for that individual in the organization.

The caution was unnecessary. All team members saw this activity as their chance to improve their professional stance and move forward in their careers. The level of excitement was the fuel to propel the process forward.

After a few weeks of this focused effort, Susan and her team started seeing concrete results. Susan found she had more time available, because her reports were acting more and more autonomously and needing less of her attention.

At some point, an interesting development occurred: the team decided that they didn't need Susan in every single team meeting. They did need to coordinate their actions in those areas in which they had interdependencies, but regular team meetings would be devoted to issues of higher-level complexity where Susan's input would be of more value or she could help resolve any conflict.

The group enjoyed their new level of autonomy. One of the team members told me, "We're feeling like kids who were given the key to our house for the first time. Now we can go in and out without having to ask Mom."

Susan was attending fewer unnecessary meetings, and things were looking up. It was time to increase our focus on the next phase.

STRATEGIC THINKING

From the beginning, I anticipated that my work with Susan was going to be satisfying. I was right. She was already making large strides to improve her straightforward, execution-oriented leadership style. Now she needed to harness that style and direct it to include a different set of tasks. By framing it this way—strategic thinking as a set of tasks—Susan's mind opened up to the possibilities. *She didn't need to develop a completely new style, but instead apply her existing style to a new set of tasks.* Susan found the idea intriguing. As she put it, she was willing to "try it on for size."

To start stretching Susan's strategic thinking muscles, I asked her to map her job. The idea was to create a graphic representation of all the areas for which she was responsible. Utilizing an off-the-shelf software program, Susan created a colorful map. On it, she organized her different areas of responsibility in nine clusters. *(See Figure 11)*

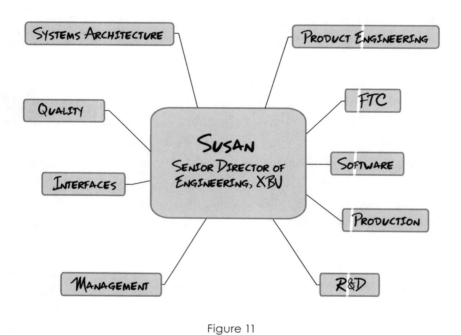

Figure 11

She then went deeper into each cluster and included the different aspects covered within each area of responsibility. *(See Figure 12)*

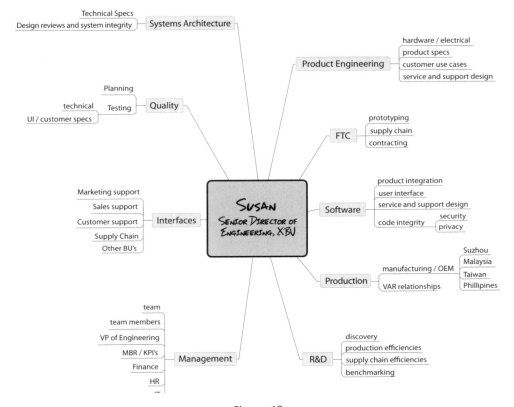

Figure 12

This exercise was intended to further Susan's capacity to look at a big picture perspective—in this case, her job—from different points of view. What follows are some of the ways in which we used strategic maps and, specifically, the map that Susan had created.

A. RESOURCES

Susan asked her direct reports to create "people maps"—maps of their areas of responsibility—and to populate every section in their maps with the names of the people working in those areas. Each person on the map was assigned one of three colors by his/her manager:

1. Green, for those who were highly proficient;
2. Yellow, for those performing well but in need of further training and professional development; and
3. Red, for those who were somewhat under-performing.

These maps were to be printed poster-size: twenty-four by thirty-six inches.

Once Susan's team members had completed this task, we taped the maps on the conference room wall. I asked Susan to step back and reflect on what she was seeing, without going into specific detail. I wanted her to develop a general impression of the "people maps" in front of her.

After looking at the maps for some time, Susan said it was obvious to her that some of the sections on these maps had too many "yellow" folks—people requiring training and further work to reach the level of proficiency needed in their jobs.

"I knew this was happening," Susan said, "but I hadn't exactly known the extent of the issue."

That explained the difficulties she had been experiencing with those departments.

As we were not focusing on strategic planning, but only assessing the big picture on different horizons, I asked Susan not to start thinking about what to do right now. Instead, I advised her to schedule a meeting with her team to address the "people maps."

Susan shook her head, gesturing toward the maps. "This is not a minor issue," she insisted, "and it needs to be resolved. I already have a couple of ideas about how to go about it. Could we look into this right now?"

Her action-oriented mind would need to wait. I tried to slow her down. "I suggest that now is not the time to start planning what to do with the insights you may be developing. Postpone this until you meet with your team and have a chance to assign responsibilities."

Susan frowned.

I added, "Of course, you need to take a serious look at your people and assess their capabilities, and you need to proactively plan for their training. But right now, let's keep moving forward. The time will come for you to revisit the areas that need urgent attention and do it *with your team*. Remember, we need to free your time for more strategic work!"

Susan glanced again at the maps, absorbing all the yellow dots. I could see that she was still tempted to push back; she wanted to start planning how to deal with the people who were underperforming *now*.

Finally, she sighed and relaxed her shoulders. "I'm starting to catch myself jumping to action and trying to do things on my own instead of maintaining a wider perspective and putting my team to work on these issues. This seems to be quite a deep groove I've dug for myself!"

I assured Susan that her bias for action was an extremely positive tendency that—paired with her intelligence—allowed her to get things done. It was just not the right tool for the personal transformation she was trying to accomplish—to develop her inner capacity for strategic thinking and then find the right people to execute her vision.

"This is what my boss has been doing all along," Susan said, with an *I-get-it-now* look on her face. "Except I've been on the execution side of that equation."

"You're right," I said. "Now you're finding a new approach, where you'll emphasize being part of the strategizing process. Then you'll be able to empower your team and delegate execution. As a useful way of practicing that, how about we focus on succession planning next?"

In preparation for the next team session, Susan asked her direct reports to identify the key people on their people map—in other words, people whose departures would cause serious disruption to the department's continuous delivery of work. There were eleven in total; Susan labeled them "key engineers." Then she asked her team members to identify the individuals who could step in to replace any potentially departing key engineer. We learned that only four of the eleven key engineers had someone among their teams who could, if necessary, fill the role.

The urgent need for succession planning became evident. It would be easy to do this in conjunction with the training effort.

Out of this modeling activity, Susan reported a deeper understanding of:

1. Focusing on big-picture perspective;
2. Identifying those areas and issues that needed attention;
3. Brainstorming with the team, and creating a plan to tackle the areas and issues identified;
4. Assigning the right people to execute on that plan.

B. TIME ALLOCATION

There were more ways to mine Susan's job map. For our next meeting, I asked her to write on the map the time she'd need to effectively work on and supervise each of the different areas covered. Some areas would need some weekly time, others daily or monthly. Eventually, we translated everything into weekly time. Finally, I asked Susan to add up all the different times in each area. *(See Figure 13)*

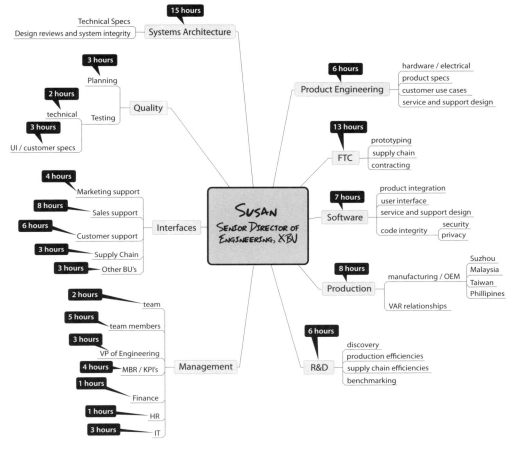

Figure 13

When she finished, she sat back in her conference room chair and laughed. "I find it hilarious and sad at the same time. How could the time required to do my job amount to 106 hours a week?" She laughed some more.

"Now I understand," she said, "why I'm chronically overloaded with work and eternally finding too much on my plate. It also emphasizes my need to delegate more."

"How do you feel about this idea of creating a map of the field and then using different 'lenses' to look at the map from different angles?"

Susan thought for a moment. "I'm starting to appreciate it as a tool to gain insight into what needs work. My natural tendency is to look at something and immediately start creating a list—in my mind or on paper—of things to do. I know it's silly, but sometimes I jump in my car with my family, start driving, and then think about where to go!"

C. JOB DESCRIPTION

The next step was going to be the clincher for the process. I asked Susan to clearly determine her job description and to create a short high-level list of her responsibilities. Then we looked into the decisions, actions and tasks needed to execute those responsibilities. We finally contrasted this list with her initial map that called for one hundred and six hours per week. Susan's insight from this activity was that she'd become accustomed to diving deeply "into the weeds" and staying at that level.

The objective of this exercise was to move Susan to the next step, where she could devote about eighty percent of her time to tactical issues and reserve twenty percent for strategic conversations, big picture thinking, reflection and dialogue about the technology, markets, competition, and the company's pipeline of innovation. I call this a "bifocal approach." At times, Susan needed to look more closely into her tasks and the execution of her deliverables; at others, she needed to view the big picture for course correction moves. This wasn't either/or. She needed to find a way to do both. She had to be tactical and strategic, continually adjusting the ratio between these two ways of working based on her current reality.

Once Susan had a clear list of the decisions, actions and tasks, I suggested that anything coming her way that *wasn't* on that list was actually a red flag. It meant that someone on her team—for whatever reason—was not doing his or her job. In that case, Susan's organizational responsibility and best use of her time was not to take care of the issue by adding it to her own plate, but to:

1. Identify the individual or team responsible for solving the issue;

2. Understand what brought the issue to her instead of it being solved at the right level of the organization (i.e., lack of knowledge or experience, confusion about the decision-making capability of the individual, dissent with another area in the organization); and

3. Coach the person through the process to resolve the issue or find the appropriate resource to do so. The issue would only be considered resolved if the responsible party *learned* how to handle similar issues in the future.

This process would call for more time from Susan to tackle issues and negotiate situations—until her staff completed most of their learning curve, thus freeing more of her time.

This was a good time to take inventory of the intense work and plan its final phase. By now, Susan and I had explored and discussed the following:

1. Her tendency to be detail-oriented, a problem solver and engage in fast-paced action, as shown on her leadership profile;

2. The feedback from many coworkers expressing appreciation for Susan's high level of competency and noticing her lack of focus on creating an inspirational vision for her team and setting a strategic path for the organization;

3. How to create more availability by better managing her time and priorities at work to mostly focus on "mission critical" and "very important" issues;

4. Coaching her team to work more autonomously and assume more responsibility, allowing her to delegate more; and

5. The need to apply strategic thinking to her role in the organization and balance a focus on execution and tactical issues with
attention to the big picture and the future direction of the organization.

Susan and I had worked together for almost four months. She
grasped all the new concepts I'd introduced, and was clear about her
new, evolving style of exercising leadership by balancing strategic
and tactical thinking. By that time, her team was acting with increased autonomy and executing well. Things were looking good.

STRATEGIC THINKING AS A PRACTICE

The next step: to incorporate a new practice into Susan's work life—
sustained focus on strategic thinking. She would hold more strategic conversations and dedicated time to look into the future and
imagine new possibilities. When we have a certain trait or tendency,
I explained to her, it reflects in our behavior in direct proportion to
its strength. When a certain trait is not predominant in our psychological makeup, we're less likely to enact it and bring it to life, even
if it's our deepest desire and aspiration. We have an insight *(I need to
be a more strategic thinker)*—and then return to our old ways *(I'm going
to make a list of things to do today)*.

Over time, Susan had developed a strong tendency toward action,
executing plans and getting things done. To incorporate strategic
thinking into her life, Susan scheduled time on her calendar, three
times a week, to focus on this new area of personal and professional
growth. In those time slots, she performed one or more of the following tasks:

1. Identifying and focusing on the most strategic aspects of her
job;

2. Conducting strategic conversations with key folks inside and outside the organization;

3. Learning more about what the company's R&D department was working on and understanding the pipeline of new products and services planned for the short- and long-term future;

4. Talking to the company's most innovative customers about the evolution of their markets and their vision of the future;

5. Identifying and researching upcoming market trends;

6. Following and anticipating competitors' moves, deepening understanding of how to gain a competitive advantage in the marketplace, and identifying new opportunities for the company;

7. Keeping abreast of the latest scientific and technological research that could affect the future of the organization;

8. Identifying potential strategic alliances with companies focused on adjacent markets; and

9. Investigating the world of start-ups to detect possible future targets for acquisition that may generate synergy with the current or future strategy of the company.

Susan embarked on these new activities with enormous energy. She told me that she was deeply enjoying the subsequent conversations and using her intellect in a different way. As I listened carefully, I could tell her voice had changed; it had risen from an all-business, practical monotone to a voice containing a lilt of enthusiasm. It was good to hear.

A number of times, we revisited the concept of not making this an either/or but a both/and practice. Susan was to dedicate the bulk of her time to creating and overseeing excellent execution by her engineering group and some meaningful time developing this new side of her, the visionary capacity to co-create the future of the organization.

CHANGING FIRST IMPRESSIONS

People often experience great resistance to seeing change in others because they are locked into their first first impressions. The next hurdle was to change the CEO and management team impression of Susan.

They currently viewed her as a no-nonsense, pragmatic, resourceful individual with great problem-solving skills, someone who would get things done. Though positive, this was not the thinking partner they would call on for assessing the direction of the company and finding new paths to success. Thus, there was a clear need for Susan to work on changing their impression of her.

I introduced this new focus for our work by relating to Susan how I got interested in the fascinating and challenging business of "updating" people's impressions of their colleagues. I started to research and seriously think on this issue after a trip to my native Argentina. I traveled to Patagonia to visit with an old friend who had moved from Buenos Aires to the south, where he'd bought a ranch. He wanted to raise his four sons in a rural, natural environment (and enjoy the great fly-fishing rivers!).

After arriving at a small town near my friend's ranch, I stopped for directions. "Hi," I said to a local. "I'm trying to get to my friend Pablo's ranch. Could you please indicate how to get there?"

"Oh, yes," the local said, smiling. "Pablo, the newcomer. Take this road another eight kilometers and ..."

"Are we talking about the same person? My friend Pablo moved to this area about seven years ago ..."

"Is Pablo tall, blond, and has four sons?"

"Yes, that's him!"

"Okay, then," said the man. "Eight kilometers straight ahead, the ranch will be on your left."

As I was driving to my friend's ranch, I kept thinking that after seven years, Pablo was still the *newcomer*. Amazing. Seven years seemed a long enough time to become part of the community and leave the newcomer moniker to more recent arrivals.

This was very similar to the problem my clients faced at times: how to alter others' first impressions after old patterns of behavior had changed.

I had a client, Harry, who received feedback from his co-workers that his listening skills were not well developed. He interrupted, cut people off, and would wait until someone else finished what they were saying just to continue with what he had in mind. Harry was definitely not a good listener. He knew this was a problem, but until he received feedback from over twenty colleagues—including his boss, peers and direct reports—he had no idea how deeply it affected people around him. He focused intently on turning the situation around and becoming someone with whom people could communicate well. After three or four months of this effort he received fresh feedback about his progress. That's when Harry realized that—to his great frustration—regardless of his earnest efforts, people were still convinced that he wasn't really listening to them.

When I researched this area, I uncovered the reasons why first impressions burrow so deeply into people's memories and are hard to change. Our minds are always looking for the most efficient and economical way of navigating the world. To do that, it records impressions with minimal initial information and uses that data from then on to make decisions. It's like pulling out a fresh 3x5 card when we first meet a person and recording what we see, hear, and perceive about this person. Once we do this, we never need to repeat the process. We have our 3x5 card readily available every time we think about this person.

Harry = bad listener. Easy, fast, and efficient.

Sometimes, the act of updating this 3x5 card can be shocking. Imagine my surprise when I reacquainted with my friend Pablo's young son, who was ten years old and 4-foot-8 the last time I'd seen him. Now, seven years later, he stood more than six feet tall. Wow! The impression recorded on my 3x5 card held such a big discrepancy with reality that it was hard to absorb. I could barely believe my eyes.

How could I help my clients change others' first impressions about them? My research discovered that we could utilize a process of cognitive dissonance. Two very different pieces of information presented at the same time would create that cognitive dissonance and force people to update their 3x5 cards in the same way I had to rapidly update my "dossier" about my friend's son.

Here is how the process works. Let's go back to Harry. For a while, he made sure that people felt heard; now he wanted them to update their 3x5 cards about him. To create the magical cognitive dissonance, he needed to begin a conversation with a colleague like this:

Harry: Hi, Joe. I'm glad we'll be able to talk this morning.

Joe: Yes, it's important that we discuss our approach regarding the upcoming board meeting.

Harry: Before we get started, could I ask you for a favor?

Joe: Sure, what do you need?

Harry: As you know, I recently went through a 360° feedback...

Joe: Yes, I'm aware of it.

Harry: Well, I received feedback that I'm a poor listener, and I'm intent on changing that. I've been working on my listening skills and paying attention to this issue. The favor I want to ask is this: at the end of our conversation, I'd like your honest impression about my listening. Would that be okay with you?

Joe: Sure. No problem.

Harry: Great! Thank you, Joe.

The conversation would ensue, and Harry would use all that he'd learned about active listening. He would make sure that he remained attentive to Joe's concerns, and he would ask Joe every now and then, "Joe, let me see if I'm getting you right. What you are saying is …" Here Harry would summarize what Joe had just said, looking for confirmation that he understood. On the other side, Joe would have the chance to clarify or amplify the ideas discussed. All in all, Harry would focus on being a good listener, not restraining himself from voicing his opinion but ensuring that Joe felt heard and understood. After some time, the conversation would end. Harry and Joe would agree to some course of action, and Harry would complete the process by asking, "So, without sugarcoating or half truths—just your honest, straightforward opinion—how was my listening during our conversation?"

At that point, Joe would face two conflicting pieces of information: his 3x5 card of Harry that reads "lousy listener," and what just transpired during their conversation, where Harry had done a good job of listening. Cognitive dissonance.

Looking back on the last half-hour, Joe would probably say something of this sort, "Harry, I believe you did just fine."

Success! Joe brought his attention to the issue of Harry's listening skills and had to write over the old notes on his 3x5 card. If Harry did this three or four times with Joe, then Joe would end up clearly seeing the new Harry, the good listener. He would update his old first impression.

There is a caveat to this process. For some time, the impression caused by the new behavior will be fragile. People may mistrust the permanence of the change. They may say, "Sure, Harry is doing a great job at listening *now*, but under pressure, he'll revert to his old ways." So if Harry does not impeccably maintain this new way of relating to other people, the change of their first impression will dissolve. It will take some time of unbroken consistency for the new impression to take hold and allow for missteps.

THE FOUR PHASES OF CHANGE

Susan and I reviewed the process of changing first impressions. She incorporated it into some of the new conversations that she held with key people around her. She reported good results from these conversations and an increasing awareness of the *bifocal approach* that we had discussed. To that effect, at carefully chosen times, Susan would connect tactical day-to-day issues with how they were impacting the big picture and the execution of the company's strategy.

I also discussed with Susan the four phases of change:

+ Unconsciously Incompetent *(I'm unskillful about something but have no awareness of that)*
+ Consciously Incompetent *(I'm still incompetent, but now I know it)*
+ Consciously Competent *(I consciously practice a skillful approach)*
+ Unconsciously Competent *(I'm skillful without even needing to think about it)*

The move from Consciously Incompetent to Consciously Competent may occur many times over the life of the personal change process. At the beginning, we can only become aware of our incompetence by exercising hindsight, so that the next time around we might be able to behave more skillfully. The move might take some time, but if we keep bringing awareness to the process, even through hindsight, we will eventually be able to catch ourselves in real time, just an instant before actually falling into our ineffectual behavior. Susan was already catching herself in real time, seeing a problem and trying to rapidly move to action instead of following a more strategic approach without losing the focus on execution (the bifocal approach). She was able to remain consciously competent about balancing her strategic thinking with her penchant for action.

Eventually, Susan found herself participating more and more in key conversations with her boss on strategic company issues—and sometimes with the CEO and other members of the management team. She was becoming a thinking partner for many of these deci-sion-makers.

RESULTS

One afternoon, Susan called me and spoke in a voice brightened by excitement. The CEO had called her into his office earlier that day and said, "Susan, you've expressed so much interest in the new busi-ness unit that we'll launch next year. Would you be interested in participating in a series of meetings that will take place over the next few weeks to discuss the pipeline of new products that we'll intro-duce through that business unit?"

Seated across from him, Susan couldn't believe what she was hearing. It was the culmination of months of dedication and hard work. She thanked the CEO for including her and wholeheartedly accepted the invitation.

By then, we were six months into the leadership development process and approaching the end of our engagement. Susan's boss was three or four months away from retiring, and the company was ready to earnestly initiate the recruiting effort for his replacement. Susan's team was more autonomous, she was thinking more strategi-cally, and she felt a growing sense of hope that she could throw her hat in the ring as a credible candidate for that position.

This is not to say that she didn't have trepidation. "What if I'm not chosen to replace my boss?" she asked me one day. We were seated in her office, and I couldn't help but think how much she'd changed in this process. Today, she was openly expressing a vulner-ability that she would likely have kept to herself six months ago. "What do I do then? Resign? It would be so embarrassing."

"Susan," I said, "what would be embarrassing is not to try, sur-rendering before fighting, hiding behind the fear of not getting what you want. It's your life we're talking about, and only you have the right answer. How do you want to show up? Wisdom is always waiting for you at some point in the future. Looking back, maybe many years from now, what would make you proud about how you acted at this juncture in your life?"

Susan was silent for a moment. Then she said, "Looking back, I want to experience no regrets."

"How does that translate into what you need to do today?"

Susan sighed. It seemed like a sigh of relief. "I owe it to myself to submit my name for consideration for the position of VP of engineering, especially after all our work together."

Susan never had to face the possibility of rejection. To her utter surprise, after a few meetings with the think-tank created to launch the new business unit, the CEO offered her the position of general manager of the new business unit. This position was even larger and more autonomous than the one towards which she'd been working for so many months. She would be responsible for her own profit and loss, and there was potential for the business unit to be spun off as its own company. If that happened, Susan would be the logical choice for CEO.

The day came where we held our final meeting in the conference room. Among other things, she told me, "When the CEO offered me the top position in the new business unit, I think it was the first time in my life that I stuttered. I didn't know if he was teasing me and I was supposed to laugh, or if he was serious and I was supposed to say something smart and inspired. I ended up asking if he was serious. He told me he was never so sure about offering a position to someone and was crossing his fingers that I'd accept it. He actually showed me his crossed fingers!" She folded her middle finger over her forefinger to demonstrate.

I felt so proud of her. Susan had fulfilled her commitment and thrown herself into the personal and professional transformation process. I could see the change written all over her face. There was a new confidence in her eyes. The exhaustion I'd seen in our first meeting had lifted.

There was nothing left for us to do but laugh and shake hands—and look forward to the successful future that Susan would help usher in for her company.

Chapter 2 Summary
Susan: Becoming a Strategic Thinker

This chapter follows Susan, a highly effective senior-level employee for a major company, a creative problem-solver and solution provider who has achieved over and over again in her career and during the 10 years with the company—but is being bypassed to replace her boss. Why?

I. CLIENT'S COMMITMENT: My approach to working with Susan, and other executive- and management-level clients, focuses on three principal questions:

1. What personal dreams and desires are driving this person? What is her unique definition of success for the coaching process?
2. What skills and competencies does she need to develop or refine for success?
3. What kind of support must be gathered to assist her on this quest?

For the process to work, the client must have the burning desire of a champion, creating the conditions for a committed, sustained process of personal transformation.

II. UNCOVERING BLIND SPOTS – The Johari Window shows "blind spots" as the areas that you don't know about yourself, but everybody else is aware of. The individual starts gaining awareness of their blind spots by completing our SELF leadership profile, in which individual characteristics and traits are contrasted against a database of more than 2,000 leaders, executives and managers.

III. THE 360° FEEDBACK PROCESS – Susan continues gaining awareness of how she impacts others through receiving feedback from co-workers on four domains:

1. Leading Self: Focus on intrapersonal areas
2. Leading Others: Focus on interpersonal areas
3. Leading the Organization: Focus on organizational and systemic issues
4. Managing Implementation: Focus on execution

III. THE DOOR OF BEHAVIOR – It takes a long time to change our personality, but we can access change by purposefully changing our behaviors to align them with desired results. Transforming a behavior into a practice anchors it, and creates lasting, sustainable change. For Susan, the desired new behaviors relate to creating the conditions to increased delegation allowing for more time to develop and exercise strategic thinking.

IV. TIME MANAGEMENT – Learning how to prioritize well starts with identifying what is mission-critical, what's very important and distinguishing from what's just "good to have" and other tasks and meetings that do not add meaningful value.

V. WORKING WITH THE TEAM AS A WHOLE – Eliminating the spoke-wheel dynamic with Susan at the center. Increasing the autonomy and self-reliance of the team, making it less dependent on Susan's continuous guidance helps free some of her time. Pushing decision-making further down the line and creating a more distributed leadership.

VI. TEAM MEMBERS' CAPABILITIES – Making sure all team members operate at appropriate capability to handle the leadership and decision-making responsibilities expected of them. Susan determines the areas each team member needs to improve and identifies the resources to accomplish that.

VII. TEAM INTERACTION WITH THE LEADER – Increased capability of team members raises their effectiveness and allows Susan more delegation. The four styles of situational leadership are discussed (Telling, Selling, Participating and Delegating).

VIII. STRATEGIC THINKING AND MAPS

1. Resources map – People Maps: The creation of maps to assess effectiveness of people in group leaders' areas of responsibility. Rapidly identifying candidates for professional development:
   a. Green – highly proficient
   b. Yellow – performing well but in need of further training/development
   c. Red – under-performing
2. Time allocation map: The amount of time Susan would need to focus on each of the areas under her responsibility. The total time needed highlights the imperative need to delegate more.
3. Job description map: Determine job description and create a short, high-level list of responsibilities. Also look at decisions, actions and tasks to fulfill those responsibilities. The goal is to arrive at a "bi-focal" approach, determining how much time is spent on tactical duties, how much on strategic planning/thinking.

IX. STRATEGIC THINKING AS A PRACTICE: The goal is to dedicate appropriate time to focusing and thinking on the future, the longer strategy. This involves:

1. Focusing on the most strategic aspects of the job;
2. Holding strategic conversations inside and outside the organization;
3. Learning more about R&D activity, and planned products and services;
4. Talking to the most innovative customers about the evolution of the markets and their visions for the future;
5. Identifying and researching upcoming market trends;
6. Following and anticipating customers' moves, identifying new opportunities, gaining competitive advantage;
7. Keeping abreast of latest scientific and technological research;
8. Identifying potential strategic alliances;
9. Investigating start-ups for potential partners or acquisitions.

CHAPTER 3

Roger: Life's a Beach

Congruency Between Intention and Behavior

ONE afternoon in early fall, I received a cryptic email from a former client: "Gustavo, I need your help with an unusual issue. Can we meet soon to discuss it in further detail?"

The e-mail came from Carol, Vice President of Marketing of a $4 billion high-tech company; we had worked together the previous year on her leadership development program. I knew Carol was straightforward and detail-oriented. It didn't seem like her to be mysterious.

The following afternoon, Carol was waiting for me in the marble-floored lobby of her building. At first glance, she looked as sharply dressed as always: crisp linen suit and simple jewelry. However, she also paced and looked at her watch, often. I'd never seen her so eager to talk!

"Gustavo," she said, shaking my hand with a smile. "Thank you so much for coming on such short notice. Why don't we go up to my office?"

As soon as the elevator doors slid shut, Carol turned to me. "There's someone in the company who is driving me and everybody else here *crazy,*" she confided in a rush. "I've tried everything I can to work on him from within, but I've reached a point of not knowing what else to do."

"Tell me a little more about him," I said, as the doors opened and we stepped out of the elevator. We crossed a large open area, and Carol nodded and smiled at several people as we passed. The efficient sound of clicking computer keys followed us to her office where Carol shut the door and gestured toward one of two leather seats.

"As I mentioned in my email," she said, "this issue is a bit unusual because the individual in question is an executive. I have no idea if this is something you can even help us with, but we're going crazy trying to reach a solution on our own."

"Let's start with who you're talking about."

Carol nodded. "His name is Roger, and he is brilliant. He's a director of our marketing group and connects key people in Research and Development with many different groups inside our marketing department. He also coordinates the work of diverse groups across different regions. He's very talented and has good ideas that support our marketing efforts, but it's hard—no, impossible—to work with him!"

"How so?"

"Where do I start?" She ran a hand through her dark hair. "He leaves everything for the last moment, which means he's late for every assignment. It feels like pulling teeth to extract a report or analysis from him when we need it. Deadlines mean little to Roger. Other folks don't want to work for him. Everybody around him is frustrated."

She paused and sighed. "At the same time, I don't want to lose him; he's creative, has good ideas and contributes a lot to our group. So, is this something you could help us with?"

"I don't know yet," I responded. "What prompted you to call me at this particular time?" I wondered if there had been a triggering incident, something that suddenly made the problem too big to ignore.

Carol nodded. "I had a meeting scheduled for last Thursday with our CEO to discuss a number of issues, including some aspects of our budget for next year. I wanted to submit to the CEO a thorough presentation that required Roger's input. I knew about this upcoming meeting three weeks in advance, so it was not a surprise meeting where I needed to improvise—I hate to improvise in front of the CEO!"

"Understandably."

"I asked Roger if two weeks would give him enough time to prepare his part of the presentation. He said that was plenty of time. I told him I wanted to receive it far enough in advance to integrate it with the rest of my presentation. I didn't want a last minute submission from him, which would force *me* to do a sloppy job."

"I called him a few days in advance of his deadline just to remind him. He said that things were fine, no problem. But three days before my meeting with the CEO, I still didn't have Roger's notes! I finally got him to send me his input about two hours before my meeting. Two *hours*. That was absolutely unacceptable."

At this point, Carol stood and began pacing the length of her office. "I'm sorry," she said. "I didn't even offer you a bottle of water." She nodded toward the small refrigerator tucked next to a side table.

"I'm fine. Carol, what would you do if Roger doesn't change within a reasonable time?"

This question, which I ask in situations that follow unacceptable and potentially damaging actions by key employees, allows me to understand the consequences awaiting the individual if change doesn't take place. When it comes to consequences, every company is different, and as a consultant, I always bear that in mind. To my utter surprise, I often find that a person doesn't have any idea that there will be negative consequences to their dysfunctional behavior, and they are flummoxed when they are eventually let go. I knew Carol didn't want to lose Roger but wondered if she had, indeed, reached the end of her rope.

It sure seemed like it.

"This wasn't the first time I had trouble waiting for Roger to deliver on something," Carol said, "but I assured myself that it'd be the last. I've also received numerous complaints from other people in our group. Everybody admires Roger's ideas, but nobody wants to work with him; it's too hard, too last minute, too disorganized. It drives other people crazy, and it drives me crazy. I'm upset that we rely so much on his coordination efforts. So, to answer your question, if he doesn't improve and become reliable, I'd have to reposition him in an area of the company where deadlines are not an issue—which would be difficult to find—or let him go."

Carol's tone and her resolute blue eyes showed me the conviction behind her words: firing Roger was the last thing she wanted, but she was determined not to face another last-minute situation.

"I'll meet with Roger," I said. Carol's sigh of relief was audible. "But until I do, I won't know if he is a good candidate for coaching or if I'm the right person to engage with him in this effort."

I have found that checking for "coachability" and fit are an essential part of the coaching process. It is only ethical to engage in a coaching arrangement if at least two conditions are met: a) the candidate is open to the process and desires personal change; and b) the coach has the capability to address the specific issues or concerns that created the need for coaching. I needed to know that Roger's situation met these criteria.

"I understand." Carol stopped her pacing and stood before me. "Please meet with him as soon as possible."

The meeting with Roger presented a few surprises. First, I thought there was a good chance that he would resent working with someone on "self-improvement" just because his manager or colleagues were unhappy with his work style. I also expected Roger would make it difficult to schedule our first meeting by canceling or trying to reschedule at the last minute. Finally, I was prepared for him to be apologetic but show up late.

I was wrong on all accounts. Roger responded promptly to my email and suggested a few possible meeting times in the same week. When I arrived at the conference room, he was waiting for me. That bode well.

Roger, with a winning smile and welcoming attitude, turned out to be a pleasant-looking man in his mid- to late-thirties. As we sat down at the conference table, he surprised me again by saying, "I've been looking forward to meeting you. I'm grateful for Carol's support and her offer to work with a coach."

"Good," I said. "Carol mentioned that you might need some help improving your work style. But I'd like to hear from you. How can I be of assistance?"

Roger took a deep breath. "As I'm sure Carol noted, I tend to leave projects and assignments for the last minute and finish under a lot of pressure."

I nodded.

"But what you don't know—what nobody around here knows—is that this is a relatively new thing for me." Roger paused, taking in my reaction. "Looking way back, all through high school, college, and graduate school, I prepared for exams with plenty of time. My grades were always in the top ten percent of the class. I saw other students waiting to the last minute to study and then do all-nighters at the end, rushing to the finish line, but that wasn't my style. I was always ready way in advance."

"Then what happened?"

"I started working at a large company—our biggest competitor today. I always had the same attitude about my work, making a point of delivering what I needed to on time. After a few years, I was recruited by this company, and I came to work here." Roger sighed, looking down at his hands. "After a while, things started going downhill. When my schedule first started slipping, it wasn't a big deal. People knew that I was good at what I do, and there was a fair amount of tolerance. But things have gotten worse over time, and I can see how my working style is hurting me now."

"What do you notice? And how is it a problem?"

"It's as if I'm not myself anymore," Roger blurted. "I'm late to meetings, I don't meet my deadlines, and I'm doing everything at the last minute. This is not who I want to be or how I want to work, but I don't know how to change it."

Roger's voice rose with frustration. He glanced out the window to view the sprawling lawn and parking lot.

"It's getting worse and worse," he continued. "By now, my boss is upset and my peers have told me in no uncertain terms that they find it hard to work with me. This new work 'style,' if you can call it that, is going to be a big hurdle for me to make progress in my career."

"What have you tried so far?" I asked. (Learning what *hadn't* been working would allow me to better grasp the situation.)

"I've promised myself a thousand times that I'll show up to meetings on time, start preparing in advance what I need to deliver to my boss or colleagues, think about the projects I'm responsible for in a timely fashion—but somehow I've been unable to do that. I don't know what's going on. It's not that I'm unaware of how badly it reflects on me; that's glaringly obvious. Yet I have not been able to change the way I work. What can I do? How can I become the person I used to be?"

I responded in a low, soothing voice, "Roger, you mentioned that this is not reflecting well on you. What do you think will happen if you don't change?" I needed to know if Roger recognized the possible consequences.

"I believe that if I don't change—and fast—I will be presented with my final salary check and escorted to the front door."

"How did you arrive at that conclusion?"

"Carol, my manager, was so distraught last time I delivered my work late that there's no doubt in my mind that one more slip means I'll be packing my things." Roger drummed his fingertips against the conference table, leaving little smudges against the glass. "I don't want that to happen, but I don't seem to be able to change. I'm really discouraged."

"You seem to have a clear desire to meet your deadlines and keep your job, but you've failed to do what's needed to accomplish that," I said. "Are you experiencing stress not related to work? Do you have any health issues or a difficult family situation? Anything stressful that might be affecting you?"

The question was crucial. It was possible that Roger wasn't connecting the dots between events in his personal life and how those issues were manifesting at work.

"Not really," Roger said thoughtfully. "My wife, Linda, and I have a great relationship. We're expecting our second child. My health is fine. My biggest source of stress is the situation I've created for myself at work! I'm sinking my own ship."

"What is your interpretation about what's happening with you?"

"I have no idea." He shook his head. "I'm totally baffled. I see no reason not to perform at work the way I used to, on time and on top of things. I've asked myself a thousand times what's going on, but each day I come to work and things are the same: I'm surfing the net and letting things slide."

"Well, so far things have worked out for you," I said. "Maybe they'll continue to work. Maybe your boss is just momentarily frustrated but has no real intention of letting you go. And if she did let you go, you could always find another job …"

I had slipped into playing devil's advocate: I needed to gauge Roger's conviction about his need to change and his motivation to go through this process. His expression was just the one I'd hoped to see: impatience with my shift in attitude.

"Gustavo, I'm clear that I need to change. For Crissakes!" he said. "I'm almost forty years old; I'm a director of marketing at a large public company. I can't be irresponsible; it's hurting my career, and I'm going to get fired! And if I just change jobs but not my way of working, I'd be fired again at my next job." He lowered his voice, grew quiet. "What doesn't let me sleep at night, is that even though I have a clear intention, I don't seem to have power over how I do things. I'm really concerned."

"At our next meeting, we will begin to tackle the issue you are presenting today. Before that, though, there are a few things I would like to discuss."

During the next hour, I opened a conversation about the difference between trying to change our personality—a very long-term endeavor—and changing our behavior, something that's within our immediate control, even if it doesn't feel that way at times. We also discussed the phases and dynamics of change, the expected evolution of a personal transformation process, and the logistics of working together. We agreed to meet again a few days later.

That evening, after dinner, I thought about Roger's case: it was not unusual. It fit a universal pattern in which a person wants to change something that is ostensibly completely under his control but, for some "mysterious" reason, he or she cannot change it. A good friend of mine had recently told me, "I hate to scream at my children. My father used to scream at my siblings and me, and I promised myself I would never do the same. Yet here I am, screaming at the top of my lungs at my kids! How could that happen? I don't understand myself ..."

Congruency between our intention—what we want to do—and our behavior—what we actually *do*—is sometimes elusive. Some are determined to delegate more in order to free time for more strategic endeavors but find themselves deep "in the weeds," focusing on details and minutia. Others want to increase their focus on creativity and innovation but keep resorting to familiar ways of doing things.

Why are we apparently at odds with ourselves? It seems that what we *actually do* should be perfectly congruent with what we *want to do*.

In reality, we find ourselves conducting our life in a certain way, while a part of us cringes and wants change. Why the conflict?

A few days later, I met with Roger again. For the second time, he was ready in advance and prepared to get started right away. He immediately rose from behind his desk and shook my hand.

"How about a cup of coffee?"

Roger frowned as we walked to the cafeteria. His entire bearing seemed stiff, contemplative, very different from his all-smiles greeting at our first meeting.

After we'd poured our coffee and returned to his office, we sat at a small round table; Roger said, "Since our conversation, I've been thinking about my predicament. The urgency has become increasingly clear to me."

"What effect has that realization had on you?"

"I think it's increased my motivation to change." Roger took a sip of coffee. "I think I enjoyed a lot of leniency from my manager and peers, and now it's 'change or bust.' Not necessarily a bad thing—if I only knew how to do that. Even this morning, I was very aware of a few things I needed to do regarding an upcoming team meeting, but I spent a couple of hours responding to unimportant emails and surfing the net instead."

"That's why I'm here. Let's see if, together, we can make a little progress on what you are trying to achieve."

I had decided that a frontal approach—confronting Roger directly about his behavior—might raise his psychological defenses. Instead, I'd decided to present him with a case study. I hoped that looking at *another* person's situation would help him access a learning mode and open his mind to possibilities.

Whatever the case, I was ready for a crucial session.

"I think it will be useful to you if we begin with an experiential exercise," I said. "Would you be open to that?"

"Sure. What do I have to do?"

"Well, we are going to reverse roles: I will come to you as a client seeking your professional services, and you will play the part of the coach. Would you humor me? I believe it will be useful to you."

Roger smiled. "It sounds intriguing. I hope I can do my part well."

"Great! I'll present you with a challenge based on a real case, a real client. My name for this exercise will be Alex."

"Let's do it!"

I left his office for a moment, just to reset our minds. Then I re-entered and sat across from him again at the table.

"Good morning, Roger," I said. "And thank you for seeing me today. My name is Alex. I came referred by a friend who spoke very highly of you."

"Welcome to my office, Alex." Roger seemed very comfortable in his new role. "How can I help you?"

"Well, it's complex and, to be honest, a little embarrassing."

"Relax. I'm your coach, and you can talk with me."

I sighed, immersing myself in my character. "Here's the situation."

I told Roger that I'd stopped working about a year and a half ago, as I took a one-week vacation. I started going to the beach with my dog, walking along the warm sand, reading, watching the seagulls. One week later, it was time to go back to work ... but I didn't. I wanted to extend my vacation and spend more time at the beach. I called the office and let them know that I would take a few more days. I also said, quite reasonably, that I didn't expect to be paid while extending my vacation. They didn't like it, but I didn't give them any options. I did this a few times, calling the office and extending my vacation until my superiors finally gave me an ultimatum: come back into the office next Monday and resume work or pick up my things. I did neither, so they sent my things to my home."

Roger's eyebrows raised. "That's a big move!" I was pleased to see that he still looked comfortable in the coaching role.

"I know," I said. "I had a lot of trepidation but felt that I couldn't do anything differently."

"What happened next?"

"I didn't go back to work. I kept going to the beach and sometimes to the hills, but mostly I went to the shore and had a great time. I kept telling myself that I needed to end the vacation and go back to work—I had to get a new job and make money again. But to this day, I haven't started my job search. I'm still going to the beach almost every day."

"How are you doing with money, Alex?" Roger inquired. "How much longer could you not work?"

"Actually, that's why I came to see you."

As Alex, I leaned forward and revealed that, with time, money had become a big issue. At the beginning, I was spending out of my savings. When the savings were gone, I withdrew from my 401(k) retirement account until I exhausted it. Then I borrowed money from my family until they essentially cut me off. I turned to my friends, each of whom lent me what they could, but finally, enough became enough there, too.

"This is really embarrassing to me," I told Roger. "I've never found myself in a situation like this. Now I have no money and no one left to borrow from. I should be looking at job opportunities on the web, going to networking meetings, or even talking with recruiters, but I'm not doing any of these things."

"So what *are* you doing with your time?" Roger was wholly engaged, his coffee forgotten between us on the table.

"I go to the beach," I said. "I just love it there! But trust me, you don't need to convince me; I need to go back to work and make enough money to get on my feet. More than that, I need to return all the money I borrowed. I have never been in debt like this. Ever!"

"Alex, what's really stopping you from seeking a job?"

I threw my hands up. "I have no idea. That's why I'm here. Instead of looking for a job, I find myself driving back to the beach every day. This is ludicrous! I need your help. Please offer some advice, something I can do to extricate myself from this miserable situation."

Roger's eyes glinted with an inspired look. "How about a job at the beach?"

"I thought about it. But, you see, I go to Half Moon Bay. Those are the beaches close to my home, and if you've been there, you'd see that there's no job; there's just mile after mile of beautiful white sand."

Roger's eyebrows furrowed. "What if I help you make a plan, day by day, hour by hour, detailing every aspect of your job search? You'd just need to follow the plan, like reading a roadmap. Would that work for you?"

"I tried that. A very good friend of mine sat down with me, and we charted on a calendar every step of a rational, well thought-out job search. 'Nothing strenuous,' said my friend, 'and very doable; just a couple of hours a day engaged in job searching.'"

"And what happened?"

"I felt so guilty. I knew I had to honor my friend's effort—he really meant well—but I would wake up, get my dog, and head to the beach."

"Wow," said Roger. "Your attraction to the beach is obviously extremely compelling."

"Yes, yes, I love the beach," I quickly responded, "but what I need desperately is to find a job, make money, and get back on my feet. I know I sound like a broken record, but I'm afraid that I'll go back home today and be back at the beach tomorrow. And I'm in a desperate situation: I owe money to everybody, I'm behind on rent, and I need to refill my fridge and buy food for my dog. This has gotten serious. Can you help me?"

Roger leaned back in his seat, lips pursed. He cast his gaze around us, seeing nothing in particular. He was genuinely trying to come up with a solution.

"Please don't give up on me, Roger," I implored. "I need your help!"

"I'm not giving up on you. We're just getting started. Now, you said a written plan wouldn't help. What about getting a friend to sit with you and help you look on the web for job openings?"

"I can't do that," I said emphatically. "My friends are busy working. It would be imposing and abusive to ask that of them. Actually, a couple of my friends offered something very similar, but I was too embarrassed to accept. I refuse to drag any more people into my own misery. What are my friends going to do, come with me to a job interview? Sit *for* me in a job interview? This is something I have to do for myself, and I need to do it now. But I'm worried that my desire for the beach is stronger than me, that tomorrow morning will come, and I'll be on my way to the shore."

"What did you do before all this, Alex?" Roger asked.

"I used to be an attorney, working at a law firm."

"How long did you practice?"

"Seventeen years."

"Would you go back to being an attorney?"

"Yes," I said thoughtfully, "I believe I would. There were some aspects of my job, like researching, that were enjoyable. But I guess I just worked too hard."

"Is there something else you could do that would make it easier on you to look for a job?"

"What do you mean?"

"Well, you know, a different kind of job that would be easier or somehow more appealing to you."

"No," I said. "I liked the legal field and being an attorney."

Roger looked triumphant; he thought he had me cornered: "So, you like the field of law, you liked being an attorney. What would it take to get you back to work?"

I gave a long silence, just like the real Alex used to do in sessions with me, and then said, "I don't have the slightest idea."

This time it was Roger's turn to be silent for a while. Eventually he said, "Gustavo, I give up. I know that this mirrors my situation to a big extent, as I want to be more organized, and I don't do it, but how can I help Alex if I don't know how to help myself?"

"Okay, then," I said, returning to myself. "Let's move on. This was great role-playing, Roger. You really tried to help Alex, and I saw you tackling the issue from different angles. It may sound hard to believe, but I stuck to how Alex responded to questions like yours at all times. I used this case study because it provides a good example of how our minds work at times: we want to do something that really *is* in our power and control to do, but for some obscure reason we don't, causing us disappointment and frustration. Some people want to do more physical exercise, for example, or lose weight, or learn a new language, and sometimes they want this for years, but they just don't do it."

"What's preventing them from doing it?" asked Roger. "What's preventing *me* from organizing my work and meeting my deadlines? How do you get out of a situation like this? And, by the way, what happened with Alex?"

I told Roger that by understanding how our inner world works, we can manage our life in a more satisfying way by recognizing and acting upon the inner dynamics at play. Each of us is comprised of distinct aspects that, together, make us who we are. We are actually a *complex self*. As the Portuguese poet Pessoa wrote, "In every corner of my soul there is an altar to a different god."

These distinct aspects have received different labels from different schools of thought. Swiss psychoanalyst Carl Jung called them "complexes," the equivalent of subpersonalities; his notion was that each part held an archetype at its core, like the hero or the warrior. Assagioli's Psychosynthesis talks about different realms of the self, while *Ken Wilber* identifies subpersonalities as "functional self-presentations that navigate particular psychosocial situations."

I've always found Eric Berne's transactional analysis (TA) an ingenious way of looking at these different aspects of self. TA identified the Parent, the Child, and the Adult, mirroring to a big extent Freud's Ego, Superego, and Id *(please see Figure 1)*. Gestalt therapy helped raise awareness of these different aspects and how to open a dialogue between them.

Figure 1

"Our everyday language already incorporates the idea of different parts of self," I told Roger. "We say things like: 'There's a part of me that would like to …' implying that there are other parts of ourselves preventing us from carrying out that desire. As in, 'There's a part of me that would love to punch my boss, but there's another part that stops me because it knows that I'd be fired!'"

Roger nodded, paying careful attention. Again, I was struck by how much he was ready to make the change he wanted.

"So imagine that there are all these parts inside you, like a small tribe,"I said. "And they're all riding a car, a vehicle representing your self." (When I had mentioned this to another client, she responded laughingly that instead of a car, she needed a van to fit all the parts of herself!)

As part of that tribe, I told Roger, he may easily be able to identify the Clown, who inspires goofing around at times; the Child, who sits on the floor ready to play with another child; the Wise Man, who gives sound advice to a friend in distress; the Warrior, ready to fight if needed; and so on. All these parts travel through life together in that imaginary car. BUT—the key realization—there's only one steering wheel. Which means that, at all times, only one part can steer, while the others are mere passengers.

"And how can we know which part is at the steering wheel?" Roger asked.

"You have to look at your behavior," I said. "The part of your self at the steering wheel is the one that gets to determine what you actually do; it has the control of your behavior."

"What's an example of that?"

I couldn't help but chuckle about what came to mind. "A good friend of mine has been saying for a few years that she wants to do yoga, but she hasn't. That's because there's another part of her that considers other activities a higher priority and organizes her time in a way that does not include yoga. The part that's complaining about wanting to do yoga is not at the steering wheel."

"How did that play out with Alex?"

"The part of Alex that was at the steering wheel, in command, was the one taking him to the beach every day. Alex and I agreed to call that part the Beach Bum. The Beach Bum had gotten a firm hold of Alex's behavior and was clearly driving the situation. Alex came up with a long name for the part that was saying 'I must find a job right away and make money.' He called it the Responsible Hard Worker, or RHW."

"So," I continued, "while the Beach Bum was having a ball going to the beach every day, RHW was sitting in the passenger seat complaining loudly, anxiously, desperate to take control. But RHW was only a disempowered passenger."

"The part of Alex that I'd embodied to role-play with you—the part that sat in front of me when I'd first worked with Alex—was the overwhelmed and frustrated RHW, willing to return to work and make some money. When we framed the conflict as different parts at odds with each other—an expression of unconscious inner conflict—the next step was to give a voice to the part at the steering wheel, the part in control of his behavior: the Beach Bum."

"When that part spoke, I discovered that Alex had been working extremely hard for many years. His job had required between seventy and eighty hours a week. RHW had been in complete control for seventeen years and had given no room—none whatsoever—to the Beach Bum. Instead, the Beach Bum had been relegated to the back seat, dreaming about a respite, some renewal time at the beach."

Alex's story was one of *unconscious extremes creating unbearable inner conflict.* He'd been exclusively listening to RHW for so many years, but once able to give a voice to the Beach Bum, the inner dictate changed. The Beach Bum said, "Look, I want to be crystal clear: I'm not giving up having a sane life. I will not go back to sitting at work for seventy or eighty hours a week. I will do anything else with my life but not that."

"Couldn't he go back to work more reasonable hours?" asked Roger.

"Using his rational mind, yes," I said. "But taken over by his emotional self, Alex *equated going back to work with working seventy or eighty hours a week.* There was no middle ground. And a neglected part of him was now firmly at the steering wheel."

"I assume Alex found some resolution to this situation." No doubt Roger was hoping that if Alex could find a solution, he could as well.

"Well, extreme situations are untenable," I said. "Nobody wins. A part of Alex associated going back to work with never again having time for enjoyment. That was unacceptable. The way out was to create a compassionate discussion between these different parts of himself and find a compromise."

"Let's compare it to a relationship. Say you have a partner who likes Vietnamese cuisine, while you prefer Italian. What's the solution? Never eating out together? You need to be creative and find acceptable compromises; maybe you find a place with an international menu, or alternate choosing restaurants."

In Alex's case, the two parts in conflict were able to engage in healthy dialogue. The goal of this dialogue was respectful integration of the self—every part of the self is honored and has a seat at the table. An integrated self has room for work, friends, fun, recreation, and service to our community.

The results were solid: RHW promised not to let things get out of hand and work excessive hours day after day. He vowed to pay attention when the Beach Bum needed a break or some time to recover and renew. The Beach Bum, meanwhile, agreed to work part-time. Also, in wanting to display the same reasonableness as RHW, the Beach Bum expressed his understanding that, maybe one or two days a month, work could require longer hours. However, in no case would that become the norm.

"Eventually," I explained, "Alex took a job with a law firm that required him to work between twenty and twenty-five hours per week. As an attorney, he was very well compensated and still found time to go to the beach every now and then. I followed up with him recently, and he was still very satisfied with the way he was balancing his work and his desire for time in nature."

Roger nodded, smiling. He felt a kinship to Alex, and I hoped that this story showed him that it *was* possible to find a solution to his predicament. "So, how do I apply the lesson of Alex's situation and resolution to my own predicament?"

"Let's follow the process step by step. I heard today from a part of you that would like to be more organized, meet deadlines on time, and bring more order and rigor to how you work."

"That's exactly what I want!"

"Well, as this is only a part of you, what are we going to call this part?" I asked.

"How about The Complainant—TC to make it short?"

"If I identify with that part, I'd say: 'It's true that I'm complaining, but I don't want to be called The Complainant; it sounds as if I only know how to whine and have no real reason to express distress.'"

"You're right; it sounds judgmental. How about EE for Efficient and Effective?" asked Roger.

"EE—Sounds good!"

Roger looked pleased.

Nearly an hour and a half had passed since our meeting began; it seemed to be a good time to stop. I suggested that Roger take a few days to reflect on our conversation before we reconvened. I wanted him to contemplate the part of himself driving the behavior he was trying to change. "Keep in mind, even if you find it disconcerting, that that part of your self has your best interest in mind. It just may be misunderstood or misguided," I said.

"You said that before," We stood up. "'Every part of ourselves is working in our best interest.' Could you explain that? How could my surfing the net or doing some other inane activity be working in my best interest?"

"What I mean is that every part has your best interest in *mind,*" I said. "What a part of you may be doing with your best interest in mind may be misguided, ill-advised, or just plain wrong, but the *intention* is always to serve you. For instance, heavy drinking when you have a delicate liver would not be helping your health and may be lethal, but the intention may be to numb your painful feelings and make being alive bearable."

"What could be the intention of the part of me that's not organized and meeting deadlines and so on?" asked Roger.

"We're going to focus on that when we meet again. Until then, trust that these ideas are working away inside you." I shook Roger's hand and smiled. "Their reasons will be ready to show up soon."

I find that it's sometimes useful to remove my client from his work environment to facilitate a new perspective, and Roger agreed. So, we met at my office. Located atop a hill, my office is surrounded by giant redwood trees. The large windows overlook the ocean, reinforcing the feeling of being removed from the daily hustle of the city.

Roger showed up on time, carrying two cups of coffee, a warm smile on his face. "Good morning, Doc." He handed me a cup.

I returned his smile. "Good morning, Roger. You seem to be in good spirits."

"Yes! I feel —hopeful."

"Did you have any afterthoughts or reflections after our meeting last week?"

"Well, I thought a lot about the different parts of myself and how, at times, I'm not aware of my own motivations and what is driving me. What I really want is to bring more awareness into how I live my life."

"In that way, you would be aligning yourself with Socrates' idea that an unexamined life is not worth living."

Roger nodded. "I thought a lot about your idea that every part of me has the intention of working in my best interest. I'm interested in having all my parts working on my *real* best interest and not an imaginary one. I want them to work with the best intentions but also be aware of what my best interest actually is."

"That sounds right," I said. "Well, last time, we talked about the part of you that is at the steering wheel: it procrastinates, does not prepare for meetings with enough time, surfs the Internet instead of doing the work you need to do. What are we going to call this part?"

"How about Lazy Roger?" He flashed a wry smile but appeared embarrassed as he situated himself on the small couch in my office.

"Again, that would be judgmental," I said, taking a seat across from him. "Judgment usually elicits resistance and defensiveness. Let's keep in mind that this aspect of yourself is also working at all times with your best interest in mind. Let's assume that that part has had, so far, an unskillful way of expressing this, but does want you to be successful."

"How was the Beach Bum working in Alex's best interest?" Roger asked, maybe feeling a bit defensive.

"By wanting Alex to work more reasonable hours and find time for renewal and enjoyment."

"But it was making him destitute and almost homeless!"

"Each part holds only his own point of view," I explained. "The Beach Bum had the best intentions and the best interest of Alex in mind but a single focus. It's only when you integrate *all* your parts' points of view that you live a balanced life."

"That makes sense," Roger brightened. "While surfing the net or reading the newspaper, I feel curious about what I'm going to find. How about we call that part Curious Roger, or CR?"

"I like it," I said. "Effective and Efficient and Curious Roger; EE and CR."

"This is fun. What do we do now?"

"Last time, we heard from EE saying that your job is in jeopardy. Would you take a moment to identify again with that part of yourself and briefly tell me what you want?"

"Sure." Roger was silent for a long moment. "I want to be the organized, planned, the 'together' person I used to be. I want to be proud of myself and appreciated by my peers and my boss. I want to role model for my direct reports getting things done. I want to meet my deadlines with enough time to research well for my presentations. I want to be Effective and Efficient."

"You're very clear about your intentions, and that will help us move forward," I said. "Now, Roger, I'd like you to take a moment to become the part of you that chooses to surf the Internet or do something else, even when you have an important upcoming deadline. This part you suggested we call Curious Roger or CR. Is that still an appropriate name?"

"Yes. It sounds just right."

"I suggest you identify now with CR and give this part a voice. Would that be okay?"

"Absolutely. What do you want to know?"

I nodded, a sign of moving forward. "Hi, CR, I'm glad we can talk for a moment. I learned that you have not been meeting your deadlines, you show up late at meetings, and you spend time online when you should be getting a market analysis ready. What's going on?"

Roger was silent for a while. He lifted his coffee cup to his mouth but didn't sip.

I waited.

"CR, take your time. Sometimes we need a moment to get in touch with what we feel. I assume that you want what's best for you: to feel good about yourself, and live a productive life. From what I heard from EE, you are having trouble engaging with work in a way that allows you to meet your commitments. I'm guessing something may have not been feeling right for you for a while. Is that so?"

Roger looked reflective. His demeanor changed noticeably, and he looked somewhat younger as he hunched a little in his seat.

"I'm not clear about it. I don't know."

"I understand you spend some time every day online. What do you mostly look at when you surf the Internet?"

"I think I'm a news junkie," he said. "I look at Google News, *New York Times,* BBC Online, and a number of other news sources."

"How do you feel doing that?"

"I have a sense of anticipation and curiosity. I wonder about what's happening in other parts of the world. I read about science and the arts. I could spend hours doing that—and do!"

I leaned forward. "Tell me more about your experience reading the news."

"It's not only the news. There are so many smart, creative people in the world. I'm really curious about our next frontiers of discovery. So I read about research in the fields of health and biology; outer space fascinates me. And my reading is not completely disconnected from our company." Enthusiasm rang in his voice and shone in his eyes. "Sometimes I find interesting research that could affect our consumer products division, and I send the information to our research and development group. Time flies when I do that."

"When did you last feel that way at work?"

"My market research always brought the same feeling," Roger said. "I read about the latest scientific developments that could eventually affect our industry. I visit some websites of university labs and learned about their research efforts. The best part was studying the competitors in our industry, understanding their strategies and anticipating their moves. That's really how you create a competitive advantage. It's a combination of influencing your R&D department to move in the right direction and moving faster and earlier than your competitors."

"How does that compare with your current job?"

"I don't enjoy what I do these days at work." Roger blinked, and looked surprised by his own words. "I feel bored."

"That's a very important insight," I said, "because it may lead you to seek a more satisfying position. What is it that you don't like about your job?"

Roger told me that his job consisted mostly of coordinating work between different groups dispersed across the world. "It's frustrating because I can't make progress by myself," he said. "These groups lack alignment because the groups' leaders do not agree on a common strategy. Things are set up so that there's no way to win, and I get tired of pursuing people to reach agreement on key issues that are still unresolved."

"CR, if the groups' leaders would finally create alignment between themselves and their groups, would that increase your level of satisfaction at work?" I asked.

Roger's leg was twitching. "That would make my work easier. But, again, I find this job boring. I want to feel engaged and not underutilized."

"It is hard to perform a boring job. It's hard to stay engaged if you're not really interested in what you're doing."

"That's why I focus on something else—anything else! I read the news online, I exchange emails with colleagues in my field, and I do anything to avoid focusing on what's really my job description."

"I see." I thought about a musician friend of mine who told me he was being paid to do something he would do anyway—because he loved music.

"What kind of job would make you feel as though you're being paid to do something that you would actually do for free?" I asked.

"I don't know." Roger fidgeted noticeably, tapping his coffee cup, biting his lip. The session had been intense; we'd reached a natural stopping point.

"This line of thinking is not easy," I said, "and you did a great job. I suggest you take some time to think about that question, and we'll reconvene in a few days. What do you think?"

"What was the question again?"

"What kind of job would make you feel as though you're being paid to do something that you would actually do for free?" I repeated.

"That's something worth thinking about," said Roger. He stood and offered me his hand. "I'll do my homework."

A few days later, Roger and I met at a conference room in his office building. He looked both troubled and excited, but bursting to talk.

We situated ourselves at the table. "I'm very excited," Roger said. "I didn't expect our last conversation to end up that way. I had no idea I was so dissatisfied with my job. Do you think that there's a relationship between that and my not meeting deadlines, procrastinating, etc.?"

"It's possible," I said, "but since this is your *own* internal process, I should turn the question to you: is there a relationship?"

Roger took a moment. Slowly, he nodded. "I believe there is. Looking back, I've become increasingly unhappy with my job and responsibilities within it. I've felt that my level of creativity has gone way down; I feel bored and exhausted dealing with something I don't want to do."

"Last time we met, I asked you about what kind of job would feel engaging to you, a job that you would be amazed that you're paid for because you'd actually do it for free. Did you have a chance to think about that?"

"Yes," Roger said. "I thought about it a lot and even talked about it with my wife. The way you described it sounds like the job I had a couple of years ago."

"What was that?"

"I was generating ideas and collaborating with our advertising agencies on ad campaigns for a few of our products."

"What did you enjoy about that job?"

"It was mostly about being *creative,*" Roger said, looking very animated. He shared how he loved engaging in a creative activity and seeing concrete results for his work. He didn't have to manage other people or coordinate the work of others. He simply arrived at the office early in the morning and worked through the day, content and engaged.

"I remember being surprised that suddenly it was six p.m.," Roger said, smiling. "The day just disappeared while I was absorbed in my work."

"Were you mostly working by yourself?"

"No, we were a small team, and we created a truly collaborative environment. We were critiquing each other's work in a constructive way, and we gave a lot of support to each other."

"Sounds like it was a good time."

"It really was." Roger looked out the conference room doors to the desks spread out outside, where his colleagues and direct reports were focused on their computer screens. "That was the kind of work that didn't feel like work."

"Well, from what I hear, it seems increasingly clear that your current position is not a good fit for you," I said.

"Gustavo, I'd hesitate to share this with my boss."

"That's a sure way of staying stuck where you are. I mentioned to Carol that eventually the three of us would meet and discuss our work."

"How would you present the situation?"

"We would share with Carol that your current position is far from being ideal for you, and we can discuss other opportunities within the group," I suggested.

Roger grew quiet. "What if the conversation goes south, and I lose my job anyway, despite having these realizations?"

"What's the alternative?"

Roger sighed. "You're right."

Shortly after we parted ways, I called Carol and arranged the meeting. Though uncertain, she eagerly accepted.

The following week, Roger and I met with Carol for lunch at a nearby restaurant. Roger wore neatly pressed gray slacks and a sports jacket; he'd put special effort into his appearance.

After some pleasantries—the swiftly cooling weather, the delicious smells wafting from nearby tables—I guided us to the matter at hand. I explained to Carol that Roger had been unconsciously acting out his dissatisfaction with his job. Roger sat very still as I spoke, nodding when I asked if I was describing it correctly, and Carol listened intently.

When I was through speaking, Carol took a sip of water. She nodded, as though engaging in an internal dialogue. Finally, she said, "I must admit—this is not what I expected."

"Me neither!"

After Roger blurted that out, we all laughed, easing the tension.

"Roger," Carol said, "I understand now what has been happening. I'm glad you discovered what you needed, though I wish it had happened earlier because you were driving us crazy!"

Roger winced, sheepish. "I know."

"Let me think about all this," she said. "I appreciate your creativity and the energy you bring to work. I'd like to offer you a more rewarding opportunity in our group."

About three weeks later, Carol reorganized the way her department managed the relationship with the ad agencies and created a central unit to align efforts. She offered Roger the position of heading the new team.

"I'm so excited!" Roger said when he called me with the news. "I have to admit, I was still a little worried that I'd have to take a hike after all."

"Do you think this will help bring balance between EE and CR?" I asked.

"I really do."

For the next several months, I checked in with Roger occasionally. Did he still feel the same energy he experienced upon receiving

Carol's offer? Was he doing something he'd be happy to do for free?

"Absolutely! The answer is yes! And I'm checking regularly with everybody on board my 'car,'" Roger said one afternoon. "Every member of my inner tribe. Now that I know they're there, I want to make sure everybody is getting what they need."

I grinned. "Good job. And who's at the steering wheel?"

"Ah! I got smart about that. I make sure we take turns so everybody has a chance to drive. We are an equal opportunity tribe."

Chapter 3 Summary
Roger: Congruency Between Intention and Behavior

The focus of this chapter concerns Roger, the director of a marketing group for a sizable company involved with R&D and time-sensitive projects. He also coordinates the work of diverse groups across different regions, a task that requires constant attention to detail and scheduling. He's very creative and always generates good ideas, but he's unable to meet the deadlines for projects or reports set by his boss. He frustrates everyone around him with his disorganization and lack of timeliness. Adding greater tension to the situation, different teams rely on his coordination efforts. This dysfunctional behavior is putting him and his company in a tough position. Does he really want to work on changing his behavior?

I. TWO CONDITIONS TO ENTERING A COACHING ARRANGEMENT:
1. The candidate is open to the process and desires personal change; and
2. The coach has the capability to address the specific issues or concerns that created the need for coaching.

II. THE FIRST ASPECTS OF CHANGING BEHAVIOR: It is necessary to understand a few of our tendencies and elements at play before being able to change our behavior, especially for something as habitually grooved into our consciousness as Roger's propensity for procrastinating and missing deadlines. Some of the aspects discussed with Roger:
1. Find out first what he already tried and *hasn't* worked
2. Know the difference between trying to change our personality (a long-term endeavor) and changing our behavior (within our immediate control)
3. The relationship between our intention (what we want to do) and our behavior (what we actually *do*) is sometimes elusive. Effectiveness is achieved when what we *actually do* is congruent with what we *want to do*.
4. Role-playing: Looking at ourselves from another viewpoint

III. UNDERSTANDING HOW OUR INNER WORLD WORKS: Several famous studies about our inner world and inner dynamics have been presented in the psychology field. I hit upon the following points in an extensive dialogue to understanding the driving force of our primary behaviors:
1. Eric Berne's transactional analysis (TA) an ingenious way of looking at these different aspects of self. TA identified the Parent, the Child, and the Adult, mirroring to a big extent Freud's Ego, Superego, and Id. Other studies are discussed highlighting the existence of sub-personalities or aspects of self.
2. The different parts or aspects of self have distinct characteristics, they act as "a small tribe." We can easily identify our inner child, the wise man or crone, the jester, the warrior, etc. They travel through life together.
3. Key realization—there's only one steering wheel. Only one part can steer

at any given time; the others are "passengers."
4. The goal of establishing a healthy "dialogue" between our different aspects is respectful integration of the self—every part of the self is honored and has a seat at the table (or an appropriate time at the steering wheel).

IV. ESTABLISHING CLARITY OF INTENTIONS—AND INTEGRATING WITH LIFE/WORK PURPOSE

1. By understanding how our inner world works, we can manage our life in a more satisfying way by recognizing and acting upon the inner dynamics at play.
2. Every part of self works with the best intentions, but because it only holds its own point of view, may fail to understand the whole picture and the best interest of the person.
3. That's why we need an "integrated self" that balances the needs of all its different aspects ensuring that each part receives attention and fulfillment.
4. Socrates: "An unexamined life is not worth living." The "examined life" brings awareness to the integration of self. Every member of your "inner tribe" receives what it needs.

V. TAKEWAY: We need to maintain congruence between our intention and our behavior. That's the path to living an intentional, purposeful life ... an "examined life."

Richard: Which Shirt Do You Like Most?

How to Avoid Thinking in (Wrong) Polarities

ONE day in mid-summer, I received a call from Peter, the CEO of a large public company focused on software development. He was referred by another CEO, with whom I had worked a couple of years before.

After introducing himself, Peter asked, "Are you available to meet this week? I know it's short notice." The urgency in his voice intrigued me. I found myself looking forward to the meeting we set for a few days later.

When I arrived at his office, Peter came out to greet me. He was an elegant man, a little overweight, in his mid- to late-fifties. His silver hair and short beard accented the determined expression on his face.

Peter showed me into his office. The walls were a soothing sandy color, and Peter's diplomas and other certificates were framed smartly across from his desk.

"I have a situation with a member of my team," he said, cutting to the chase, "and it's complicated."

"It usually is. What's going on?"

RICHARD

Peter sat in his high-backed leather desk chair, four fingers of one of his hands repeatedly drumming the chair's arm. "It's Richard, my VP of sales. He's a top player, a brilliant executive with lots of experience and good ideas. He's someone who understands sales. I like Richard; I personally hired him about three years ago and I haven't regretted bringing him on board. He knows our technology and what our customers need, but some of our most important clients find him abrasive and hard to deal with. I've also gotten numerous complaints from other members of the management team."

"What kind of complaints?"

"Richard seems to be always on an 'output' mode," Peter said. "He's opinionated; inflexible, and he's loud. Richard is not shy to jump in and blast another team member with his own point of view instead of conducting a conversation, a civilized dialogue. And I say *blast* because last week, my VP of engineering said that he felt 'sand blasted' by Richard."

"Even if the answer to this question seems obvious," I said, "I'd like to understand your motivation. Why do you feel that you need to do something about this?"

Peter nodded. "Every time I see Richard acting bigger than life, overpowering other people with his unconscious impersonation of Tony Soprano during our team meetings, I cringe. It's not my style, and I don't think it's respectful. But by doing nothing about it, I feel I'm condoning his behavior, sending the wrong message to the team and to other people in the organization."

"Have you talked with Richard about this?"

"I did, but not very successfully." Peter paused. "I was clear with him about the way he conducts himself in our meetings not being okay with me, but I haven't seen any change. I don't think I was very effective in communicating with Richard."

"You mentioned that it would be very hard to replace him. What if—"

"Absolutely!" Interrupted Peter. "I do not want to be put in that predicament. We need Richard to keep leading Sales!"

"What if other members of the team leave, upset about Richard?"

"That would certainly be a problem. Why do you raise the question?"

"I'm thinking that you may feel hostage to the situation. The company needs Richard, but at the same time, the way he relates to others is not aligned with your beliefs."

Peter was nodding emphatically. "That's exactly right. I do feel hostage and resent that I can't openly say, 'Richard, change your ways or you can't be part of our team.'"

"Peter, that 'change or leave' ultimatum sounds like binary thinking," I said. "We could explore other ways to encourage Richard to modulate how he relates to others."

"I'm afraid that's beyond my capabilities," he replied, laughing wholeheartedly. "I know technology. But working to change Richard, that sounds like something up your alley."

"Point well taken. I suggest that I meet with Richard and work on creating a more conducive context for this work."

"I will send an email to Richard right away to introduce you. When can you get started?"

I appreciated Peter's way of taking in information, processing it rapidly and moving forward.

"I will suggest to Richard that we meet sometime next week. I will keep you posted."

"Good luck," Peter said, smiling. "You'll need it."

RICHARD: PRISONER OR VOLUNTEER?

About a week later, I met with Richard—at my suggestion—at his office. I wanted the opportunity to look around and try to understand Richard through not only his words but also his working environment: is it orderly or chaotic? What's important to him?

Family photos were prominently displayed on the walls. The frames were simple, solid wood—nothing ornate or pretentious. The desk and side table held several photos of Richard on a golf course, wearing a determined expression as he held the club. His desk held organized stacks of folders and papers.

Richard had just celebrated his fiftieth birthday, and he was married with three children, two still living at home. He was tall and imposing—roughly 6-foot-2 and around 220 pounds—energetic and well dressed. I assumed immediately by his handshake that he was confident and self-assured; I was just glad his grip didn't break any bones in my hand!

Richard had been the vice president of sales for the company for a little over three years and had eight people reporting directly to him. After we sat down and exchanged pleasantries, I asked him to tell me about his communication style.

"Well, Gustavo," he said, "I was born and raised in the Midwest. I have firm family values, and what you see is what you get. I believe I have a straightforward communication style."

"Keeping that in mind," I said, "what is your take on this leadership development effort your CEO wants to engage you in?"

"I think the timing may not be right for this initiative," he said, nodding and leaning forward. "Also, I'm sure some of my colleagues in the management team are better candidates for this, some need to shape up and get their act together."

Hmm, I thought, watching him straighten a sheaf of paper on his desk. It was obvious that Richard didn't think *he* needed to focus on his own professional development.

"As you know," I said, "feedback illuminates our blind spots, and a feedback process will be part of the effort. When was the last time you received feedback from your colleagues?"

"I get feedback all the time. You look at people in their eyes, you speak frankly and let others speak frankly, and—one way or the other—you get feedback every day."

In my experience, people generally have trouble giving direct feedback to a strong, self-assured character like Richard, who towers above most others. He would be a big presence in any room and may come across as intimidating to those less confident. I needed to engage Richard if we were going to have any chance of working together.

"Richard, at the beginning of an effectiveness engagement like this, I look at a potential participant as either a 'volunteer' or a 'prisoner.'" Recalling the photos of Richard on the links, I thought some golf metaphors would be appropriate. "Volunteers are usually not fully satisfied with their game; they realize they could swing or putt better and want to improve their handicap. Volunteers embrace the process, and see their handicap diminish as their swing and their game improve."

"On the other hand," I continued, "prisoners are happy with their handicap, don't see any need to improve, and consider the time required by a leadership development effort as a waste of time, money, and energy. I find it dishonest to work with prisoners because they typically fulfill their own prophecies, and the effort ends up being what they anticipated: a waste."

Such a clever approach, I thought. I was proud of myself for presenting Richard with these choices. What respectable golfer would not want to improve his game?

Richard was unfazed.

Very politely, he said, "I completely agree with you. It *is* silly to not want to improve. I always want to improve. But I also see," he extended his pointer, "one—that we are super busy right now and this effort will take time and take our eyes off the ball; two—that this effort should be directed to Sam, our VP of Marketing, not me; and three—why fix what's not broken?"

"Richard, you seem to be a man who would not shy away from looking at yourself and addressing anything that could work better. Is that a fair assessment?"

"You got me there." Richard nodded vehemently. "If there's anything I could do to improve myself, I wouldn't hesitate to grapple with that."

"Good, this is what I suggest. Let's look at your leadership profile and the 360° feedback that we'll collect from all your key colleagues at work. Call it a swing check." I stuck fast to the golf metaphor. "If you are satisfied with what you see, that will be the end of our work together. If you see a need to work on something, then—and only then—we'll roll up our sleeves and get to work together on that."

Richard smiled. "You're tricky, but it sounds fair."

We discussed logistics and agreed to review his SELF leadership profile at the next meeting. He would complete it online beforehand. Meanwhile, we would launch the 360° feedback with the list of respondents that Richard would provide.

RICHARD'S LEADERSHIP PROFILE

A week later, Richard and I met again with his leadership profile in front of us. There were a few very clear red flag areas, or aspects of his leadership style that could be making him less effective as a leader. The first: Dogmatism.

Richard was certain about his ideas. As he'd said during our initial meeting, he had "been around the block and knew his way around." His clear and deep convictions enabled him to be unwavering in situations that would be difficult for other, less experienced folks to resolve.

People with deep convictions have the advantage of being decisive, but they often run the risk of seeing things in terms of black and white and becoming dogmatic. Strong beliefs about how things should be often eliminate the curiosity to understand how things actually are.

Perhaps not surprisingly, Richard didn't think that this was a problem; he viewed this tendency as an asset. "What you may call dogmatism, I call knowing where I stand on things and what my values are," he said. "It's a strength that I wish more of my people possessed."

"Why don't we look at dogmatism in the context of the rest of the report?" I suggested.

Richard's expression was impassive as he reviewed the other traits that could cause problems for an executive. His score on Emotional Stability was quite low, indicating a tendency to be reactive and to readily show emotions. A person with this tendency usually says, "I'm intense" as if their intensity is something to value, while others might say, "He's explosive and intimidating, he lacks emotional control." There is an obvious and troubling difference between the two perceptions.

Meanwhile, Richard's score on Stress Management suggested that he could get easily frazzled, agitated by difficult situations or events. To complicate matters, Richard's level of Defendence—his resistance to receive criticism—was high, so I expected him to discount feedback about his leadership style.

Richard seemed to be taking all this information in stride—perhaps *too* much in stride. He showed no concern about how these traits might be affecting his performance or the quality of his leadership. I couldn't help but wonder how he would respond to the 360° feedback report, which would be completed in two weeks. He hadn't gone through this kind of feedback process during his three years as VP of Sales at this company, and everything indicated it would be seen by the organization as a great opportunity to provide feedback to Richard. I suspected that the feedback would be harsh, as resentment had probably been accumulating in folks for some time.

After reviewing hundreds of feedback reports and seeing how people come forth when they have a chance to safely provide feedback, I still marvel at how we are willing to live for so long in a mild (and sometimes even acute!) state of unhappiness. It seems to be such a generalized predicament that people are unable to confront others with issues that are hard to live with until they find a safe opportunity to provide anonymous feedback without fear of repercussions. The operative word here is *anonymous*. A big part of our culture is deeply rooted in conflict avoidance, and the majority of people seem to lack the skills to successfully confront other people in graceful, dignified ways.

"I guess we'll see what they have to say," Richard said about the 360° feedback process after we finished reviewing his leadership profile.

LOOKING AT THE FEEDBACK

Two weeks later, back in the same conference room, Richard was again well dressed in neatly pressed slacks and a tailored sports jacket. And, once again, his too-powerful handshake made me wince.

"Let's do this," he said as we sat down.

More than thirty of his colleagues provided feedback on the 360° survey, including the CEO, a large number of peers, his eight direct reports, and other people in the organization with whom Richard interacted frequently. As expected, the feedback was nothing short of a glaring cry for Richard to change the way he related to others.

The question in front of me was how to help Richard open up in response to this feedback. How could I make this a learning experience that would enhance his emotional intelligence and make him more effective with others? After all, the 360° feedback process is not intended to be a demoralizing experience, but an opportunity for personal and professional growth. The key is that the subject find a way to open his mind and heart to the praise and recognition he receives—*as well as* to the plight and suffering he may be unintentionally creating around him.

As I started reviewing the 360° feedback with Richard, I looked for that opening. I was also intent on including three elements: compassion (for all the painful circumstances in Richard's life that had created the guarded man he seemed to be today); a firm attitude about our moral obligation to treat well the people around us; and clarity on how to skillfully communicate with him.

As on many other occasions, I found that the data was generally impactful but when we got to the *normative* data—where Richard's scores were contrasted with the population in our database (over 2,000 executives)—the results were shocking. On some competencies, Richard's scores plummeted to the lowest possible percentiles. If Richard ranked in the second percentile on a competency, then *ninety-eight percent* of the 2,000-plus executives in our database were more competent than him.

The competencies where Richard was particularly low were:

A. Emotional Control

B. Listening

C. Flexibility

D. Conflict Resolution

E. Partnering/Relationship Building

F. Teamwork

Meanwhile, his scores were very high on:

A. Accountability. Meeting commitments and deadlines.

B. Self-Confidence

C. Assertiveness

D. Decisiveness

E. Effectiveness. Getting the job done.

In the comments section, there were many mentions of Richard lacking emotional control and coming across as intimidating and abrasive. He was managing using fear as the main way to motivate and mobilize people.

Richard reviewed the feedback quietly, but his jaw clenched and unclenched as he processed the information. It was apparent that the data affected him, but I couldn't quite tell *how*. "What do you think?" he asked me.

"Richard, I sometimes find it helpful to relate this list of strengths and weaknesses to my client as a short story," I said. "Let me try that. Now, here's a man—Richard—who delivers. He understands the marketplace, meets his commitments and deadlines, and gets the job done. He does that with confidence, decisiveness, and assertiveness. Richard delivers a strong performance. To accomplish that, however, he sometimes loses his temper, alienates people around him, and gives rigid directives. He also creates unresolved conflict and resentment, foregoes building strong working relationships, and destroys the possibility of creating teamwork and a collaborative environment. People don't respond to this man's leadership but to his outbursts and their own fear as they relate to him. He is a good example of leadership by intimidation."

If I'd thought that Richard would be shocked or aghast at this description of himself, I would have been disappointed. Richard stared at me coolly, then he stood and started pacing, towering above me in my seat.

"Gustavo," he said, "I know this doesn't look good, but I focus on getting the job done. That's my highest priority. Others in the company may be better liked, but they don't get the job done the way my department does—the way *I* do." Richard's voice was rising, his neck beginning to redden. "This company would do well to have more people like me. To get results, you need to bite the bullet and deliver. And to make things happen, I have to frequently choose between being nice and being effective. What would you choose if you had to? Being nice or being effective?"

After his earlier aloofness, Richard was having an intense emotional moment. I could easily see how young, junior employees might feel intimidated by this big man. It would be a good idea to de-escalate the situation and reason with Richard instead of challenging him. If he were emotionally charged, Richard would probably bypass his reasoning mode, making it difficult, if not impossible, for him to listen.

In a soft, calming voice I said, "Richard, over years of work, I have met many people with deep convictions and clear values. People like you. It's a delight to find someone who knows right from wrong and brings forth his sense of integrity with clarity and force. I'm all for that. The downside for people who feel so strongly about things is that sometimes they don't modulate their emotions well, which affects how they communicate what they think and feel. Therefore, they may sometimes become their own worst enemy by being too forceful, too intense; other folks might experience them as intimidating or scary. Have you found, at times, that your intensity backfires and makes you less effective with some people? I'm sure that people who care for you would have told you so at some point."

"Well, yes," Richard responded, noticeably calmer. "My wife, Ellen, tells me that all the time. But that doesn't take away from my question. 'Would you rather be nice or effective?'"

"Richard, my response has to be a bit long here."

I told him that we often think in terms of polarities—good versus bad, high versus low—making it easy to imagine a continuum between the two extremes.

"So," I said as I stood up and approached the whiteboard, "you are now describing your choice between a particular polarity." I drew the following image: *(see Figure 1)*

EFFECTIVE _____ NICE

Figure 1

"But sometimes," I continued, "our mind plays a trick on us, creates a false polarity, and we believe that our only option is to choose from one of these opposing alternatives.

129

"This trick resembles the shrewd salesman's tactic to never ask, 'Do you like this shirt?' because you may respond 'Yes' or 'No,' and if you say 'No,' there's no sale. The sly approach is to present two shirts simultaneously and ask, 'Which shirt do you like the most—the green or the blue?'"

"I believe the nice-versus-effective choice is a false polarity. It indicates an attitude that treating people well is ineffective in the business world, and that the only way to truly be effective is to lead with harsh 'command and control' or abrasive communication," I said.

Richard sat down. He took a long sip from the bottle of water he'd brought with him to the meeting. "Go on," he said.

"The truth of the matter is that you're dealing with two polarities at the same time, two different axes, which creates four different possibilities. You could be one of these four possibilities." I began adding to my original diagram: *(See Figure 2 and 3)*

INEFFECTIVE_____ AND _____ NICE

OR

INEFFECTIVE_____ AND _____ LET'S SAY, A JERK

Figure 2

"Or you could be …"

EFFECTIVE_____ AND _____ A JERK

OR

EFFECTIVE_____ AND _____ NICE

Figure 3

"So, let me turn the question to you now," I said. "Looking at these options, would you rather be Effective and Nice, or Effective and a Jerk?"

Richard didn't respond but seemed to be paying attention, so I continued. "Behind all this resides the false polarity source of all this confusion." In large, clear lettering, I wrote: *(See Figure 4)*

RESULTS _____ PEOPLE

Figure 4

"The line in between Results and People illustrates a continuum," I said, "indicating that there are different degrees of focus on results versus focus on people.

"Of course," I added, "in this logic-impaired framework, the more you focus on the people, the less you are going to achieve the results you are seeking. Conversely, if you are deeply focused on achieving results for your organization, you must let go of considerations about people.

"But in order to be accurate," I continued, "we have to see that we are talking about two different axes, two different variables."

I changed the diagram to a two-variables equation. *(See Figure 5)*

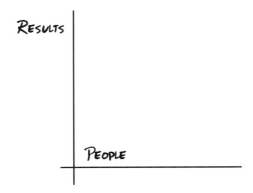

Figure 5

I explained to Richard that one could either be high or low on each of these dimensions, so it's more illustrative to see it as four quadrants. *(See Figure 6)*

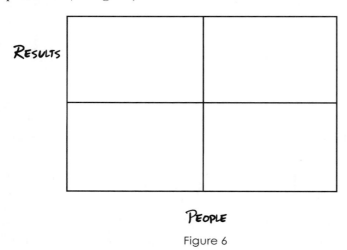

RESULTS

PEOPLE

Figure 6

"If you operate on the top left quadrant, you forego focusing on people to get results. It's like saying: "I don't care how you feel; just show me your numbers!" There are companies that are run that way. Usually, their staffers are well compensated but not engaged. They dream of leaving at some point, loyalty is low, and it's not a pleasant work environment. Solid research shows that people unengaged and not passionate about their work are less productive than people who invest their hearts and minds in what they do.

"If you operate on the bottom right quadrant, then people are important to you, and you are well-liked and popular. However, you are low on results, and your organization is not sustainable. In this case, you are an Ineffective Good Guy. Those types of organizations are out of balance and not sustainable, as they don't obtain the necessary results to thrive.

"Once you start seeing these two variables in this way," I told Richard, "it becomes obvious that you want to operate on the top right quadrant, where you get the best of both worlds: you create a sustainable organization that accomplishes top results through motivated, engaged people." *(See Figure 7)*

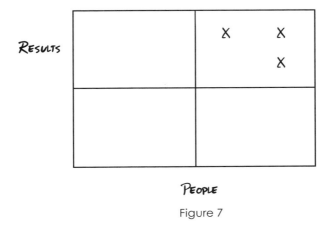

Figure 7

Richard seemed reflective as he stared at the four quadrants. "I see your point," he said. "I have to think about all this."

I nodded. "We learn how to be in the world from people we admire. Where did you learn to manage and lead people the way you do?"

Richard responded with no hesitation. "My first boss, Bob. I'm a 'softie' compared with him. People around him were always on their best behavior, and nobody dared to let him down. He made things happen."

"Was he injecting passion and enthusiasm in his people or getting things done out of fear?"

Richard paused, eyebrows furrowing. "Looking back, sure, I have to admit that fear wasn't unusual around him, but that's not the point. Things got done, and we kicked our competition's rear. I remember staying until late at night if I had to report to him the next morning because he could ask me about minute details, and if I didn't have an answer, he wouldn't hesitate to berate me in front of the whole team … it wasn't pretty! But boy, was I well prepared!"

"I wonder about the consequences," I mused. "There are always consequences to creating that kind of work environment …"

Richard was silent for a long moment. His eyes grew distant, as if peering into the past. "I focused so much on how he consistently got results that I never dwelled on that." After another long pause, he added, "We got results, but people were stressed out. Some folks— not me! —were always talking about leaving our department or even our company. It wasn't easy in those times to land a job, but those folks were always looking for other opportunities. Every now and then, someone in the team would leave for an easier situation."

"What about you? How did you deal with all that?"

"After working with Bob for about two years, I learned to live with his way of leading us and how to be mostly on his good side. You know," Richard added, more quietly, "my own father wasn't too different than Bob—demanding, severe—but looking back, I appreciate his high expectations for me."

Richard's revelation made me pause. I decided to further explore his experience with Bob.

"At some point you obviously left your job with Bob," I said. "Why?"

Richard cringed. "I developed gastritis. Then ulcers. My doctor finally said I needed a less stressful job, which my friends had been saying for quite some time. My wife even threatened to leave me if I didn't change jobs," he paused for a moment, "I guess she wouldn't have, but she sure was adamant about the need for me to work in a less pressured environment."

I nodded. "Being that Bob's style was so similar to your father's, would it be okay to ask how your relationship was with your dad?"

"Sure," Richard said, shrugging. "After I left for college, I didn't communicate much with him. I used to go back home once or twice a year, you know, studying hard, and then after graduation, I got a job. I never slowed down again. We were okay, but we didn't have a 'fuzzy' relationship. Just not his style. Probably not mine, either." He chuckled.

"So, it seems that you had two very strong role models with Bob and your father," I said. "And we know that there are always some consequences to a harsh leadership style, just as there are with a hard parenting style. Richard, what consequences are you experiencing because of your style?"

Richard clenched his jaw again; it probably wasn't even a conscious action. "I'm not sure I know the answer to that question. But I'll think about it."

INTRODUCING A CHALLENGE

We were approaching the time to end this session. I knew Richard would benefit greatly from becoming a more engaging leader who would *inspire* people to achieve ambitious goals rather than lead by inducing fear. Creativity and innovation, which both Richard and the CEO wanted for the company, inevitably involves trial and error, but what sane person would risk error and failure with Richard? Still, he wasn't yet a "volunteer," and I wouldn't work with him as a "prisoner" of the CEO's leadership effort. That would not foster change in Richard nor support his personal and professional development.

What *would* create an opening in Richard that would allow him to consider other ways of relating and working with people? I had one more card to play: his family.

"Richard, we agreed that after looking at your leadership profile and your 360° feedback, we would determine whether you want to work on the competencies that people rated you low on. But I'm not sure we've completed our homework."

I let the sentence trail. "I'm listening," Richard said.

"I know you care deeply about your family. It seems unfair that you requested feedback from your colleagues at work but haven't asked for any from your own family." I paused to gauge his reaction and then added, "As if you don't care what they have to say …"

Richard looked puzzled. "What do you propose?"

135

"I propose that, to be fair, you meet with your family and in an informal, easygoing way, ask for their feedback."

"What would I be asking them?"

"How they feel about you as a husband and a father. Usually families talk about that at a funeral. Why wait until you're gone for your family to express how they feel about you? And if your family is important to you, and there's anything you could do to be a better father and husband, wouldn't you want to know what it is?"

Richard was quiet for a while. "I'll seriously think about that."

"The only suggestion I have—again in the spirit of being fair—is that if you decide to go ahead and get feedback from your family, you also offer them the possibility of giving you feedback anonymously."

"Like I said, I'll think about this." He stood, and his face was, again, impassive. He was stonewalling.

"Let's meet *at least* once more, and we'll take it from there," I suggested, purposefully leaving the process open.

Richard nodded, crushingly shook my hand, and then we parted ways.

THE FAMILY MEETING

Richard rescheduled our next meeting twice. I couldn't help thinking that he might be deliberately postponing to avoid difficult questions about his leadership style.

We finally met three weeks later. He looked somber and subdued, perhaps anticipating a difficult conversation. I shook his hand with dread; I still didn't enjoy his overbearing handshake, but it seemed to be his only mode of greeting. We met at his office, and his desk was uncharacteristically covered with folders and piles of paper. Even his mismatched attire seemed out of place.

With no preamble, Richard said, "Last time we met, you suggested I also ask my family what they think about me, rather than making them wait to say it at my funeral. I kept thinking about that, thinking if that was the right thing to do."

Rather than sit across from me at his desk, Richard sat on one of the two chairs in front of it; I took the other.

"So I called a family meeting," he continued. "Gustavo, I can't tell you how surprised they were."

Richard related that the family meeting had taken place on a Saturday afternoon. Attending were his wife Ellen ("We have been married—she has put up with me—for twenty-six years!"); his daughter, Liz, twenty-four, married and living in the area; and his two teenage sons, Richard Jr. and Tom, seventeen and fifteen. Liz and his wife sat beside each other on the leather loveseat, while the boys stretched their gangly limbs out on the rug.

Richard said he was pacing; his nerves surprised him. "The CEO of my company just launched a team effectiveness program for the management team," he told his family. "As part of the process, I received feedback from a number of work colleagues."

He paused. "And?" Ellen asked.

"Well, people at work, particularly those who reported directly to me, see me as smart, knowledgeable, hard working," he said. "But they also think I'm rigid, dogmatic, and a harsh boss who loses emotional control at times."

The boys looked up at Liz and their mom, and they all exchanged a half-smiling look. Richard was convinced that they would have a kinder impression of him.

"It was humbling," he explained to his family. "I found out that I'm placed extremely low compared to other executives. In some cases, almost everyone had higher scores than me!

"But this has all made me think," he said. He finally stopped pacing and sat in a big chair facing his family. "I want to hear from you all about your experience of me as a husband, as a father. I'm not going to focus on people at work and not hear from my family."

With his next words lodging unexpectedly in his throat, he said,

137

"I don't want any regrets."

A long silence followed. Richard looked at each member of his family, but they avoided his gaze. "Come on guys," he said, laughing. "I know you have something to say. I need to hear from you!"

After another silence, Richard Jr.—Ricky—said, "Dad, could you ask a specific question?"

Richard felt a quick stab of frustration. Then it hit him that maybe his family was like his team at work, requiring some specific questions to provide feedback.

"It was somewhat shocking for me to receive feedback that people at work perceive me as abrasive, harsh, and intimidating," he said. His wife looked at him, puzzled. "I know that sometimes I get upset when people are not thinking about what they are doing or don't learn from their mistakes, but I was floored to read about how people around me feel intimidated. So my question to you is, as a father and a husband, do you perceive me the way they do? From one to ten," he said, "ten being the highest, how do you rate me on the scale of abrasive, harsh, and intimidating? How about on losing emotional control?"

Richard felt he'd provided the structure they needed, so he was perplexed when his questions were followed by another long, tense silence.

"Look," he said, "the feedback at work was anonymous and confidential. I know that's why it was so candid."

Richard jumped up from the chair and hurried to the kitchen, where he pulled the magnetic notepad from the refrigerator and tore off a few pages. Back in the living room, he said, "I'm going to pass out a page to each of you. Don't write your name; just write a number for each of my questions: from one to ten, ten being the highest, how do you rate me on being harsh, abrasive, intimidating? And how do you rate me on the scale of losing emotional control? Don't be shy. I really want to know."

There was some nervous chuckling, and then Richard's family

began to write. He watched the expressions on their faces become serious, and he felt a flicker of worry. When everyone had put their pens down and looked up, Richard said, "All right, now turn your papers face down and hand them to me."

Pages in hand, Richard shuffled to show his family that he wasn't trying to determine their individual ratings. He was playing fair. Then he turned each small piece of paper around: 9 and 9; 9 and 8; 9 and 10; 10 and 10.

Richard was floored, speechless. How was it possible that his family perceived him as harshly as his work colleagues did? How could an intelligent and dedicated family man like him be so unaware?

"I didn't say a word for a while," Richard told me. "Then I asked them to give me some time to reflect and we'd talk again soon, but I didn't know what to say. My wife has talked to me a number of times since then, telling me not to take it so badly, but it's been hard for me to digest this. It's not that this is the first time I heard someone saying that I was too harsh—my wife has actually told me that many times—but I never thought my own family would see me under such a negative light, as if I'm an ogre. I was raised this way. I am the way I am with my children because I care about them."

Richard's voice was heated, but there was a begging sense about him. Was it possible that the opening had been created?

"What do you want to do now?" I asked.

"I feel defeated," Richard said simply. "I put my family above everything, and to learn that they see me this way is demolishing. Now I understand the feedback from people at work, and I feel as if someone ran a bulldozer over me. I feel flattened and angry at the same time."

"Richard, your family's feedback—and how much you care about them—gives you such a big motivation to change."

"But can I actually change who I am? And if I can, can I change fast, before my two sons leave home for college?"

THE FOUR PHASES OF CHANGE

Great question! That very question could be the beginning of engaging Richard in this process. I said, "If you're willing to focus on *who you are,* then here's the answer: maybe you can change, but over a long period of time. Now, if you focus intently on *who you want to be,* then the answer is yes, absolutely yes, you can change! And in a very short time."

I continued, "Usually change in ourselves occurs in four distinct steps or phases. The first phase could last a long time, sometime years or decades. In that first phase, we have developed a blind spot, something that inevitably happens to all of us. And during that phase we are Unconsciously Incompetent (UI)." I began to draw: *(See Figure 8)*

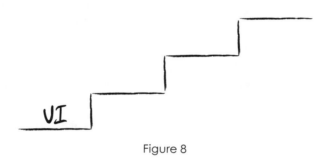

Figure 8

"We are unskillful or incompetent about something, but are completely oblivious about it and its cause. We have developed a blind spot.

"Then one day," I continued, "we receive feedback, irrefutable evidence about our lack of skill or competency, and we move to the next step: we become Consciously Incompetent (CI). We are still lacking the skills, but now we know about it." *(See Figure 9)*

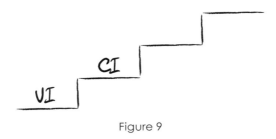

Figure 9

"So we seek help. We read articles and books about what we need to learn. Or," I added, smiling, "we get a coach. And eventually we learn about the process that will correct our lack of skill; we find the path to a more competent way of approaching the situation. And that allows us to move to the third phase, where we find ourselves able to be Consciously Competent (CC)." *(See Figure 10)*

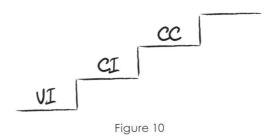

Figure 10

I explained to Richard that this step takes a lot of awareness, intention and purposeful action. We know what to do, but it's not our natural tendency to do it, nor is it a well-practiced skill. But if we practice hard enough, we will eventually internalize our new competency to the point that we move to the next phase: Unconsciously Competent (UC). *(See Figure 11)*

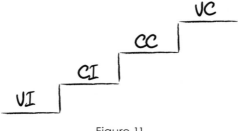

Figure 11

At this point, we have incorporated this new skill into our way of being in the world and don't need a special effort to keep it going. Deeper parts of the brain take over, and the process becomes automatic. If you have been driving for a while now, you know that's the way we drive, with very little effort as our mind is free to think, plan, worry, and even talk on the phone!

"A memorable experience I had with these four phases of change came about while trying to improve my backhand at tennis," I said to Richard. He glanced quickly at one of his golf photos as I shared my story.

Most of the time, when I hit the ball with my backhand, it would go too high and to the right, and I'd lose the point. I went to see a tennis instructor, who said: "Let's play and I'll watch your backhand and give you feedback." After just a few minutes, the instructor stopped the rally, approached me, and said, "Gustavo, the problem is that at the very last moment, just before hitting the ball, you whip your hand. You bend your wrist abruptly—whipping—just before hitting the ball."

Sensing Richard's interest, I continued to share my tennis story with him.

After the coach gave his diagnosis, I thought for a moment, picturing my movements on the court. I shook my head. "I'm sorry to challenge you, Coach," I said, "but I don't think I do that!"

"You definitely do," my coach said. Not a hint of doubt in his voice.

"I don't think so …"

My coach picked up his racquet from where it was leaning against the net. "Let's play again for a few minutes, and I'll have someone shoot a video," he suggested.

I smiled. "Let's do it!"

About half an hour later, we were comfortably sitting at the club cafeteria. "You ready to see this in slow-motion?" the coach asked, finger hovering over the Play button on his camera.

"Absolutely," I said confidently.

And I saw myself, *whipping the ball!*

I could not believe my eyes, but at the very millisecond before the racquet hit the ball, my wrist bent abruptly every time, whipping the ball and sending it high and off the court. A humbling experience. I was now officially Consciously Incompetent: Conscious because I was now keenly aware of my faulty stroke, and Incompetent because I had no idea how to correct it.

I learned that if I wanted my backhand shots to go straight and low, just above the net, I had to keep my arm straight as a rod while hitting the ball. I learned to focus on my right arm holding the racquet while thinking, *straight arm, straight arm, straight arm.* And then, more and more often, I would hit the ball correctly and it would fly low and straight, just as I intended, and hit the other side of the court beautifully.

"I was happy," I told Richard, "but the problem now was that I could only think about holding my arm straight. I didn't have any idea about where the opponent was or what to do next. I had no anticipation of next moves—just a nice straight arm. I had to practice and practice until I could hit the ball with a straight arm and consider all the other factors of playing tennis. But by practicing again and again, I eventually became Unconsciously Competent."

"What is my equivalent of your straight arm?"

"Richard, as you know, the interaction with people around you has more dimensions and is more complex than playing tennis. If we work together, after a few adjustments to how you relate to others, you would start seeing a deep change in how others relate to you. We will focus on your work environment, but eventually this will also affect in a positive way how you relate to your family."

"I still have reservations about spending a lot of time on this," he said, "but I want to inspire people, not intimidate them."

A little resistance on my part, I thought, could test Richard's determination, engage him more deeply, and increase the chances of a successful transformational process. "As we discussed before, for our effort to be successful, you have to be convinced that you want to do this work," I said. "The work done to improve ratings is like cosmetic work: things would change a little bit on the surface, but the core would be the same. Only work done in earnest yields results."

Richard's eyes narrowed just slightly. "Gustavo, if you don't think I'd put all my energy into this process, you don't know me at all. What I learned from my family had the effect of a lightning bolt to my head. I've become my father! Even worse, I'm a caricature of who I want to be. I toss and turn at night now instead of sleeping, as I consider the person I have become. I don't like who I am …" He cleared his throat, looking away. "That's not easy to admit. But the experience with my family shed a different light on the feedback I received from the people who work with me. I want to get results but not at the cost of people hating me or needing to tiptoe around me. I've always thought that I'd rather be respected than popular. Now I see it differently. I'm not respected; I'm feared. I want to change that. Please help me."

I remained quiet for a moment to let his passionate words reverberate inside both of us. Then I said, "Richard, I hear you, and I can see your resolve. I can work with that."

"How?"

"We will work on your competencies as a leader of people and how you relate to people at work," I said. "We will work on how to sustain excellent results while creating a great place for your team."

I paused for a moment, switching gears. "Regarding your family, may I give you a suggestion?"

"By all means, please!"

"As we focus on the issues at work, I suggest you engage a family counselor to work with you and your family. Even just a couple of meetings could facilitate better dialogue and resolve old family patterns."

"Good idea. I even know someone to ask for a referral. Thank you!"

His openness surprised and pleased me. We stood and shook hands. This time, I suggested he treat my hand a bit more tenderly. We both laughed. Our working agreements had been set.

When we met again two weeks later, Richard showed up in good spirits. He was waiting for me in his office with a bottle of water and a cup of coffee. It was a nice gesture, and I thanked him for it.

"Let's start working," I said. "Before we shake hands, keep in mind that handshakes could also be graded."

"What do you mean?" Richard asked.

"Handshakes can be placed among a continuum that goes from ten, which can be crushing, down to one, a "dead fish." Somewhere between a six and a seven could be called firm and polite. When you go beyond that, you run the risk of being inappropriate, and you're sending a probably unintended message."

"The message being …?"

"I'm more powerful than you. You should fear me," I said bluntly.

Richard nodded. "I should start looking more carefully at how I approach people."

"Not a bad idea. 'An unexamined life is not worth living,' said Socrates." I extended my hand. Richard shook it firmly.

"Good job, Richard. That was about a seven on the handshake meter."

"I'll remember this," Richard said as we walked to his desk. "I still bench-press two hundred pounds, and I'm proud of keeping strong, but it's not my intention to instill fear in anyone."

"That's good." I took a sip of the coffee. "So, how are things going with your family, if I may ask?"

Richard smiled. "We've met with a family counselor. I think we're on the right track."

We were ready to start the next leg of our journey together. I shared with him my plan of action: to tackle a few issues revealed by the 360° feedback that commonly have a big halo effect, as they influence a number of other competencies. When people see low ratings in a number of leadership competencies, often they want to work on all of them simultaneously. The reality is that they need to find the "themes" that are driving why and in what ways people see them in a negative light. There are usually two or three such themes at most; sometimes even lacking one core competency can taint all other scores. (Quick example: try behaving without integrity and see what happens.)

With Richard, I suggested we start by focusing on two competencies: Listening and Emotional Control. The plan was to work on these two areas for some time and then—if enough improvement was made—conduct a brief feedback process focused on tracking how people perceived his progress.

LISTENING AS A SKILL

Richard was a bright individual, and he rapidly grasped the principles of effective listening and the idea that listening was not just about hearing what other people have to say, but also making them feel heard. We talked about active listening and how, by reiterating to people the gist of what you've just heard, you can:

1. Confirm the accuracy of what was said and understood;
2. Get clarification when it is needed; and
3. Make the other person feel heard.

We role-played a few situations. Richard was eager to learn and practice, but he interrupted, jumped to conclusions, and sometimes even finished my phrases—often not on target with what I was intending to say. I suggested that he remain curious about his style of communication, so we would interact for a few minutes and then stop the action to analyze the effectiveness of his style.

Eventually, I pulled a small video camera out of my briefcase and asked Richard if he was ready for prime time—a little trick that reminded me of my tennis coach. I suggested we choose a somewhat difficult topic and talk about it for a few minutes while we videotaped our interaction. Then we would watch and evaluate it. Richard agreed, and we launched into a conversation where I role-played one of his reports coming to him to discuss a course of action for the remainder of the quarter and ask for clarification about some aspects of the plan. Richard briefed me rapidly so I could have a context to speak intelligently about it.

From the start, I tried to give Richard a bit of a hard time. My reasoning—as his direct report—was slightly slow, and I displayed some difficulty in "getting it." I also asked a few challenging questions and expressed some doubts about the team being able to implement the plan on time and hit the sales numbers he mentioned.

Eventually, we stopped the conversation and watched the video on my laptop.

Richard seemed fascinated; he was watching the screen with a childish expression on his face. He was able to see himself in the mirror, experiencing himself in ways that weren't accessible to him before.

What he saw was not flattering—and he mentioned it. He was being impulsive, his mind racing as I spoke, getting bored if I talked a bit too slowly. He reported that at the beginning of the exercise, he promised himself he would be tolerant and respond calmly to my questions, but in a very short time, he felt impatient and irritated. He was enthralled at the experience of just being himself and then objectively observing his own communication style.

Richard was a determined learner. We practiced again while videotaping and eventually, he was able to slow down his mind, focus on the subject of our conversation, and ask good questions. At some point, I noticed he was getting tired. "This work is harder than selling to a tough customer," he confessed, "but I'm determined to go back home with the order!"

ENROLLING THE TEAM

Before the end of our meeting, I asked Richard if he would be willing to try a daring experiment with his team that would test and improve his listening skills. I also anticipated it'd be a high challenge.

"I like challenges," he said, his eyes glinting. "I'm game."

"Are you familiar with soccer?"

"Of course. My sons play soccer, and I had to get familiar with it or die of boredom watching them play in weekend tournaments."

"What happens when a player commits a malicious foul?" I asked.

"The referee gives that player a yellow card."

I smiled. "On your next team meeting, I suggest you follow a five-step process regarding the feedback you received from the team. This should not take more than a few minutes."

"Okay." Richard reached for paper and pen. "I'm taking notes."

STEP 1. EXPRESSING GRATEFULNESS. Your team invested some time to think about you and write useful comments to help make you a better person and executive. Acknowledge that and thank them for their time and effort.

STEP 2. WHAT I LEARNED FROM THE PROCESS. Share with the team what you learned from the feedback, your insights. This is an overview of the strengths and weaknesses uncovered by the feedback process. It's also your way of saying, "I heard you, and I'm paying attention."

STEP 3. ACTION PLAN. Share with the team what you are planning to do differently because of the feedback received.

STEP 4. SUPPORT NEEDED. You are not going to be able to change long-term, deep-seated traits without the support of your team. Ask for support about the competency that you are working on: skillful listening.

STEP 5. REQUESTING FEEDBACK. At the end of the working session, ask for feedback from the team about the meeting. Inquire about what worked well for them and how these meetings can be improved.

I asked Richard to let me look at his notes. This is how they looked. *(See Figure 12)*

PROCESS TO FOLLOW AFTER RECEIVING FEEDBACK

Step 1:	THANK YOU FOR YOUR TIME AND EFFORT TO GIVE ME FEEDBACK.
Step 2:	HERE ARE MY INSIGHTS FROM THE FEEDBACK.
Step 3:	THIS IS HOW I'M GOING TO CHANGE THE WAY I DO THINGS.
Step 4:	THIS IS WHAT I NEED YOU TO DO TO SUPPORT MY PERSONAL CHANGE EFFORT.
Step 5:	PLEASE GIVE FEEDBACK ON HOW THESE MEETINGS CAN BE IMPROVED.

Figure 12

"Wow!" he replied, looking over his notes. "This will test me, and I know it's not going to be easy. What I'm not clear about is this: what kind of support am I asking my team for?"

I smiled. "Timely question. You are going to give a small yellow card to each of your team members. A 3 x 5 yellow card just like the ones the soccer referee hands out to the players who commit a foul. They are to raise the yellow card every time you are communicating

149

in a way that is not working for them—whatever that means—or if somehow they don't feel heard. They don't need to say a single word. They just need to raise that yellow card. It's your real-time, on-the-spot feedback sign. The instruction for *you* is that if someone raises a yellow card, you can only say, 'Thank you! What do you need?' You cannot get defensive; you cannot push back. Do you think you can do this?'"

Richard laughed. "I love it. I know they're going to chuckle and tease me—the whole idea is a little quirky—but I'm intrigued, and I'm committed to following through."

A HEALTHY SUSPICION

When we met again, Richard was smiling. From the doorway of his office, he shook my hand firmly and said, "That's one more thing I'm tracking now—not crushing people's hands."

"Excellent," I said. "And how are people reacting to that?"

"Funny that you ask," Richard said, grinning. "A few times I mentioned, after shaking people's hands, that I'm working on my handshake, and some people just laughed. Others said they were always bracing, expecting a hard time! I had no idea that this was happening."

"That's why we call it a blind spot," I responded. "It's a crude example, but imagine a good friend telling you that your breath is less than optimal. Once you know, you can brush your teeth and put a mint in your mouth."

We settled into our regular seats at his desk. "So, tell me about what happened with your team and the yellow cards."

Richard beamed. I hadn't seen this kind of vibrancy—even joy—from him before. "I've been looking forward to telling you. At last week's meeting, I went through the steps you described. I thanked the team, and they seem surprised—and glad—that I was expressing appreciation."

Richard walked to the whiteboard when he shared what he had learned from the feedback process.

"I don't believe that they expected that level of transparency," he said. "But I felt that it was good for me to role model honesty and candor. Finally, I communicated what I was planning to do about it, and I asked for their assistance."

There was a long silence, Richard said. He related thinking about the scene in his own family room.

"I thought they were stunned by my presentation," he told me. "I put a lot of effort into making it impactful. I even prepared a set of slides. I wanted them to see that I was taking this seriously."

The team asked what Richard meant by them "supporting this process." With a smile pulling at his mouth, Richard distributed the yellow cards and explained how they were used in soccer. Then he gave the team the instructions on how to use them.

The eight men and women seated at the conference table laughed. "Are you serious?" one asked.

Richard laughed too, gamely. Then he said, "I'm dead serious. I'd be extremely grateful if you show up and help me work better with you."

"I think they loved that I was asking for their help, and they seemed to go along with my suggestions," Richard told me. "We got down to business, and I started the meeting with an overview of our plans for the next few weeks. Then we went through our usual reporting process, and our action planning. I follow a template for these meetings that allows us to cover a lot of territory in short time."

At the beginning, Richard said, he was expecting the flash of a yellow card at any moment, but he eventually forgot about the challenge. It was only at the end of the meeting when he realized that nobody had raised a yellow card even once!

"Before we broke the meeting," Richard said, "I made a point of mentioning that nobody had raised a yellow card. I wanted to make sure that they hadn't forgotten about it, the way I had. You know what they said? They said that everything was fine! I guess nobody saw a need for a yellow card. I felt so relieved!

"You know," he continued, smiling, "I think we've overblown this issue of me not listening. I've always had an open door policy, and if anyone has something to say, I'm all ears. Anyway, I feel relieved to hear that this is not an issue."

I now understood the source of Richard's jubilation: he felt vindicated, the way I had expected to feel watching the video of myself playing tennis. But I could not avoid feeling a healthy suspicion about this sudden change of heart among Richard's team members. In their anonymous online feedback, they were adamant about Richard's inability to hear their concerns and engage in constructive dialogue, and mentioned feeling intimidated at times by him as he "shut down" people who objected to his ideas or slowed down the meeting. Now they were saying everything was fine? I knew in my heart that the team members were lacking the courage needed to challenge Richard regarding his communication style.

I shared with Richard my concerns and the possibility that this "flight to health" could be motivated by one of the issues uncovered by the feedback process: people feeling intimidated by his powerful presence and shying away from confronting him. To verify or refute this, I suggested I facilitate the next team meeting, with a focus on observing and improving the team dynamics.

"I don't think that would make any difference in how we talk to each other," Richard said.

"That would be a good thing to confirm," I said, "but in any case, the discrepancy between the feedback report and your experience with your team warrants a second look at this. Understanding the team dynamics is well worth the effort."

Richard sighed. "I trust your judgment, and I promised myself I'd remain open to this process. Come and join us at our next meeting."

GATHERING COURAGE

The team meeting was scheduled for 9 a.m. I showed up a few minutes early, the first to arrive. I wanted to meet the team members individually as they walked in. One wall of the conference room was a giant whiteboard extending from wall to wall and floor to ceiling.

A couple of minutes before the scheduled time, Richard's team members began trickling in; I imagined him to be a leader quite unforgiving of tardiness. As they situated themselves around the table, I observed this lively group of young individuals. They seemed intrigued by my presence.

At exactly 9 a.m., Richard entered the room. I suspected it was his way of making a point about punctuality. Richard introduced me as his coach and mentioned that, as part our work, I was "shadowing" him in some meetings to focus on making them as effective as possible. I thanked the group for allowing me to observe and asked them to conduct the meeting as usual. As we had agreed in advance, Richard reminded the group about the use of the yellow cards and supplied cards to those who hadn't brought theirs to the meeting. We were ready to start.

Without hesitation, Richard went to the front of the room. He started at a fast pace and never slowed down, writing on the whiteboard as he spoke. He outlined sales trends in various regions, breaking down all that information by industry and addressing issues of pricing in some of the different product lines. A staggering amount of information flew onto the board. About fifteen minutes into the presentation, I noticed that some of the individuals in the room were squirming and others were exchanging looks with one another. I had the impression of a wide disconnect between Richard at the whiteboard and the group sitting around the table.

I raised my hand, and Richard stopped for the first time since he started. I asked if we could interrupt the meeting for a moment and huddle, as is common in many sports games. Richard agreed and sat down. I mentioned that the huddle time was what allowed teams to

153

reorganize their thoughts for a moment and strategize about the next few minutes of the game.

I decided that to encourage the team members to talk and disclose more about themselves, I needed to talk for a while and create the right climate for them to open up. I asked, "Are you interested in learning the 'secret sauce' of the best-performing teams?"

Everybody nodded.

"If you survey a large number of teams and ask what they need to improve as a team, chances are that the top answer for most will be communication.

"The secret sauce of the best teams in the world is that they communicate well, in a way that generates deep trust within the group. They accomplish that by frequently engaging in meta-communication, and they do that in real-time and courageously. *That's* the secret sauce: meta-communication and trust, real-time feedback and courage."

Some members of the group looked puzzled.

"Meta-communication means communicating about communication," I explained. "The team will take time every now and then to talk about how they are experiencing the team interaction, what's working well and how to leverage that, and what needs to improve about how they relate to one another. In this way, they are able to regularly revisit their dynamics and continuously improve. I call this process 'cleaning up the pipes,' and I've found that it's needed regularly. Have you done something similar in this group?"

They looked at one another, their glances falling on Richard. Eventually, someone said, "Not really."

"Today could be the day you get started," I said. "What do you think, Richard?"

"That's why you're here! Absolutely!"

"Great! Another powerful element of improving how a team works together is real-time feedback," I said. "You see, it's not very useful if you tell me that you didn't like how I discounted your suggestions during a meeting that took place a month ago. I don't remember what I had for breakfast yesterday, so how could I remember our conversation from a month ago? That's not very effective feedback."

"Real-time feedback allows me to correct my course in real time—right now, as it's happening. If I'm not being as effective as I could during our conversation, and you let me know what I'm doing that's not working well for you, I can immediately change my approach to our dialogue. You tell me I'm too loud, I lower the volume of my voice. Too fast? I slow down. We then have effective real-time communication."

Everybody seemed to be listening closely. "As we're honest about our communication, and we see each other being responsive to one another's requests, we develop trust. What we are not allowing to grow is resentment. Every time something is not working well for one of us, we express it in the moment—in real time—and find the best possible way of addressing that concern. How does resentment grow? Something is not working well for me and I say … nothing! The first time is mild annoyance, but by the twentieth time I'm really exasperated, and the last thing I want is to work with you."

Richard gave me a wry look, maybe wondering how his team was reacting to all this. I nodded back at him encouragingly.

"Finally, a key element that supports this process of meta-communication, building trust, and real-time feedback is courage," I said. "Every time we speak up, we take a risk—the risk of looking foolish, the risk of being misunderstood, or the risk of the other person not seeing our good intentions and getting upset with us. And taking risks always requires courage."

"If you engage in this process and there's good faith on both sides, trust increases over time—trust that it's safe to share your point of view and that you will not be penalized for providing feedback. In this way, it becomes easier and easier to be open, honest, and direct to a point where this way of communicating becomes part of the

DNA of the team. You have then set up the conditions for a high performing team."

Next, it was time to share my observations with the team. I mentioned that Richard had just presented an enormous amount of information in a very short period of time—so it seemed to me—and that people had been squirming in their seats, maybe showing signs of uneasiness with the pace.

"Did I misinterpret what was happening?" I asked.

A long silence ensued. Ten seconds, then twenty. I was determined to wait until someone spoke.

Still more silence.

I held my commitment.

"Come on guys, speak up!" said Richard.

Silence. Some shifted in their chairs.

I signaled to Richard to wait. This might become a turning point for the team.

Tom, one of the youngest members, said, "Well, I had some questions while you were presenting, Richard, but it didn't feel right to interrupt."

"I had no idea," Richard said hesitantly.

"How could you have known?" I asked. "You needed real-time feedback about what was happening."

Then, addressing the group, I said, "No one in this room is a mind reader. If we are not aware of something, we need to be told. And that's why you have a yellow card: to raise it if you have a question or if anything in Richard's communication is somehow not working for you. It'd be easy to blame the poor communication on Richard. You could say he was going too fast, and it would be true. But whose responsibility is to initiate change in this interaction? It couldn't be Richard's, because he had no idea that he was going too fast. The responsibility is yours to speak up, to be courageous and raise the yellow card and tell Richard you have a question or ask him to explain whatever you need to make this presentation work for you.

Then the responsibility shifts to Richard to respond appropriately."

"Please bear with me," I added. "It's such a luxury to be able to replay a situation searching for how to make things work better. Many times, we don't have this opportunity in life. I suggest you give yourselves that chance and re-start today's meeting."

Immediately, Richard stood up, went to the whiteboard, and erased everything on it. I was impressed with his way of bringing leadership to this moment and his willingness to create a learning experience for the team.

"Good morning again, team," said Richard. "Let's get started."

Everybody laughed, and the humor eased whatever tensions or uncertainties had arisen.

Just like earlier, Richard started talking about the sales trends and inventory issues while writing on the board. He was presenting at a slower pace, but just a few minutes later, that pace began quickening.

Suddenly, a yellow card went up. It was Tom again, with a big smile on his face.

"What?" asked Richard. But then he remembered and said, "Thank you! What do you need?"

"Richard, you're going too fast, and I have a couple of questions," said Tom.

Eventually, other members of the team joined the conversation, asking questions and making comments. I felt grateful for Tom's presence.

Eventually, Richard resumed his presentation. After a few minutes, three yellow cards were up.

This time, Richard found it easier to respond. "Thank you! What do you need, guys?"

"You're still going too fast," said another team member. Everybody nodded. A few had questions about the data on the board and about Richard's suggested solutions for the pricing issues. Others voiced suggestions that Richard considered good ideas, because he began writing them on the board.

After a few of these interruptions, there was a deep shift in how the meeting was developing. Instead of Richard presenting to a group of people taking notes, it became a dialogue, a discussion, as other folks walked to the board to write and draw out their ideas. He eventually sat down as people took turns going to the board and adding their pieces to the emerging plan. There were some heated moments and lively interactions. I was thrilled; it looked like a very different group than the one that started the meeting earlier.

At the end of the meeting, I suggested we review how the team had interacted and discuss how to improve future meetings. Excitement filled in the room, with people laughing and teasing one another.

Once more, Tom was the first to talk. "This was our best meeting ever," he said.

"What made it a good meeting?" I asked.

"I'm walking out with all my questions answered, and I feel clear about what I need to do next."

Someone else said, "I was able to express my doubts about our ambitious sales goals, but I'm walking away with new ideas on how to approach my clients. I'm eager to test this new approach. I feel good about it."

"Me, too," still someone else added. "I'm glad about your suggestion, Steve, to go together to two or three of my clients. Your experience in their industry will help me with those sales, and I hadn't thought about that possibility before."

I had the impression that Richard was waiting to speak to allow the team to express its feelings. After a while, he said, "Guys, I enjoyed our meeting, and I had a realization. To be honest, at the beginning I was annoyed by the yellow cards. As you may know, I hate interruptions."

Everybody laughed. They knew it all too well.

"But then," he continued, "at some point, I got it! I was giving you marching orders, telling you what to do while what you really wanted was to ask questions, share your suggestions, your objections, and even present possible scenarios. I got it! You wanted to have a conversation. I know, I know, it seems obvious, but still, it blew my mind!

"You see," Richard continued, "a long time ago, I was in the Army for a few years."

Eyebrows rose at this revelation. It was plain to see that Richard typically shared little about himself with his team.

"I trained as an officer, and that's how I learned to interact with the troops: our captain would give us our marching orders; we didn't engage in conversation. You see, we had to be sure of what we were going to say or ask if we raised our hands, or our captain would chew our heads off for not being attentive or for asking stupid questions.

"Later, I was part of two different start-ups, always in charge of sales. In those start-ups, I had green folks working for me, and they didn't need a conversation; they needed thorough training and crystal-clear marching orders. And I was very comfortable doing that; it wasn't any different than in the Army."

Richard paused, looking around the room. "Now, what's different is that you're a seasoned sales team, and you know what you're doing. You're battle tested. You don't need marching orders; you want to be part of how we strategize as a group. Of course you do!"

Richard explained that he'd always thought he knew how to listen. However, he operated mostly in output mode and received no input from the team; there wasn't any dialogue. Consequently, he said, the team probably perceived him bulldozing through their meetings.

"Why would I listen?" Richard asked. "I didn't think that was the point."

"Good Golly Miss Molly!" blurted Tom.

Richard looked puzzled.

"I'm sorry," said Tom, "but out of the blue, I just remembered Little Richard." And he started singing "Good Golly Miss Molly!" The team joined him. I thought it was their way of expressing how glad they were with Richard's realization.

At our next session, I asked Richard how he felt about the team meeting.

"I had such a profound realization during that meeting," he said. "I'm still reeling from it. Since then, my team has been the most enthusiastic ever. A couple of key clients mentioned to me recently that they were getting great support from our salespeople. New ideas are bouncing around the team, and there's a high level of energy. And you know the best part? The next few days, as I walked through the hallways, every time I crossed paths with some of my guys—without me saying a word—they raised their yellow cards! And we all chuckled. I have never had such a collegial, fun relationship with my team. I'm planning to play 'Good Golly Miss Molly' at the beginning of our next meeting." He laughed.

"Richard, I'm so happy for you. Good job!" I said. "That could become a ritual for team meetings that only they would understand—a secret cue. Now that you engaged in conversation with your team, you can easily see the dotted line that connects listening with dogmatism. When you came across as dogmatic before, you probably had good ideas to share, but without the dialogue and the listening, people felt talked *to* instead of talked *with*.

"Let's celebrate that this is working and build on it. Next time we meet, we will start working on the second challenge: emotional control."

"Could we start today?"

"Will you chew my head off if we don't?" I teased him.

Richard laughed; it was contagious.

"I want to introduce more humor into how I relate to my guys," he said. "I love it! I want more humor at home, too."

"Richard, you accomplished something extraordinary with your team, a brand new way of relating to them. You said that you saw them being more enthusiastic, more engaged. Let's talk about how to sustain momentum and discuss ways to firmly establish this new style of yours."

We discussed the new practices that Richard would incorporate as pathways to a new culture for the team and a new way for him to relate to others.

As I was leaving, I said, "Richard, you might consider playing 'Good Golly Miss Molly' at home."

"I love the idea! I'll call another family meeting and hope they get intrigued. My only purpose would be to dance with them!"

"There's no such thing as too much fun at home," I said.

We shook hands and broke the meeting.

WHAT IS "EMOTIONAL CONTROL"?

The feedback Richard received at the beginning of the process indicated that he was prone to emotional outbursts and acting out a wide range of negative emotions on the continuum of anger, from slight irritation or annoyance in his voice to outright yelling and pounding the desk. That was a big part of why people had been tiptoeing around him, feeling intimidated when they conveyed disappointing news.

I started our next meeting with a brief introduction to emotions, highlighting the difference between *expressing* and *acting out* our emotions.

"We all use the expression 'emotional control,'" I said. "Our company's 360° feedback mentions it as an important competency of self-management. But emotional control is a misnomer. In reality, we do not *control* our emotions. What we control is our behavior. Our emotions flow from our hearts and bodies as we encounter different situations in the world. I hear your appreciation for me and feel gratefulness. I experience your lack of attention to me and feel rejected. I see that you didn't deliver what you promised and experience frustration."

Richard nodded. "With you so far."

"Where we exercise *control* is over our behavior," I said. "It is a healthy practice to express our emotions—even our negative ones—and that is a powerful way of communicating. When I express how I feel to you, I become vulnerable and authentic, real. Your knowing what I'm experiencing now connects us. Most importantly, when I'm respectfully expressing how I feel about something that's relevant to both of us, I'm instilling trust in our relationship. As I become transparent, you don't have to guess how I'm feeling, and my sharing is an invitation for you to do the same. You know where I stand, I know where you stand, and now we can fully collaborate with each other without any waste of energy trying to maneuver around each other.

"But it's not a healthy practice to act out our negative emotions. When I express my emotion, I'm letting you know—in a respectful way—how I feel about something. When I act out my emotion, I'm hostage to how I feel, and lose touch with my intention and real purpose. I could express feeling rejected instead of turning my back to you; I could express feeling frustrated and angry instead of slamming the door or raising my voice. In *expressing,* I'm communicating to you how I feel; I'm exercising my freedom. In *acting out,* I'm letting my emotions take over my behavior. I'm indulging in my feeling, allowing my emotion to enslave me."

I stopped and paused. "Richard, you've been listening for a while. What is your reaction to what you've heard so far?"

Richard leaned back in his desk chair, pensive. "I'd never thought about the distinction between expressing and acting out. It makes sense. I can see how it's more respectful to express my frustration instead of raising my voice the way I sometimes do."

I decided to build on that. "I can imagine someone feeling intimidated if you yell or pound the desk, while I can imagine the same person feeling concerned if you are expressing frustration or disappointment. If you are disappointed, I want to do better; if you yell at me, I just want to get out of here."

"It makes sense." Richard's eyebrows were drawn together over the bridge of his nose. "To be honest, I thought that emotional control would be more like putting a lid on what I felt, and I don't know if that would be possible for me."

"That would be unhealthy. If you bottle it up or put a lid on what you feel, your emotions will eventually leak through the seams. And by the way, you'll have some reflection of that in your body. Your blood pressure could go up and make you a candidate for gastritis or ulcers, which you experienced while working with Bob. We need to express how we feel to keep ourselves sane. We just need to do that in a skillful and respectful way.

"Sometimes, what makes the act of skillfully expressing our emotions difficult is that, if we feel anger or fear, we get a shot of adrenaline from our adrenal glands. That increases our heartbeat, engages our primitive response of 'fight or flight,' and makes it difficult to engage our cerebral cortex. We are literally *not thinking straight.*

"That's why someone really angry is capable of irrational behavior," I said. "The mind is barely working. We are not thinking about consequences; we are taken by our emotions."

"That sounds like me when I see someone not making their best effort or not thinking," said Richard. "I don't suffer fools lightly. What should I do in those moments?"

"The most powerful tool is part of common knowledge," I explained. "When people say to take a deep breath and count to ten? It's an accurate remedy. You may need a little more than that, but that's thinking in the right direction. Interrupting the pattern is what works. Our mind knows that we are experiencing a strong emotion because it's 'reading' our body. It's very useful to understand what our mind is reading in our body because those are cues for action. Let's say you're in a meeting and something someone said is making you angry. What do you experience in your body?"

"I haven't thought about it, but you're right. My cheeks and ears burn, I feel hot, and my stomach tightens. Oh, and my armpits get sweaty right away, too."

"That's it!" I said. "Those are your cues. When your cheeks and

163

ears get red, your stomach tightens, and you get sweaty, those are the cues for action. The first action should be to interrupt the pattern and—for a moment—remove yourself from the situation."

"Sometimes that's not possible," he said.

"You can always excuse yourself from a meeting to use the restroom for a moment. That's actually your chance to walk away for a few minutes, wash your hands, maybe your face, and give your body a chance to lower the adrenaline level in your blood. Then, when you return, you are able to engage the full power of your mind to ask yourself *how you want to respond to the situation*. Figure out a purposeful and intentional way to show up. Determine the most skillful way of expressing what you're feeling."

"What if the other person is saying something really stupid? Some folks at work really frustrate me," said Richard.

"You are still responsible for your reactions. You can't make other people responsible for your reactions as if you are an automated machine: press the green button, Richard is happy; press the red button, Richard is upset. People will still do their own thing. What you have control over is how you react to that. I'm suggesting you assume responsibility for how you want to be in the world, including how you want to react to people who—using your words—say something stupid."

"That makes sense." Richard gazed over my shoulder at the framed photos of his family, and I gave him a moment to think before I spoke again.

"Richard, remember—we are not working on knowing more about who you are, but on discovering who you want to be. We talked about anger or frustration as a cue for action and discussed the first action, which is to interrupt the pattern, remove yourself from the situation, let the adrenaline level go down, and come back calmer—and ready for the second action."

"The second action requires an understanding of the main role of anger and frustration," I continued. "It is a very powerful reframe

164

to understand anger and frustration as positive forces in the same way that hunger and thirst are positive and necessary. If we don't experience hunger or thirst, we'd die starved or dehydrated. If we don't experience frustration and anger, we will be okay with poor performance—our own and that of people around us—and we won't strive for excellence. Frustration is the same energy that has driven many individuals to come up with ingenious solutions and inventions to solve problems. Frustration about the performance of others is a cue to engage in the second action: coaching for performance. The more you coach your people for better performance, the more you can expect higher levels of excellence in your group. Get upset and yell and you get a tiptoeing, walking-on-eggshells organization; coach your team and you get a learning, high-performing organization. Your choice."

"Wow! Put that way, I've been quite effective at creating tiptoeing." Richard's face was sheepish. "But I do want a high-performing team."

"We look back to learn. We look forward to succeed," I said.

SUSTAINING INTENTION

During our meetings over the next few weeks, we continued focusing on how to strengthen Richard's skills at managing his emotions, and then harnessing that energy in a positive, intentional way. We role-played a few situations that would normally elicit strong emotions, and Richard had a chance to practice skillful expression of his emotions.

Richard's main concern—shared by his reports and people around him—was that he would relapse. Despite his best intentions, they feared, something would inevitably go wrong, and he would fly off the handle, setting back the whole process to square one. Even worse, people would realize that any change was only temporary, and stress would force Richard to revert to his old ways.

I knew that life wouldn't take long to present Richard with an opportunity to practice this new skill. Sure enough, two of his re-ports each lost a valuable customer—in the same week.

Richard had been feeling great pressure to meet the sales goals for that quarter, so the loss of customers couldn't have come at a worse time. Still, when the first report tentatively rapped on Rich-ard's door and sat down to give the news, Richard did everything we practiced in our role-playing. "Give me a second to think," he said, and then took a deep breath. He focused on something calming with which he was familiar—the rolling, vibrant green lawns of a golf course—and counted silently to ten, then twenty.

Finally, his heart stopped pounding and his face cooled. He felt more capable of having a constructive dialogue with his remorseful report.

"I could see the relief on his face," Richard told me later. "I knew he was expecting me to throw a fit, yelling and banging on my desk."

After the salesman left, Richard further calmed himself by im-mersing in some strategic planning. He set short- and mid-term goals for how to recoup the loss. Though he still felt tight with frustration, he was also proud of himself.

Just a couple of days later, Tom reported losing a key customer. The stress proved to be too much.

Tom walked into Richard's office with, Richard described to me later, an odd expression on his face: dread in the tight set of his jaw, but also trust in his eyes, as though he believed that Richard would be disappointed but ultimately understanding about the news.

However, the capacity to understand and respond rationally seemed far out of Richard's reach. With Tom sitting across from him, all Richard could feel was a wave of fury. He spun his chair around to face his computer, forced his hands to relax from their fisted position, and counted to ten. Then he reached twenty. Thirty. It was no use. Richard felt heat surging through his face and leapt from his chair, sending it crashing back against his keyboard.

"Is your position too much to handle?" Richard yelled.

Tom, stiff in his seat, said, "Richard—"

"Because I could replace you in seconds. You think you're the only one who applied for this job?"

The diatribe continued like this, with Richard yelling and pacing around an increasingly subdued Tom. Finally, twenty minutes later, Richard scathingly told Tom to take the afternoon off.

A week after this incident, Richard and I met, and he told me about it. His face was awash with mortification. "I felt agitated for hours," he said.

He told me that late that night, he woke and reflected on what had happened. Twisting in bed, the sweaty sheets tangled around him, he felt the fevered embarrassment of failure.

"I went back to work the next day, and—new to me—I apologized to Tom."

"How did he respond?" I asked.

"Graciously," Richard said with humility. "And with surprise. I think he was expecting me to fire him. But the truth is, he's been with us for three years and has never produced anything but great results. That's what I told him. Then we discussed ways of turning the situation around and decided that the best way to understand the situation would be to go together and visit the client who'd canceled his order."

"And what happened there?"

"We managed to uncover the real problem, work around it, and recover the sale. Only, instead of feeling happy about it, I felt even more of a failure."

"Why?"

"I'd lost my temper unnecessarily," he said simply. "I treated Tom horribly for no reason."

"Richard, you know my way of seeing these situations," I said. "We look back to learn. We look forward to succeed. Through hindsight, you developed awareness of your way of showing up in the situation, you apologized, and you managed to turn the situation around. Were you able to coach Tom?"

"Yes, at least I remembered that," he said. "I made a point of sharing my reasoning with Tom so next time he would know how to further explore ways of serving our clients and be more creative when shoring up a difficult sales situation."

"So, I give you half a point, because you had to learn through hindsight and after losing your temper," I said. "But remember, according to your previous style of handling these situations, you'd have received zero points, and there would have been no learning opportunity for Tom. Next time, you may catch yourself in real time and move into the coaching mode earlier in the process. That's when you will get a whole point."

"Okay, I feel a little better then," Richard smiled, catching my attempt to inject some lightness into the moment. "But here's what I worry about: What could I do to not repeat my outburst?"

"What you can do, Richard, is listen to the story I'm about to tell and let it work through you. A story often has the power to provide learning in a way that is not otherwise accessible to us. This is about Milarepa, born in Tibet about 900 years ago."

Richard situated himself more comfortably in his chair and nodded, seemingly ready to absorb the story.

"A great Tibetan poet and sage named Milarepa studied and meditated for many years. He traveled the countryside, teaching the practice of compassion and mercy to the villagers he met. He had faced, in his life, many hardships and sorrows, but had transformed them into the path of his awakening.

"Finally, it was time for him to return home. Much to his surprise, upon entering, he found his house filled with demons—terrifying, monstrous demons that would make most people run. But Milarepa was not like most people.

"Slowly inhaling and exhaling a few times, he turned toward the demons, fully present and aware. He looked deeply into their eyes, bowing in respect, and said, 'You are here in my home now. I honor you, and open myself to what you have to teach me.'

"As soon as he uttered these words, half of the demons disappeared. The ones that remained were grisly, horrific, huge monsters. Milarepa bowed once more and began to sing a song to them, a sweet melody filled with caring for the ways these beings must have suffered and interest for what they needed now and how he could help them. As the last notes left his lips, all of the demons disappeared into thin air—except one.

"Its fangs dripped evil, its nostrils flamed, and its opened jaws revealed a dark, foul black throat. Milarepa stepped closer to this huge demon, breathed deeply into his own belly, and said with quiet compassion, 'I must understand your pain and what it is you need to be healed. Please teach me.' Then he put his head in the mouth of the demon."

"In that instant," I said to Richard, "the demon disappeared and Milarepa was home at last."

Richard looked as engaged and enthralled as a child.

"The lesson," I said, "is that when life circumstances see us going back home—inside ourselves, to that place where emotions reside—we will find our own old demons waiting for us. I face this frustrating situation. I go inside and what I find is—anger! That old demon of mine! We may call it frustration, aggravation, irritation, or disappointment, but it is all the same psychic energy. So the inner demons will never disappear once and for all. They will be waiting for the right circumstances to show up at our home again.

"One choice we have is to push them out of our sight and out of our awareness," I continued. "We may repress and negate them. If we do, they become what Jung called our shadow: the parts of us that we dislike and disown. With this approach, our demons will only be gathering energy, building up steam to come back roaring, stronger than ever. They would be waiting for us at home. In this case, it is warranted to fear a relapse; it is bound to happen."

"What's the alternative?" Richard asked.

"A more skillful choice is to acknowledge our emotion and

channel it in a productive way. *Our emotions are energy that always contains a positive aspect.* If you do not deliver on your commitment or do substandard work, and I experience no reaction to that, I would be indifferent, uncaring, and you would learn nothing from our interaction. But if I feel angry or frustrated by your actions, I can use my anger as energy to help you. My anger becomes the fuel that motivates me to show you a new approach—a way to become successful. Anger or one of its expressions—frustration, dissatisfaction—is the origin of all inventions. We are challenged by having to move heavy things, so we invent the wheel. We are frustrated by cold, so we invent ways of making fire. Anger and frustration become the drivers of innovation, change, creativity, and many of the good things we enjoy today."

A look of comprehension bloomed across Richard's face. He nodded. "What you're saying is that I'm bound to experience anger at different times. But I can harness that energy and make it work for me."

I couldn't help but smile. Without realizing it, Richard was practicing one of our earlier exercises: reiterating the gist of what I'd said to make sure he understood. I definitely felt heard.

He was learning.

CLOSURE

After five months of working together, Richard took stock of the progress he'd made and its impact on business results. He had several occasions to practice successfully what he'd learned about managing his emotions. He reported that meetings with his team were more productive, the overall productivity of the group had increased by different metrics between twenty percent and thirty percent, and there was a renewed sense of camaraderie. He felt good about how he was able to respond to frustrating circumstances and engage people in dialogue looking for solutions to mitigate problems.

We launched a brief feedback process to assess the impact of Richard's progress on his team and other key people in the organization.

"Uh oh," Richard said jokingly before we reviewed the results. "The moment of truth."

There it was: the new feedback showed remarkably positive changes in how Richard was exercising influence. Though some folks still expressed concern it may have been a temporary improvement and that Richard may revert to his old ways under stress, most of his colleagues agreed that he'd improved vastly. In response to those who doubted the permanence of his change, Richard expressed his deep commitment to continue on the path he started on and to not waver, even under stressful circumstances. After all, primary to his heart, his family relationship had improved enormously. That was a deep source of happiness for him.

In our last meeting, Richard said, "I'm absolutely determined to be the new man I've become."

I smiled back, thinking his words were nothing short of profound.

"And by the way," he added, mischievous as a teenager, "We are still dancing at home to 'Good Golly Miss Molly'!"

Chapter 4 Summary
Richard: Which Shirt Do You Like the Most?

This chapter concerns one of the most difficult types of situations for any CEO: Confronting a successful Vice President of Sales who knows the technology and customer base, and is exceeding projections, but is abrasive, inflexible and lacking on interpersonal skills. The lack of emotional control of this individual may cause morale issues that are potentially toxic to the management team and the entire company. An additional objective: to create a better working relationship between Richard and his team.

I. DEALING WITH UNWELCOME FEEDBACK

1. Creating a positive atmosphere in the face of critical feedback
2. Reframing the learning experience, creating an opportunity for personal and professional growth
3. Working to create compassion and clarity
4. Goal: to open mind and heart to praise and recognition received—*as well as the plight and suffering unintentionally created around him.*

II. THE QUESTION OF NICE VS. EFFECTIVE: The "nice vs. effective" issue is a
false polarity. It indicates an attitude that treating people well is ineffective in the business world, and that the only way to truly be effective is to lead with harsh "command and control" or abrasive communication. A focus on results should not preclude a focus on people's issues.

III. FOUR PHASES OF CHANGE: Stepladder to complete awareness and competency

1. Unconsciously Incompetent: Completely oblivious about my incompetence in a certain area. A blind spot.
2. Consciously Incompetent Still lacking the skill, but know about it.
3. Consciously Competent: Have learned the skill, but still need to intently focus on it while performing the task.
4. Unconsciously Competent: The new skill is fully incorporated. Deeper parts of the brain take over, the process becomes automatic.

IV. LISTENING AS A SKILL: The art of active listening and playing back what
you heard to others:

1. Confirms the accuracy of what was said and understood;
2. Enables you to get clarification when it is needed; and
3. Makes the other person feel heard.

V. ENROLLING THE TEAM: A great way to ingratiate the team to a two-way communicating and listening process, this 5-step process of responding to a 360-degree feedback on the supervisor includes:

1. Expressing gratefulness
2. Describing what you've learned from the process
3. Presenting an action plan to introduce desired change
4. Identify support needed from the team for this process
5. Requesting further feedback—and acting on it

VI. 4 STEPS OF IDEAL COMMUNICATION WITHIN TEAMS

1. Meta-Communication: communicating about communication
2. Building trust
3. Providing real-time Feedback: Correct course now, as it's happening
4. Displaying courage: Take the risk, trust will build over time

VII. PRACTICING EMOTIONAL CONTROL: There's a difference between *expressing* and *acting out* our emotions.

1. Taking time to let emotions cool and allow reason to enter the moment
2. Assuming responsibility for our own reactions
3. Skillfully expressing emotions instead of acting them out
4. Reframing anger and frustration as a positive door to identify what's not working and introduce corrective change

VIII. SUSTAINING INTENTION: The height of effective leadership

1. We look back to learn. We look forward to succeed.
2. Emotions are energy that always contains a positive aspect.
3. See anger as a fuel that motivates toward a new approach, a new way to become successful.
4. See anger, frustration and dissatisfaction for its ultimate positive: the origin of all innovation, change, creativity and invention.

John: The Decision Algorithm

Leadership and Courage

JOHN called me one late afternoon. After reminding me that he had attended one of my leadership classes at Stanford the previous year, he wanted to know if I remembered him.

"Are you tall, wiry, wear glasses and have a dry sense of humor?" I asked.

John's laughter was contagious. "Yes, that certainly sounds like me."

"I remember you. It's good to hear from you. What's on your mind?"

I heard a brief pause on the other end of the line, followed by a sigh. "Well, I am the Chief Marketing Officer of Tech-Tel (a large public telecommunications company). I am facing a situation that calls for some of the leadership skills mentioned in your class, and I thought I'd seek a consultation with you. Could I invite you to lunch and see if this is something you would be interested in helping me with?"

A few days later, we sat at Il Fornaio in Palo Alto. With a somber expression on his face, John looked definitely worried. The restaurant hummed with a hundred conversations and several deals in various stages of development. It felt almost like being at a business forum. While we looked at our menus, I couldn't avoid overhearing a few words from the surrounding tables. To my left, a possible merger was being discussed, while to my right, a young entrepreneur showed colorful graphics on his iPad, likely pitching his idea to a potential investor.

John mentioned that he arrived recently from one of his frequent business trips to Europe. "You know," he said, "call me old-fashioned, but our company has a few European partners, and I would rather meet with my counterparts face-to-face when I can, than through video conference or phone."

"I relate to that," I said. Then I remembered something that I always liked about European business lunches. "I wonder, what did you notice about business lunches in Europe?"

"Oh yes. The most noticeable difference with us Americans is that Europeans enjoy their meals and get to know each other over lunch, and then only discuss business at the end, usually over coffee."

I smiled. "For us today, would you like to have a European or an American lunch?"

There was no hesitation. "Definitely European!"

We enjoyed our Italian meal while discussing the benefits of "slow food." I learned that John was married, had three children (two girls and a boy), was born and raised in New York and moved to California to attend Stanford University almost twenty-five years ago. Always fascinated with technology, he studied computer science and earned an MBA from Stanford. John was also keenly interested in hearing my stories about fly-fishing in Patagonia. He was well grounded in education and family, focused in his thoughts, and enthusiastic about adventures, both his own and others'. I imagined he was the type of businessman who got things done and savored a good challenge.

Eventually John got quiet, a serious expression on his face. "Our coffees are here, and I guess it's time for me to tell you why I called you. By the way, I find it extremely refreshing to enjoy an 'European lunch' and forget worries and business issues for a moment while enjoying each other and our food."

"I believe we are sharper and smarter when we can come back fresh to focus on work, instead of thinking about it all the time," I said.

John related that his company had recently lost its number two position in the market, and was now relegated to a distant third—a position not unlike that perpetually faced by CBS in the battle of the traditional TV networks. Ken, the CEO, was extremely distressed about this development, and so was the Board of Directors. The press had been merciless pointing to the latest company mistakes, and the stock had been pummeled by a constant influx of bad news.

For the past four months, John and his team had been working on a marketing campaign for a new product line, which was still under wraps. A lot was at stake. His department identified this new line as the one with the potential to bring his company back to the number two position. If it really took off, they surmised, it could possibly challenge the archrival company that held first place in the market. However, to do so, the marketing campaign must be a resounding success.

The time came for John to present the new campaign to Ken, the CEO, and the management team.

"It was Monday morning last week, just a few minutes before eight," he told me. "I walked into the big conference room, filled with enthusiasm and energy, confident that I had an exciting campaign to introduce to my colleagues. My team had spent the last few weeks working almost exclusively on this campaign and the previous weekend had pulled an all-nighter to make sure that the presentation would be top-notch and nothing could go wrong. I met with the team Sunday afternoon, all of us stealing time from family for a final review. Everything was ready."

I settled more comfortably into my chair, John was a good storyteller. "John, you are good at building suspense. What happened then?"

"I was the first one to show up at this meeting. One by one, the other nine members of our management team arrived, ready for a full agenda. Some brought coffee cups with them, while others started animated conversations. I was a little nervous, but I felt that the energy level in the room was good, and I could expect a good reception to my ideas."

"What about your CEO? Was he there?"

"Ken likes to make an entrance. He was the last to show up. The moment he came into the room, everybody grew quiet. They all knew that Ken would not waste time starting the meeting. After a few routine items were discussed, Ken took the floor."

John changed his voice to imitate Ken, a tact I found very appealing because it brought John directly into the CEO's skin. "Ladies and gentlemen, it's time to move to the next item on the agenda. Let's discuss our new product line and how to introduce it to the market. We invested our best R&D resources and quite a bit of time and money creating this new family of products, and I firmly believe that it will bring us back to a position of leadership in the market. We've also learned from experience that regardless how good the technology is, if we don't find the right way to introduce it to the market, we will fail. John, let's hear from you."

I noticed John's forehead pearling with perspiration while recalling the moment, even though the room temperature was comfortable, even a shade cool. "That would certainly put a lot of pressure on you," I suggested.

"I felt the pressure. But I was ready. I bolted to my feet, I was so excited that I couldn't remain seated. I started my presentation using a very short but impactful set of slides. I think I was very crisp. As I went through it, I felt again that the ideas were well thought out and innovative. I felt reassured that the campaign would be successful. At the end, the team applauded."

"It sounds as if you did a great job!" I suggested, "But I'm still waiting for the punch line."

John continued with the story. After showing the slides, he opened the conversation to the group. After he fielded a few questions about

178

different aspects of the campaign, the room fell silent.

Everybody looked at Ken. As the CEO, he always waited until the end to express his opinion, "so as not to influence the team too soon," as he put it. Finally, he said, "You know, my first reaction was just like all of you guys; I like the campaign, and it does feel snazzy and cool. But I wonder if we are drinking too much of our own tea. There's so much at stake! The market hasn't been kind to us lately. For the last few quarters, our competition has been beating us, and our market share has shrunk. Let me paint to you the most likely scenario if this marketing campaign misses the mark."

Ken elaborated on how bad the situation would be if the new campaign were to tank, how much was at stake, and how difficult it would be to turn the situation around. He noted that if the marketing campaign tanked, the company would face "irreparable damage" and that the company would not have the time or the resources to reverse the situation. As John put it, "Our stock would probably be hit so badly that we would become a likely acquisition target."

"You know, Ken was on a tear. He reminded the team that when a company like ours gets acquired, there's an immediate redundancy of people—and the ones more likely to go were the folks in the 'acquired organization.' Us."

John took a deep breath. "After this long talk, everybody got really somber and reflective. The mood of the group changed in just a few moments."

"I guess fear had entered the room," I said.

"Absolutely. Then someone said that the campaign might be too flashy, too edgy. Someone else wondered if it wasn't too provocative. A third person recalled a competition's campaign that failed for those same reasons. The CEO expressed his own doubts and acknowledged how hard it was to walk that thin line between 'too conventional' and 'too out there.'

"My conviction wavered. I went from being elated to frozen and worried. I felt—almost physically—the weight of the responsibility.

179

What if I wanted so much to succeed that I convinced myself that the campaign was great? What if it failed? The job market is extremely difficult right now, and I can't imagine having to go out looking for a new job—maybe for many months. I have two children in college and one more joining them in a few months. I can't take unnecessary risks," John added.

I nodded in agreement, my empathy and compassion working as much as my strategic mind to understand John's situation. "What happened next?"

"I tried to look upbeat, but I felt dead inside. We have spent so much time trying to be creative and push the envelope. Eventually, I suggested that my team and I would go back to the drawing board and rethink the campaign. I mentioned that the discussion was excellent and thanked everybody for their contribution."

"What a big swing within the same meeting. What were your thoughts after the meeting?" I asked.

"I felt tired and defeated," he said, his diminishing voice painting a vivid picture. "What a contrast with the way I went into the meeting! My mind was swaying back and forth. I still thought that the campaign designed by our team was excellent. And yes, it was provocative and jazzy. Many times those characteristics are exactly what make a campaign a success. But what if it went too far and the market rejected it? What if people liked the campaign but didn't buy the product? I remembered an ad campaign from a few years back that was a smash hit; everybody was singing that jingle and repeating a funny expression, but nobody could remember what the product was. On the other hand, a middle-of-the-road campaign would not be memorable and would not have the impact needed to move the market in the right direction. All this was going through my mind, back and forth."

John related that he went back to his team and explained what transpired during the management team meeting. He also talked about the current challenging situation for the company, the recent market share loss and the risks involved in botching the launch of the new product line. He suggested they take a fresh look at the campaign and focus on weighing the risks involved. He urged them to make it more conservative and less flamboyant while still retaining the impact value.

The team was discouraged. After all, they had invested so much time and energy in the creation of the launch campaign—and as anyone in the market development world knows, creativity breeds some of the most exquisite and positive energy in business. For many, it's addictive. However, in a testament to the respect John received as a good leader, his team also expressed understanding of the precarious position of the company and what was at stake.

John made a big effort to instill enthusiasm again. He made it clear that he wasn't dropping the original ideas, but he wanted to have two distinct, viable options from which to choose.

The team worked intensely for next few days to create a new, "moderate" version of the campaign. They changed the content as well as the look and feel, this time with a more conservative, less risky approach—a "dialed down" version of the original campaign, as one team member put it.

There it was—a very tough situation involving a crisis of confidence in a good leader. "John, you were very articulate relating all of this. I can see that you are not facing an easy situation. How do you think I can help?"

"Well, my team has all the technical capability and resources we need to create a great campaign. We have all the tools and processes we need. What's missing? I know it's something subtle, and it's in the leadership domain. It's the capacity to look at all that our creativity had conceived, make a *sound decision* and stand by it in front of the CEO and the management team. We need the capacity to develop a deep conviction in what we believe instead of wavering between 'too risky' and 'too dull.' Ambivalence is killing us. Does that make sense?"

"Absolutely. If I've got you right, you want the following:

A. To know that you made the best possible decision with the elements that you have in your hand;

B. a decision-making process that will allow you to feel no regrets, no matter what happens afterwards; and

C. you want to do all this quickly and right away.

Is that right?"

"Well said. How are we going to get to that?"

"Let's work together on a decision-making process, and then introduce it and run it by your team."

John and I met a couple of days later. This time, there was no casual European-style lunch discussion. He drove directly to what was worrying him. "I still feel torn between our first bold ideas for the campaign and going with a more traditional but safe approach."

"That's precisely why we are meeting today," I said. "Would you be able to suspend thinking about this and approach our work with an open mind?"

As I prepared for the work ahead, I knew this was not an uncommon situation. Sometimes we find ourselves in a tough predicament and our minds are ringing with just one obsessive question: "What should I do?"

It happens to all of us. We search for a decision-making mechanism but miss the precise "algorithm" for that search. We search Google for an answer, but we must search inside ourselves for a decision.

Over the next couple of meetings, I asked John to run through a personal search algorithm to find the decision he sought.

The next time we met, John and I discussed how fear and passion play key roles in our inner life and the fundamental difference between moving from fear versus passion. Our life includes many moments when we find ourselves walking a tightrope, holding a long pole with one basket at each end. One contains fear and the other passion. The basket that weighs more will sway our emotions and with them, our decisions and behavior.

A Cherokee story expresses this beautifully. At all times, we have in our heart two wolves facing each other; one white, the other black. They are always at odds, trying to prevail over each other. The white wolf represents everything that's good and inspired, wholehearted, generous and courageous. The black wolf represents the opposite forces—jealousy, envy, fear and petty thoughts and intentions.

This tug-of-war continues throughout our lives, and features numerous battles. Who wins these battles? *The wolf you feed the most.*

THE DECISION ALGORITHM

I walked to the whiteboard in the conference room where we were meeting and drew the following: *(See Figure 1)*

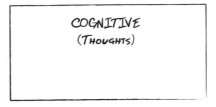

Figure 1

"John, let's focus for a moment on your thinking. When you think about a marketing campaign, what elements do you consider important?"

"My number one is 'know and respect your customer.' Our team made a religion of this principle. We try to consider everything we create as seen from the customers' perspective. I also believe that to effect change in our customers—and a decision to buy is a manifestation of change—we need to stir their imagination. We can't offer 'more of the same.'"

The objective of this Thoughts exercise was to bring logic and rationality into the picture as elements that would eventually inform the final decision. Within this step, we looked at facts and objective data points.

John and I created a decision tree and a comprehensive analysis of risk elements embedded in the planned campaign. We weighed all the risk factors and then compared the results between moving forward with the original campaign and proceeding with the more conservative approach. For each risk factor, we created at least three risk-mitigating strategies.

As I expected, the outcome was not conclusive, which should not be interpreted as a flaw in the process. The fact is that sometimes concrete and objective data is not enough to arrive at a final decision. Regardless of how much you think about the data, you will not resolve the issue with data and logical thinking alone. Other criteria must be brought into play.

Fortunately, we still had a number of other processes to address. We moved to the next step of the algorithm: Values. *(See Figure 2)*

COGNITIVE (THOUGHTS)	VALUES

Figure 2

In this step, John identified the values that he held dear to his heart. His top five were: Integrity, Creativity, Courage, Spirit of Service and Accountability.

We then reviewed his current circumstances, and how different action paths could and would be in or out of alignment with those values. This involved intense work, which required John to look deeply at how to inform his decision-making process with his own personal values. Few are the leaders who don't face this situation on a regular basis, as they deal with decisions that cut across the grain of their values but potentially move the company forward. Yet, we determined that John needed to reconcile his personal values to his decision-making process a little more closely.

We formulated the thrust of this work as a response to the following question: How could John keep his sense of personal integrity, be of service to others, act courageously, make himself accountable and sustain creativity through his choice of a course of action?

That led us to Step 3: Wants and Needs. *(See Figure 3)*

COGNITIVE (THOUGHTS)	VALUES	WANTS AND NEEDS

Figure 3

This step relates to the exploration of an area we leave unvisited many times. What did John want? What did he need? What about his team? What did they want and need?

We have to distinguish wants from needs, to avoid unnecessary problems. The difference is quite stark: I need to eat to stay alive; I want a colorful salad. The need has to be met for a vital reason, while the want may be satisfied with a wide variety of options (i.e. substituting steamed vegetables for the salad).

We spend such a big percentage of our lives at work. It is our moral obligation to seek fulfillment and satisfaction from what we do. By looking and attending to our "wants and needs," we remain engaged and fully available to do our best work.

To better understand John's predisposition, I said, "You mentioned at our lunch that you fly often. So you've heard a statement like this many times: 'If there's a sudden depressurization of the cabin, an oxygen mask will drop in front of you. If you are traveling with a child or an elderly person, please ... do what?"

"Put on their mask first," blurted John.

"Are you sure?"

John looked confused. "Oh, you're right. They say, 'Put on *your* oxygen mask first!'"

"But, you see, your tendency, your knee-jerk reaction would be to put their mask on first. In which case, you may faint while trying to do so. While if you put on your oxygen mask first, you can then help a lot of people."

It makes sense. I nodded and smiled. "Taking care of our needs may seem selfish, but it makes us sustainable and better able to help others."

Throughout this step, John gained clarity about his own wants (aspirations) and needs (what sustains him) and reflected on those of the team in relation to the situation we were considering. This process highlighted that the team needed to preserve a high morale and level of engagement, and any decision must reflect that.

We then moved into identifying John's Success Patterns. *(See Figure 4)*

COGNITIVE (Thoughts)	VALUES	WANTS AND NEEDS
SUCCESS PATTERNS		

Figure 4

186

I asked John to narrate a couple of different instances, somewhat similar to his current challenge, in which he was able to face the obstacles in front of him, navigate them well despite their difficulty, and achieve success.

Then, we looked at the common elements in his stories to extricate the patterns that allowed him to prevail in the face of threat and danger. An interesting discovery that comes with this process is that:

1. We have our own patterns of challenge (what we experience as challenge or threat, even though others may breeze through); and

2. We all have our own, personal patterns of success (the unique way in which we seek allies, manage our internal resources and overcome challenges).

The idea behind this process is to recognize our own unique way of identifying challenging circumstances, and then approach them in a way that allows us to succeed. Even if we're not aware of it, we all develop a special pattern of our own design, our very own **formula for success**.

There are a number of elements, or markers, that form the building blocks of that personal "success pattern." When we know what these elements are, we can identify our own "success pattern," and then **purposely replicate it to create predictable success**.

The main elements of John's personal challenges and success patterns were easy to recognize and included the following:

1. A fork in the road with a "bold, daring" option; and a more "middle of the road, conventional" approach.

2. The stakes are high, the risks costly.

3. There is time pressure to make a decision.

4. The search for a credible external advisor, who has no personal investment in the outcome of his decision, to provide an unbiased opinion.

5. Focused research of similar cases to draw from others' experience.

6. An integration of "synchronistic" data and events into the process (in his words, "signals that the universe sends that point to a specific way of approaching a situation").

7. A team approach to the preparatory stages and—rejecting a "decision by committee"—the assumption of personal responsibility for the final decision.

8. Exercising influencing skills over key people with power over the situation.

As the last step for this part of the process, we applied John's unique success blueprint to his work situation, focusing on how to enter his "pattern of success." Some of the insights gained through this process were that he had not sought advice from an external expert neither paid enough attention to conducting case studies research. These were key pieces needed to inform a sound decision. John continued taking notes on immediate actions to be taken by him and his team following our meeting.

Next, we moved into the **Emotional** or "feeling" perspective. *(See Figure 5)*

COGNITIVE (Thoughts)	VALUES	WANTS AND NEEDS
SUCCESS PATTERNS	EMOTIONAL (Feelings)	

Figure 5

When you need to make a decision, if you focus primarily on logical and rational processes, you may end up ignoring how you actually *feel* about your decision and its consequences. You may act in a way that "makes perfect sense" but betrays your emotional world. An example comes to mind: one of my clients readily accepted an offer of a job inside her company that came with a promotion in both status and compensation, but required moving across the country. It was a big advancement. The logical thing to do was to accept it, which she did right away. She dismissed the fact that she felt awful about moving to a small town in the Midwest—a very different cultural world from Northern California—and being far away from her extended family and friends. She lasted nine months at her new job before she returned.

When I work with people focused on technology or science, it is not uncommon to see the person's eyes glaze for a moment when I ask, "How do you feel about the current situation?" The most frequent response I hear is, "What do you mean?" Probably reflecting the person's inability to immediately access his or her feelings.

John and I also discussed how he typically coped with fear and stress. Through the exploration of his emotional/feeling inner world, we built the bridge between heart and mind that would enable him to move closer to making decisions in an integral way.

I asked John to reflect on the success stories that he evoked on the previous step. In each of these cases, he was facing extremely difficult circumstances. Fear was part of the equation. At some point or other, John had experienced doubts about his success and fear of failure. Our reflection process included identifying how he was able to successfully contain fear and exercise courage in a way that made him successful.

Also, with the idea in mind of managing fear while evaluating risks appropriately, I suggested a continuum between extremes with progressive stages in between:

A. Paralyzed by fear (no action is taken)
B. Extremely cautious (ineffective action inspired by fear)
C. Playing it safe (half-hearted action lacking power and conviction)
D. Timidly sticking your neck out (a good beginning but not quite there)
E. Letting passion inspire your work (action propelled by enthusiasm and courage)
F. Risking it all, betting the farm (action unfiltered by prudent consideration of risks)

I do not advocate a "risking it all" action where we simply disregard the risks involved or act recklessly. Exercising passion also calls for judiciously assessing risks. But, for those of us in fluid, competitive situations—translation: the 21st century business world—"playing it safe" leaves us in the uninspired place of the conventional, "more of the same" approach that impedes true creativity and innovation.

Like many other continuums, we need to find the right point of balance that maximizes our chances of success. For a deeper understanding of the risks involved, the task for John was to identify a few possible options that would fit into each point of the continuum. Afterwards, we applied the insights to his situation at the company.

INTUITION

Often disregarded in our decision-making is **Intuition**—our immediate knowledge of a deeper reality that rings true, and circumvents rational processes. *(See Figure 6)*

COGNITIVE (THOUGHTS)	VALUES	WANTS AND NEEDS
SUCCESS PATTERNS	EMOTIONAL (FEELINGS)	INTUITION

Figure 6

Most of the processes at work require left-brain activity. That's the seat of our logical, rational, inductive/deductive thinking. When we need to inject creativity and innovative thinking, we tap into the resources of our right brain, the one that imagines, and brings disparate things together in new ways. Poetry comes from our right brain.

Our culture emphasizes rational and logical processes, often ignoring our "gut feeling" (because it isn't "logical"). I found that many times, without understanding how or why, we "know" if what we are attempting can work. We also experience the power of intuition when we have a profound insight while, say, in the shower or cooking. My best insights come while cycling!

We witness the power of our intuition when we follow what our mind is telling us and ignore our "gut feeling." Most of the time, we learn that the immediate "knowing" contained a mysterious accuracy, while our mind was plainly wrong all along.

With this step of the process, John recollected some instances in which his intuition served him well. He practiced accessing his intuition while silencing his mind chatter. He then applied this skill to the situation we were considering, adding one more piece to the puzzle that would eventually support his final decision.

WISDOM

We were ready to tackle the last station of the Decision Algorithm: **Wisdom**. *(See Figure 7)*

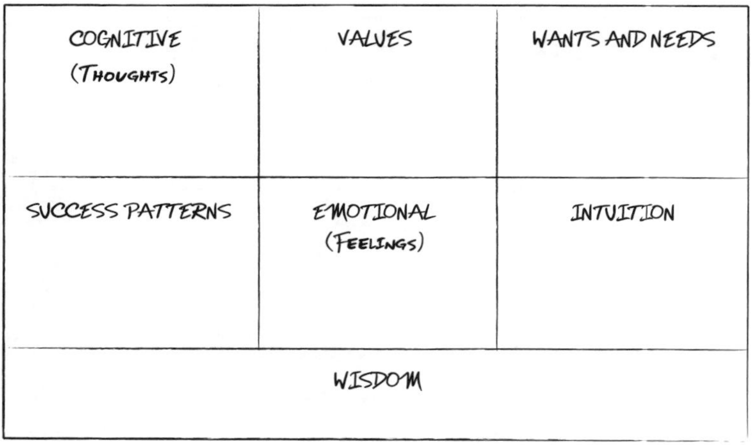

COGNITIVE (THOUGHTS)	VALUES	WANTS AND NEEDS
SUCCESS PATTERNS	EMOTIONAL (FEELINGS)	INTUITION
WISDOM		

Figure 7

"How do I access wisdom when pressed for a decision?" John asked.

"When under stress, two things become hard to access," I said. "Humor and wisdom."

"Interesting. When I'm under stress, you're right: my sense of humor is gone."

"That's not funny!" I blurted and we both laughed for a moment.

"Wisdom lies at the vantage point where you could see your life from the largest and widest perspective. Now, instead of telling you about it which may leave you still in your head and thinking, how about you have an experience?"

192

John felt hesitant. "You mean, right now?"

"Right here and now."

"All right. What do I have to do?"

"We'll engage in a guided imagination exercise. The only thing you need to do is to sit comfortably and relax. Because this is an inner experience, it may be beneficial if you close your eyes, just for a moment, while you listen to my voice."

I was expecting more resistance, but John launched into this part of the exercise without hesitation. He sat in a very relaxed position, his face flashing a hint of amusement about the new situation in which he found himself.

"John, I suggest you relax and connect with a sense of curiosity and openness to whatever you may experience as we tap into your imagination. Imagine that you traveled through time and that you find yourself far in the distant future, a safe place where you can relax and feel at peace. You're sitting on your front porch in a comfortable rocking chair. You realize that—as you gently rock in your chair—that you are 95 years old. You feel good, still healthy and strong. It feels great to be 95 and in good health. Please tell me if you can see yourself there in your mind's eye."

"Yes" responded John. His face appeared deeply serene and relaxed; he looked younger, a boyish expression replacing the earlier worried grimace. I almost could not recognize him.

"From this quiet place on your front porch, please look back over your life and recall that time when you were working at Tech-Tel. Remember for a moment the time when you were working hard with your team to create a great marketing campaign for the new product line. You also remember that Ken, your CEO, cast some doubts about your proposal being too edgy. Remember that?"

John nodded in assent.

"So many years have passed by. Now that you're a 95-year-old you can see things in perspective. Back then, you were doubting between an edgy, provocative version of your marketing campaign and a more 'dialed down,' conservative one. The first one made you feel excited, but really conscious of risks. The second one felt safer, but maybe a little boring. Hindsight allows us to see so clearly. (I paused here for a moment to allow John to slow down and experience the moment.) Take your time. Now that you're 95 years old, what would make you feel proud about how you acted?"

After a while John said, "From my rocking chair, this what I see. We invested creativity and imagination on our first campaign, and then it was all about fear. I can see the fork in the road where we either follow our inspiration—or respond to fear and shrink away from greatness. They look like two possible paths in two different but parallel universes. I guess fear was inevitable, and we had to learn to deal with it."

"So, from this vantage point of your front porch so far in the future, what advice could you give to your younger self?"

John reflected for some time. "You only live once. Live fully. Live in a way that you will not feel regret when you are 95. It's okay to make mistakes. It's not okay to shrink from life for fear of making mistakes."

"Anything else comes to mind?"

"My team. To that younger John, I'd like to tell him not to leave his team out of the loop. They are a loyal, hard-working group. Let them share in your process. Take a risk. Let them participate in the decision-making process, whatever the consequences."

"Great. Thank you. I suggest you find a way of expressing your gratitude to this wise part of yourself and—knowing that you could visit with this aspect of yourself anytime—find a way to say goodbye for now."

I waited a few moments before asking John to come back to the here and now.

Often, when we find ourselves in a difficult situation, the first question that comes to mind is "What should I do?"

Sometimes, we are able to find an immediate response and see the path to follow ahead of us. But other times we feel confused or torn between options. By carefully examining the seven areas of the Decision Algorithm (our Thoughts, Values, Intuition, Wants/Needs, Success Patterns, Feelings and Wisdom), we can achieve the clarity we need to move forward, as our next step becomes transparent and accessible to us.

At this point, John was of the idea that, if further validated, his most sound decision would be to move forward with the original bold plan, and introduce the new line of products as a disruptive new technology.

THE TEAM

John was elated to find personal clarity. Still, he was intent on hearing from his team before making a final decision. He wanted the group to experience the process that he went through with the idea that it could become a new way of informing key future decisions.

There wasn't any time to waste. John needed to get back to the CEO and the management team as soon as possible. We met with his team a couple of days later.

John spoke to the group in poignant terms. He said that he did not believe in "decisions by committee" but that, as the leader of the group, it was his responsibility to hear from every team member and then make the tough decisions. It was also the most efficient way of making timely decisions and remaining agile as a group. He proposed that the team go through the same process he just experienced so he could incorporate the team's ideas into his thinking.

Working on the seven areas with the team proved to be quite an experience. The people on John's team had been working together for some time, but had never explicitly explored their common values, feelings about their work or professional "needs and wants." The meeting was considered by the group to be an "amazing team building experience." One aspect that came out of the discussion was that, while keeping the original campaign intact, two or three items needed some reworking to convey a more engaging message.

INFLUENCING THE CEO AND THE MANAGEMENT TEAM

Energized by the reaction of his team and reassured by the careful exploration of the issue, John prepared again to present the campaign to the CEO and the management team. He was committed to remain truthful to his own style and candidly share the process through which he arrived at his decision.

John woke up earlier than usual that morning and again went over all the major points of his presentation. He felt ready.

During the management team meeting that day, John tried to concentrate on what was being discussed while feeling the excitement of his upcoming presentation. When the time came, he stood up gingerly and said: "When I left this room a few days ago after our discussion about the marketing campaign, I felt frustrated and confused.

"Frustrated because I couldn't be more articulate and better represent the original ideas informing the campaign that my team and I have developed. Confused because, at some point, I lost contact with the enthusiasm and passion I felt for many weeks while working with my team on this campaign, and instead I got in touch with the weight of the responsibility on my shoulders. I was keenly aware of the risks involved, and was overtaken by the fear of failing."

He paused for a moment before continuing. "I believe that fear will lead us to mediocrity and a 'more of the same' approach. Fear will make us lose touch with creativity and the winning attitude that we need to prevail again in the market.

"After our meeting, I reflected deeply on all the aspects of this campaign. I also took my team back to the drawing board to de-construct and re-examine all the elements involved in this project. We created alternative options taking into account the concerns I heard from this group."

Next, John brought out his punch line, "After careful consideration, I firmly believe that to become again a predominant force in the market, we need to gather our courage and make a bold move to wake up our customers. I firmly believe that 'good enough' will not be good enough. We don't want to stay in the game. We want to *win* the game."

Following that bold proclamation, John proceeded to outline the updated marketing and ad campaign. His enthusiasm was contagious.

A few months later, John was featured on the cover of an industry magazine that wrote about his groundbreaking campaign. The new product line was very successful, and the company was already focusing on the next generation of products.

At the conclusion of our work together, John shared with me that he also used the Decision Algorithm to resolve a difficult family issue. It was satisfying to hear him say, "I'm committed to make future important decisions examining all the aspects we explored together."

Chapter 5 Summary
John: The Decision Algorithm

John's back was to the wall: he and his team had spent months developing a new marketing campaign designed to catapult his telecommunications company out of a distant #3 position in the marketplace. If it succeeded, the company could look forward to closing on the #2 spot. If it failed, the company would, in the words of its CEO, suffer "irreparable" damage and probably become a candidate to be acquired. Under pressure, courage failed—when John presented the marketing campaign, fear gripped the CEO and he deflated the room, leading others in the management team to say the campaign was too edgy and risky. In their eyes, it missed the only mark that mattered: reclaiming once loyal customers. In his assessment, John felt the only thing lacking from the campaign was its greatest intangible: a leadership component, a vision and the courage to bring it forth.

I. THE DECISION ALGORITHM: We examined the marketing plan, and looked at how to improve the decision-making process in its development, to instill more confidence from the team as a whole, and to feel no regrets moving forward. The interplay of fear and passion is never greater in business than when making decisions that involve big risks and big rewards.

The Decision Algorithm includes the following elements:

1. Cognitive-Thoughts: Bring in logic and rationality, facts and objective data points. Use of a decision tree.
2. Values: Identifying and applying the personal values to the process (integrity, courage, creativity, etc.).
3. Wants and Needs: Distinguishing between what is necessary and what is merely desired.
4. Success Patterns: Using our success stories to uncover how we handle challenges, adversity, manage internal resources and work with others to achieve results. The goal: to create predictable success.
5. Emotional (Feeling) Perspective: Integrating the emotional component into our decision-making process.
6. Intuition: Incorporating the immediate knowledge of a deeper reality that always rings true and circumvents rational thought.
7. Wisdom: Seeing life or a project from the largest and widest perspective that allows access to wisdom.

II. MANAGING FEAR AND EXERCISING COURAGE IN THE PRESENCE OF RISK: THE CONTINUUM OF DECISION-MAKING

1. Paralyzed by fear: No action
2. Extremely cautious: Fear-inspired, ineffective action
3. Playing it safe: Half-hearted action lacking power and conviction

4. Timid, but willing to try: A good beginning
5. Letting passion inspire work: Action propelled by inspiration and courage
6. Risking it all: Action regardless of risk. Betting the farm

III. WORKING WITH THE DECISION ALGORITHM: The Decision Algorithm provides the seven-pointed clarity to move forward, after factoring in market conditions, strength of product or campaign and its innovative qualities. When brought to the workgroup, it enhances teambuilding, input from every team member, and a perspective that overcomes fear with courage and passion for the work. Many leading technologies and products, such as John's campaign, arise from this approach.

Brian: Developing Executive Presence

Looking in the Mirror

I WAS ready to call it a day and start the weekend. Just before I closed my laptop on this Friday afternoon, I heard a ping and wondered if I should read the incoming email or wait until Monday. My curiosity won.

The email was from Michael, a former client with whom I had worked a few years before. I remembered Michael's dark eyes and sense of intensity, his tall frame and lanky, dark hair. He looked Latino but was of Irish descent, "Black Irish" he had told me proudly.

When we met, he had been in his late forties, and at the helm of a large division of a public company. He was bright, a good leader always desiring to get better, and aspiring to eventually become CEO of his company. I remember his biggest challenge, translating his visionary ideas into specific goals and objectives so that his people could understand and execute them.

In his email, Michael asked to get together. He didn't sound urgent. I noticed that his email address was not from the company where I had met him and wondered what challenge he was facing now.

A couple of weeks later, we were sitting at Café del Doge on

University Avenue in Palo Alto, sipping what I consider arguably the best coffee in town. "Michael" I said, "you look way more relaxed than when we were working together some time ago. When was that, three years ago?"

"No, five. Time goes by quickly, eh? It's no wonder I look and feel more relaxed. Almost two years ago, I left the big company I was working at when we worked together, and I'm now heading a small startup, still in the high-tech field. And I'm now the CEO."

"Congratulations! That sounds a lot like you, always entrepreneurial and doing something new. What does your company do?"

"So far, nothing. We are still in the design stage, so it doesn't feel as if we are doing much, but we are working hard. We are designing what's hopefully going to become the next generation of web-based networking tools."

"It sounds intriguing, and you sound excited about it."

"I am. Thank you for focusing on me for a moment, but I contacted you about someone else," said Michael.

"Well, I'm glad you are well and happy about your work. Tell me about the 'someone else' you have in mind."

"I remember the work we did together. It changed my life at work for the better. Before I met you, I never found someone that could understand how my mind works and show me how to translate my ideas into executable plans. It was magical work! Now I want you to work your magic with someone else. This is the situation: I have a person on my team, Brian. He is hardworking, intelligent, good with people and gets things done. You can't ask for someone better to be your right hand man."

"It sounds like someone very capable."

"He is. I have been relying on Brian for a long time. You actually know him. He was working with me, also as my right hand man, at my previous job."

I quickly remembered. "Oh, that Brian! Of course I know him. I like Brian, and I agree with you. He is very competent. I remember that people liked working with him."

"He has been with me in the last three companies I worked at, including the current one. Which brings me to the reason why I wanted to get in touch with you. Lately, I started feeling that I owe Brian a chance to be more than my right hand man."

"What do you have in mind?" I asked.

"Well, Brian has been such a loyal and dedicated employee and has worked for me for so long that I'd like to help him move upward and forward. I'm happy as the CEO of my company, but Brian has extremely limited opportunities here. He deserves to be a vice president or at least a senior director at a substantial company. A position like that would imply larger responsibilities and also better compensation and overall benefit package than what we could offer at our start-up company."

"Michael, it sounds as if it'd be okay with you if Brian leaves."

"Yes. I'd greatly miss having his help and his great attitude around here, but like I said before, after so many years assisting me, I feel I owe it to him to help him get to the next step in his career. I thought I'd try to recruit your help because he lacks one important thing to be successful somewhere else."

"What's that?"

"Executive presence. I know first-hand how capable Brian is, but without executive presence he will not get the position he deserves. He would be a great asset to any company, but they wouldn't know it by just interviewing him. Even knowing how good he is, if he doesn't improve his sense of presence, he will always be offered a lower position than the one at which he is truly capable of being great."

I needed to clarify a couple of things with Michael. "We both know what 'executive presence' is, but would you mind elaborating on that in relation to Brian?" I asked.

"It's hard to put my finger on it, but he just doesn't come across as a credible top executive. It is not because he can't deliver great work, and it's not because he's not strategic enough. I can tell you all the reasons that are NOT causing him to not have a strong sense of presence, but I can't tell you exactly *why he doesn't have it.*"

"I am not surprised. Sense of presence or executive presence is created by subtle details. Like beauty, harmony and many other subtle things, we know when we see them but it's elusive to define them."

"Gustavo, do you think you can work with him? Could you help him improve on this indefinable executive presence?"

"Only if he really wants it. It is a process that could get enormously challenging, and it will require, among other things, humility and a good sense of humor."

Michael raised his eyebrows. "Humility and a sense of humor? I wouldn't have thought about that!"

I elaborated on these two attributes, which many great executives possess but which somehow get overlooked when young managers and executives-to-be try to climb the corporate ladder. Sometimes humility is misperceived as a lack of confidence by those who are ego-driven and who can feel at ease when facing Wall Street analysts and their own shareholders at difficult times, like during a down cycle. Humility and a sense of humor are needed to transform self and acquire executive presence, not to display it. We need humility to see ourselves in the mirror with compassion, while exercising the capacity to be critical of what needs to change. That's the challenge, to see all that needs to be different about yourself without damaging your self-esteem. That's where a good sense of humor comes into play. We need compassion and being able to laugh at ourselves, our quirks, what makes us human.

"Well said. How would you get started?"

"Have you discussed any of this with Brian?"

"No, not yet," responded Michael. "Brian has a stubborn streak, and I didn't want to talk with him about this and see him dig his heels in opposition."

"That's where I would get started. I suggest we both meet with Brian and make all this explicit to him. Then, I'll meet with him alone and evaluate his motivation and readiness. That will help determine his chances of success."

"Sounds like a plan," Michael responded. "By the way, if there's something else that he could improve, it is being less stubborn."

"As you know, if Brian and I engage in this process, part of it will be to administer a 360° feedback, and we'll see what comes out of that."

"Great! I already feel better about supporting Brian in this way. As I said before, I owe it to him."

"You are a good person, Michael. I appreciate your being supportive of your people. Let's see if we could make this really work for Brian."

MEETING BRIAN

A few days later, Michael and I met with Brian at the company's office, located in a small industrial park in Menlo Park. Still in the startup phase, the company had a little over forty employees. As soon as I opened the front door, a woman seated behind a large desk covered with paperwork greeted me. "Gustavo!" she exclaimed, "It's so nice to see you! Do you recognize me?"

"Kerry! I could forget many things, but not you. You look great. It's nice to see you still working with Michael."

"Oh yes, wherever Michael goes, Brian and I follow. This is the third company that I have worked at with both of them."

"Good for you. You must be doing something right!"

Kerry showed me the way to the conference room. Three walls were covered with white boards, and there wasn't any white space on them, every inch covered with graphics, numbers and acronyms, a true piece of Silicon Valley techno-art. A few minutes later, Michael and Brian joined me.

Brian was the smiling, pleasant man I remembered, now with a little more gray hair and a few more pounds. We shook hands effusively and sat around the conference table.

Michael explained what he had in mind. He didn't mince words. He said that he was grateful to Brian for all the years of working together, and he wanted to support Brian moving into the next phase of his career. To do that, Michael believed that Brian needed to hone his leadership skills and develop a stronger executive presence, hence my presence in the room. Michael invited Brian to consider engaging with me through a coaching process and, eventually, to consider applying for an executive position with a large high-tech company in Silicon Valley.

Brian was silent for a long moment. "I'm flattered and grateful for your offer, Michael," said Brian, "but couldn't I continue my career here, at your side, at this company?"

"Of course you can, that choice is always open to you. But this is a small private company, with no external financing. At this point in my career, I'm okay with that. I'm the CEO here, I'm following my own personal plan, and I'd be happy leading a successful, profitable small enterprise. You, my friend, could aspire to run a division of your own or become the vice president of engineering of a large organization. Here, you have five people reporting to you and a total of fourteen in your department. You could do so much more! Ultimately, it is your choice. I just want to make sure I support what you want."

"Again, I'm grateful. Thank you."

"Okay, gentlemen," said Michael, "I spoke my piece. I will let the two of you discuss if you want to move ahead with this and in that case how you'd work together." He looked at Brian. "Whatever you decide, I will be okay with it. Of course, my selfish preference is that you stay here and keep doing the great work you do. But if it's time for you to open your wings and fly higher, I want to make sure I fully support you in that."

Michael left. Brian and I sat at the conference table in silence for a while.

"What would you like to do, Brian?" I asked.

"There's no doubt in my mind that I need to move on. Here I am, working at a small company with good people but with no prospect of really advancing my career. That's something important to me. I'm forty-eight years old. If I don't move on now, my career is shot."

"Is that true?" I asked.

"Oh, yes. At least, I feel that way. Once I reach fifty without a senior executive position at a large company on my resume, my chances to be hired for a position like that are less than slim."

"I'm not quite sure that's always the case, but I understand your position. At some point you need to have been a senior executive to get a job as one."

"Exactly. You need to show that you had that experience to be credible."

"Brian, what's your point of view about not having enough executive presence?"

"I agree with Michael. I am always the one on the execution side. Need something complex and highly technical done? Give it to Brian. Need a VP of Engineering? Look for someone else."

"What do you attribute that to?" I asked.

"I don't have a clue. For me the whole concept of executive presence is like a Zen koan. No, I don't know what the sound of one hand clapping is. And I don't know why in the last three companies I worked with Michael, people gave me excellent feedback about my good work, but the few times I applied for an executive position, someone else got the job."

"That must have felt frustrating …"

"You could say that. A couple of times I had people reporting to me promoted to positions that I'd have been happy to get. Why was I passed over?"

"That's what we should uncover. But I have to forewarn you:

207

working on your sense of presence could be a challenging process. If you want to look at your executive presence not as an interesting exercise but as a transformational process, it will imply looking at everything in yourself: how you dress, how you talk, how you address another individual or talk to a group, how you relate to authority. We are talking about a process that will demand that you look yourself in the mirror with no distorting lenses. And sometimes the image that the mirror may reflect will not be a complimentary one. Are you up for that?"

"It doesn't sound like a walk in the park. I do feel some trepidation. At the same time, I feel grateful that I have this opportunity to work with you. What are my chances of success?"

"How do you define success?" I asked.

"I don't know—being perceived differently, developing more credibility. I guess the ultimate proof of success would be to land a meaningful position at a reputable company."

I told Brian that if he dedicated himself in earnest to this effort, he would improve his self-awareness significantly—and that would change in a positive way how he impacted the people around him. That's what happens in any sound transformational process—the transformation extends beyond the individual, like a force field, to those who interact with him or her. Does it guarantee the future position or opportunity an individual might want? No, but it surely improves the odds.

Brian nodded and smiled. "That I will improve is all I need to hear. I learned a long time ago that there's nothing guaranteed other than death, taxes and my in-laws visiting every other weekend."

"Nothing I can do about that." We both laughed.

I felt delighted to have this challenging work ahead of us and excited about helping Brian overcome any limitation. We discussed the feedback process we would set in motion to gather data about him from his colleagues, how often we would meet, and other logistics of working together.

GETTING STARTED

A few days later, Brian and I sat around the same conference table. It was still early morning, and Brian was smiling while we enjoyed a cup of steaming coffee. "Gustavo, I've been waiting for this for many years. I want to make it work," he said.

"Earlier this morning," I replied, "I was reading the newspaper while having breakfast at the kitchen table. I saw an ad that made me think about the process that we will be engaging in. The ad read: 'Organize your garage … instantly!' with a generous use of exclamation marks."

"That's funny," said Brian. "I know exactly which ad you are referring to. Why did it make you think about our work together?"

"Because there's a great appeal for the American consumer to attain something instantly. 'Instantly' has a connotation of 'no effort,' and results obtained with 'no effort' sell. Imagine trying to sell 'after many hours assembling our shelving system and many more hours transferring all your boxes and loose items to the shelves, your garage will be nicely organized.' If that's how you're going to sell garage organizers, I wish you the best of luck."

Brian laughed wholeheartedly. "That's really funny. You're right."

"If 'instantly' would be on one extreme of a continuum, then the process that we are starting today would be close to the other extreme. I'm mentioning this because I want to prevent you from feeling disappointed if you don't see 'instant' results."

He nodded. "Good point. I'm forewarned, and I promise not to expect overnight improvement."

"Great. We are going to meet every other week for six months. That will give us twelve meetings to go over everything we need to cover. That will be the ramping up period. After that, we will meet once a month for another three months to sustain progress and deepen the learning."

"I trust that you know what you're doing."

"I do," I said, and we both laughed.

Brian and I paused for a moment. We were both ready to start the journey.

"Brian, we are extremely complex beings. We are like an onion with many layers. In our work, we are going to start with the outer layers and move deeper as we make progress. And as we do that, we are going to leave no stone unturned, and we will look underneath for the changes that will help you move ahead with your career. We are going to move through this one issue at a time; otherwise, it may become overwhelming and then nothing would get accomplished."

"That's what I want," said Brian.

"Knowing that you are action-oriented and have been focused for a long time on execution and getting things done, I anticipate that at times you will want to go faster. Not very different from when you have a to-do list and want to execute the different items as fast as you can to move on to other things."

"You are describing very well how I operate."

"Well, this time that style would not work. We need to tackle one issue at a time until changes have been created and only then, we will move on to the next."

"You are at the helm of this process. I understand your cautioning me," said Brian.

"Good. I may remind you of this at some point. Remember I mentioned that this work could be difficult and uncomfortable? That we may need to look at some aspects of yourself that may be unflattering and difficult to look at?"

"Yes. You were very clear about that."

"Well, today we are going to talk about something that probably nobody at work would dare to mention—your weight."

He blushed noticeably. "Oh yes, I know I'm overweight."

"The way I interpret your blushing is that there's a level of embarrassment, or plainly, shame around this."

Brian looked pensive for a moment. "I'm actually very excited that obviously you are not going to leave any stone unturned. You're right about nobody at work ever mentioning my weight, and I find it enormously encouraging that you did. Ah … and yes, I feel embarrassed about being overweight."

I then elaborated on the relationship between embarrassment and self-judgment, how one goes with the other and creates lower self-confidence and self-esteem—none of which helps a man aspiring to become a senior executive. Embarrassment lets us know that there's judgment about an issue.

"What do you mean?" Brian asked me.

"Brian, you probably would not feel embarrassed if I mentioned you are wearing a blue shirt. Is that right?"

"Yes."

"That's because you don't feel judgmental about that. Judgment makes a person feel inadequate and prevents work on issues that demand openness and a sharp focus."

I looked squarely in his eyes. "I suggest that while we work together, we both suspend judgment to look as objectively as we can to what's supporting of and what's detracting from you, your professional persona and your career."

"I agree. Thank you for picking up the judgment in me."

"As your coach, I will function at times as a mirror and occasionally the image coming back will not be what you want to see, but it still needs to be looked at if anything substantial is going to change."

"I understand and welcome that."

"Our work will not focus on your losing weight—that's not my role—but I need to point out this aspect as it impacts your professional persona. I believe that—from a social perspective—a little overweight may be okay. For millennia, it indicated prosperity—only wealthy people used to be able to gain extra weight. But today, unless you are dealing with a medical problem or immovable genetics, being heavily overweight takes away from your credibility. I assume that if you are an executive you know how to take care of yourself, and if I don't see congruency in your behavior, even unconsciously I may feel that your credibility is undermined. It's like seeing a medical doctor who is overweight and a smoker. If he's not taking care of himself, how could he credibly take care of my health?"

"Without a doubt, you have a point," said Brian.

I asked him his height and weight: Brian was 5-foot-10 and 245 pounds.

"Okay, let me look at my iPad for a moment. I found this website that has a table of healthy weight for men. Even if we consider you 'large framed' your healthy weight range is 158 to 180 lbs. Let's be lenient and say 185 lbs. That will make you 60 lbs. over your ideal healthy weight. Would you consider losing at least some of those extra pounds?"

"I'll try ..." said Brian in a tentative tone.

"Brian, our work will not be about weight loss but about executive presence. If you don't feel up to it, we could stop here, and there's no harm done. I wouldn't even bill for my time so far."

"What did I say? Please don't give up on me. I said I will try to lose weight."

My research shows that when people "try" to do something, there's only about ten to fifteen percent chance of success. When people "commit" to doing something, that success rate rapidly goes up. "You do not have to commit to lose weight. It's your choice, like all the changes I will be suggesting," I said. "But every change we'll seek, small or large, will point to you coming across as a credible and influential executive ready for the next opportunity."

Brian's eyes traveled to the window, and he looked lost for a moment, maybe weighing an inner conflict. I appreciated that he was reflecting on the issue instead of jumping to show commitment merely to please his coach.

Finally he said, "As you may imagine, I've been wanting to lose weight for quite some time, and I'm afraid of committing and failing."

"If you commit to it, you will not fail. If you *try* to do it, though, failure is almost guaranteed. Please, bear with me and follow my directions for just a moment. You have a cup of coffee in front of you. Please try to lift it."

Brian lifted the cup of coffee a few inches.

"No Brian, you did not follow my directions. You lifted the cup of coffee. I'm asking that you *try* to lift it."

Brian looked at me dumbfounded.

"Okay, let me show you the action of 'trying to lift the cup of coffee.'" I grabbed the cup of coffee and, while grunting, made a face to simulate the intense effort of trying to lift an object that weighed a thousand pounds. The cup didn't budge. "This is 'trying,' Brian. This is how it looks."

Brian was looking attentively, so I continued. "Now, let me show you 'lifting' instead of 'trying to lift'. This is how it looks." I lightly lifted the cup above the table.

"Gustavo, I believe I 'tried' to lose weight for the longest time. I would like to commit to doing it."

"Great. Don't do it alone; seek help. I suggest you engage a nutritionist, even if it's for a couple of consultations to guide you through the process."

"Good idea. I actually know of one, and I will seek her assistance. What else are we going to discuss today?"

We were finished, and I told him so. I explained how our process would be conducted at marathon pace, rather than sprint speed. We would focus on one thing at a time and keep building areas of focus as we made progress. Also, I told him that at some point, we would initiate a 360° degree feedback process that would involve feedback from a large number of his colleagues at work.

"You mentioned that will be part of our work, and I welcome the opportunity to receive feedback. Could I include people from the previous companies I worked at?"

"Absolutely. Please start preparing a list of people from whom you want to receive feedback, and we will launch this in a few weeks. I will see you in two weeks."

Brian and I shook hands effusively. He knew that I would not skirt difficult issues to help him. I knew that he was committed to his own success. Our working alliance had been sealed.

LOOKING IN THE MIRROR

"I can't wait to tell you," said Brian while shaking hands with me.

"Tell me. I like your enthusiasm!"

"In the last two weeks, I lost seven pounds." Brian looked at me with obvious pride on his face.

"Congratulations! I'm really glad that you are being supportive of your goals. It seems that you have what it takes to undertake a personal transformational process. I'm happy for you."

"Thank you," Brian responded, still a glowing smile on his face. He sipped from a bottle of water he'd pulled from the small refrigerator in the conference room upon my arrival.

"As I told you before, I will not coach you on losing weight. That will not be my role. But I believe that losing weight will boost your self-esteem and your self-confidence. And if you persevere, that will be one solid step towards gaining the sense of presence that you need to succeed at work."

"It makes so much sense. What are we going to do today?"

"First, I'm going to remind you that we are looking at you with a critical eye but with no judgment."

"Is that possible? Isn't a critical eye the same as judgment?"

"No. There is a substantial distinction. A critical eye allows you to see something that needs correction but does not imply fault. The painting is crooked; it needs to be straightened out. Judgment would imply that you did something wrong, say, by not seeing that the painting is crooked. *What kind of person has a crooked painting in his office?* That's a judgmental question."

"I realize that there's a strong judgmental voice in my head," said Brian. "And mostly judgment about myself."

214

"That's why I'm intent in reminding you to silence judgment. With judgment present, every coaching session will be a demolishing experience. With a critical eye and no judgment, you could make the changes you want to make to gain a deeper sense of presence and keep your self-esteem intact."

"As in 'just straightening my crooked paintings'?" asked Brian, a twinkle in his eyes.

"Exactly," I said, relieved to see Brian tapping into his sense of humor. "I love that you bring a sense of humor. Humor is the lubricant of personal transformation."

"And I love your metaphors."

"Great. Keep your good sense of humor at hand. Today we are going to talk about clothing."

"Clothing?"

"Clothing. And not just clothing in general but your clothes, how you dress. Remember I compared our human complexity with the layers of an onion? We begin our work by focusing on the outer layers. Last time, we talked about your weight and how our physical image projects a message about ourselves. I mentioned a health care practitioner having to not only *be* credible by displaying specialized knowledge, but he or she must also *look* credible, projecting the image of someone that knows how to take care of self."

"What about the way I dress?"

"Again, this is something that—for many different reasons—people would notice but tell you nothing about it. You do not look sharp."

Brian's eyes opened in surprise. "I don't?"

"No, you do not," I responded. "Who irons your shirts?"

"Nobody. I buy wrinkle-free shirts." Brian looked perplexed.

I walked towards the door. "Come with me."

"Where are we going?"

"Not far. Please follow me." I walked outside the office into the building's lobby. I noticed that there was a large framed mirror between well-tended potted plants. I looked around and saw that we had the whole lobby all to ourselves.

I stood in front of the mirror and asked Brian to stand next to me. "Remember, Brian, this is not about judgment but about developing a critical eye. Please, look at my shirt then look at yours. What do you notice?"

"Yours looks new and mine doesn't," said Brian timidly.

"Okay now, please look at my pants. Now look at yours. Now look at my shoes, and look at yours. What do you notice?"

"Same thing. Yours are new and mine aren't."

"We are practicing your 'critical eye.' Let's go back to the conference room."

As soon as we sat again at the conference table, I said, "Brian, please let me share what I see with my critical eyes turned on. My shirt, my pants and my shoes are NOT new."

"They're not?"

"You look surprised. No, they are not new. My shirt and my pants are well ironed, and my shoes are polished. I polish my shoes every few days. Now, yours do NOT look less than new, they look sloppy. Big difference!"

"Wow! Nobody ever told me that. Yes, I did see the difference but never paid attention to it."

"Brian, in my eyes you will never be a better person just because your clothes are well ironed and look sharp. For myself, I look into my friends' hearts and souls, not at their clothes. But that's not the norm in a business or corporate environment. As you meet with people through the day at work, you are projecting an image and creating an impression on them. What do you want that image to be? Sloppy or sharp? If you want to develop executive presence, this is one more detail to pay attention to. It may feel like a lot of things to keep in mind, but once you get there, these things will feel natural and part of your new routine. Walking around with a trim figure in sharp clothes will project an image of someone really 'put together.' What do you think?"

"I can't argue with that. I guess I just dress every morning thinking 'practical' and looking at the weather. I just haven't thought about what kind of image I'm projecting."

"That's what you have a coach for. We will look deeper than weight and clothes, but we have to start at the beginning. When you meet someone, *before* you open your mouth, you are already being appraised by how you look. Make sure you look right."

"It makes sense," said Brian while looking reflective. As he nodded I assumed he was integrating these ideas.

"Now, let's not stay with the obvious. You seem to readily accept my suggestion about dressing sharp. And we know that's a big change for anyone. Let's slow down for a moment. How do you really feel about focusing on how you dress?" I asked.

Brian reflected for a while. "I feel somewhat rebellious about the idea. Why would I care if people look at clothes or shoes to determine who's relevant or who should be promoted? I don't."

"I'm glad you are insightful and able to tap into your feelings about all this. I asked because *if you go unconsciously against your grain, the changes will not stick.*"

"So, what should I do?" asked Brian.

"I believe the situation calls for some soul searching. Imagine there's a game called 'The Corporate Game.' You may or may not participate in it. It's completely your choice. BUT, if you decide to play it, you will have to play it according to the 'rules of the game' to win. Otherwise, you will be disqualified or at least consistently lose the game."

"I believe that's what happened to me. I see your point. I will think about this. If I decide to play the game according to the rules, what should I specifically do?" asked Brian.

I loved Brian's willingness to be reflective and learn. I respect the choice not to participate in the "corporate game"—but for every person who is hesitant or reluctant, another of equal or lesser intellectual or strategic ability gets the plum position or promotion because he or she plays the game like a chess grandmaster.

"Well, if you decide to move forward this is what to do: celebrate yourself," I said. "You have the means. Go to a nice store; get a few fresh shirts, pants and shoes. While you are at it, get a couple of nice jackets. Even if what you buy is wrinkle-free, send it to the cleaners and have it professionally laundered. Polish your shoes. Remember, from now on, if you take the challenge, you're going to look …"

"Sharp," said Brian smiling.

"And you will never again look …"

"Sloppy!"

As I was leaving, I said, "By the way, if you decide to move forward, don't buy too many new items if you are planning to keep losing weight."

Brian laughed wholeheartedly. "I'll keep that in mind."

HOW DO I COME ACROSS?

In my work, I focus on genuinely accepting whatever my client sets as his goals and choices—it's not about my personal preferences. But I must confess that I felt pleased when I saw Brian two weeks later. He looked sharp—and a few pounds lighter.

"Tell me," I asked, "how did you arrive to a decision about how you want to dress for work?"

"Well, your words kept resonating with me. 'If you want to play the game and win, you have to play by the rules' Then I remembered pictures of Bill Clinton 'before and after' becoming president that I saw a long time ago on the web. It was quite a transformation; his consultants made him look 'presidential.' That impressed me. I decided I want to move my career forward, and I guess that implies 'playing the game.' So, here I am, in my new look."

"I even noticed that you cut your hair."

"A whole new look."

"Great. Today we will move to the next area."

"Should I worry?" asked Brian with a mischievous look in his eyes.

"This will be fun. I brought my tiny video camera. I suggest we go through an exercise where I record you talking for a few minutes, and then we can look at the video and discuss how you are coming across. How do you feel about that?"

"Sounds good. What should I talk about?"

"Please let me pose a scenario. I want you to make this as realistic as possible." Then I described the situation: "The management team of your company has been meeting for the last couple of hours. To further their discussion and make some key decisions, they realize that they need more information about a project you are working on. Could you think about a project that your management team would like to know more about?"

"Certainly, I'm working on a technology project that may change how we interface with our customers."

"Great." I carried the scenario forward: "Someone just went into your office and let you know that the management team is requesting that you join them. You walk into the conference room, and once you learn what they need to be briefed on, you walk to the front and get ready to talk about the status of that project you are leading."

"I don't have to use a lot of imagination, because I had a similar situation a week ago—in this same room—updating our top team."

"That's even better," I said. "Okay, I'm going to roll the camera, and when you are ready, please pretend that the management team is here and present to them again as if it were the first time. I will play a member of the team and may ask you some questions. Ready?"

Brian talked for about five minutes, and I asked a few clarifying questions every now and then. After that, we sat side by side at the table to replay the video on my laptop.

"Wow! That's how I come across? It's awful!" exclaimed Brian.

I stopped the video. "Remember what I said about judgment? It will impede or seriously slow down your transformational process. Please gently switch to a scientific point of view that has a keen critical eye able to distinguish what supports your leadership from what detracts from it. Then you could rapidly move to implement the changes you need to make. Judgment will just make you feel bad about yourself and discouraged."

"Thank you. I need to remind myself of that all the time. Why am I so judgmental?"

"Let's not be judgmental about that!" I said, smiling. "Just notice when it happens, set it aside and move on. You can't be judgmental and curious at the same time. Just remain curious and in a learning mode. What did you notice when you saw yourself on the video?"

"I'm not sure. I didn't like seeing myself, I didn't sound very convincing, and I don't know even where to start to change that."

"There are a number of things that you may adjust to be more impactful and influential when presenting to a group. But this is like eating an apple; you do it bite by bite or you will choke. My suggestion is that today we concentrate on only three things. Then I'll ask you to try again, focusing on only those three things. The next time we'll meet, I will ask you to sustain the change, and we will focus on additional aspects of your presentation and slowly work through the process of becoming really good at this."

"That sounds manageable."

"It is very manageable," I said. "These are the three aspects that I suggest you focus on today. Here's the first one: when someone asks you for the time, you do not tell them how to build a clock. Keep your responses high level and to the point. You provide too many details. Don't go there unless you're asked about it.

The second one: at the end of a sentence, the pitch of your voice goes up. That makes you sound tentative, almost as if you are asking a question instead of making a statement."

"I had no idea I do that," said Brian. "May I see the video again?"

"You will in a moment. Before trying a new style I want you to clearly see what you actually do. Then, you'll be ready to implement changes. Finally, the other aspect I suggest you focus on is very simple. Every now and then you said 'Uhh' and 'Ehh,' which reinforces the tentativeness. It's as if you need to fill the silence because you are uncomfortable with silence. If you need to think about what you are going to say next or your response to a question, that's okay, but think in silence. Silence is okay. You remain authoritative, not tentative, when you're thinking silently for a moment."

We then replayed the short video and Brian was able to isolate those moments when he was going into too much detail, or "Uh … ing" and "Eh … ing" and ending phrases on a higher pitch. He raised his finger every time he caught himself doing that.

At the end I asked, "No judgment?"

"No judgment. And yes, I was totally unaware of what you pointed out, but I was able to see it clearly now."

"Great." I then offered up an explanation to put his mind at ease regarding how difficult it may be to change a behavior. "When shooting a movie, directors move through dozens of takes in virtually every scene, even with the most accomplished professional actors, shooting the same scene many times until it comes out right. Why? Directors are ironing out things like the 'Uhs' and 'Ehs' in speech and movement. Their critical eyes are sharp as eagles, but they don't judge the actors at all, because they know eventually the actors will get it right. One of the masters of theater improvisation shared his secret to his being so good: 'Rehearsal, rehearsal, rehearsal.' Let's try it again."

It took us quite a few attempts but eventually Brian was able to focus on the big picture, make statements, not questions, and felt increasingly comfortable with the silence between one set of words and the others he was formulating.

Finally, he looked over at me. "Gustavo, I'm exhausted."

"Working on self is hard work. You did well. Let's call it a day. For the next couple of weeks, please just focus on sustaining what you've accomplished so far, so we can move forward."

"Keep losing weight, stay sharp, focus on the big picture, don't make statements sound like questions and no more 'Uhh' and 'Ehh'. How's that?"

"You got it right. No wonder you're good at getting things done. We are going to continue to work on presentation skills but at this time, I suggest we launch the 360° feedback process."

"Sounds good. I will email you the list of people I want to receive feedback from. I have about forty names on that list," Brian said.

"Great. I look forward to reviewing with you the feedback report next time we meet."

Maybe I was imagining things, but as we shook hands, I swear I was starting to see a new light in Brian's eyes, a nascent sense of confidence.

THE FEEDBACK REPORT

On our next meeting, Brian and I reviewed his feedback report. Thirty-eight people responded to his request for feedback and wrote copious comments about Brian. The report's tone offered a unanimous acknowledgment of Brian's dedication and hard work. He scored in the 90-plus percentile in the vast majority of the competencies that our 360 instrument measures, indicating that very few people were perceived to be as good as him. The very few competencies where Brian scored low were like glaring red lights, demanding our attention.

Two of the low scores were related: Flexibility and Conflict Resolution. I recalled Brian's boss, Michael, mentioning that Brian got stubborn at times. Rigidity would certainly explain his difficulty negotiating and resolving conflict.

All the other low scores were related to low sense of presence: Self Confidence, Inspirational Vision and Influencing Others. What made this really intriguing was that the low scores were coming neither from his direct reports nor from his peers, but from his managers.

"This is peculiar," I said. "It seems that for your team and co-workers you are great; they rated you high on all accounts except for one item. Meanwhile, all the other low scores are coming from your current and previous managers. What is that about?"

"I do have an issue with authority. I strive to give my best to my team and to my peers, and I expect my managers to do the same with me. When that's not the case, we lock horns and things get difficult," said Brian. "What is it that my team rated me low on?"

"Remarkably, only one item, Inspirational Vision. What do you make out of that?"

"I'm always focused on execution, and I don't spend the time on vision."

"Would you like to?"

"Yes. I see that as a flaw of mine, like a one-track mind always focusing on getting things done. I do understand that people need to feel inspired. And it is part of my role to do that."

"I'm glad that you see it that way. I agree. And as you aspire to be a leader with bigger responsibilities you will need to connect with your own visionary capacity, align it with the vision of your organization and communicate it in a way that will bring meaning to people's work."

"That's what I want!" exclaimed Brian.

"Your increased sense of presence and your well-honed communication skills will allow you to create that. I suggest you incorporate a new practice. How often do you meet with your team?"

"Once a week."

"My suggestion is that once a month, you dedicate a portion of your meeting to refreshing the vision of your organization and the particular way in which your team interprets and owns that vision."

"I like the idea. What exactly would I say?"

"Your mind is well trained to focus on execution. Execution

comes from a strategy. Strategy comes from a desire to fulfill a vision. We are going to use our remaining presentation skills training sessions to practice linking all these things together in a way that makes work meaningful and satisfying."

"That will take care of that aspect with my team. What about my relationships with my bosses?"

We switched gears, since his low marks were so different from the one competency that scored low with his team. "Tell me more about lack of flexibility or coming across as stubborn with your managers," I said.

"Well, with my current manager, his thinking at times is flawed—particularly on technical issues—and I strongly push back. I assure you that I almost always end up being right, and I bite my tongue not to say 'I told you so' to my boss."

"I see, your current boss rated you low on four items[2]. I believe we could use one stone to hit all four birds."

Then I gave him these suggestions:

+ Next time that a situation presented itself where he possessed a different point of view, instead of "pushing back" or behaving as if "my boss should know better," employ a didactic, coaching mode. Explain the reasoning behind your point of view.
+ Exercise the same patience he exercises with his reports. Turn conflict into an instructive conversation.
+ Have that conversation in an articulate, confident way, utilizing his better communication skills.
+ Once resolution has been achieved, talk about the link between the issue at hand, even if it's a pedestrian one, and the larger vision for your team.

---

[2] All ratings and comments on the 360 feedback are anonymous, except for those received from the individual's manager.

"Wow, I wonder if I could do that. That's not who I am," said Brian.

"We are not here to focus on *who you are*. That's not intended to sound harsh, but it's accurate. We are here to support *who you want to be*. You don't have to do this or follow any of my suggestions. It's always your choice how you want to show up in any given situation. But if you want to become a thinking partner with your manager and eventually take a post yourself with higher responsibilities, you will have to stop thinking about upper-management as 'them,' but as 'us.'"

Brian smiled. "It sounds as if you're saying I have to grow up."

"You could say that," I said, as I got ready to wrap up our meeting. "I also want to congratulate you again for the well-earned positive feedback, and if you agree, next time we will continue with your communication skills."

"I'm enjoying the process. I'm committed to sustain what I accomplished so far and build on it."

THE PROCESS OF CHANGE

When I met Brian again, he looked disheartened. "What's on your mind? You look a little subdued. How are things going?"

"I feel down. I have not lost any weight since you and I met last time. I met a couple of times with my manager, Michael, with mixed results, and I didn't have a chance to practice being more inspirational with my team."

Brian fell victim to unrealistic expectations about the coaching process. After our last session, loaded with new energy and behaviors to practice, he expected his days to run like any of his technology projects—continuous improvement with no breather or down times. It was obvious that he needed to:

A. Become more realistic about the process of personal change;
B. Develop more compassion and patience about his progress; and
C. Receive some support to sustain morale and momentum.

"I was waiting for this moment," I said. "This is good."

Surprise stretched across Brian's face. "How could it be good? I feel awful and discouraged that I'll ever be able to change!"

"Brian, unwavering progress is a problem. It's like the housing market, only going up. You start wondering when the market is going to crash. A gentle rising with some ups and down ensures long-term results. It's a poor metaphor; maybe it's better to think about how we got accustomed to wanting a soup and opening a box or a can. Immediate satisfaction. Who has time to plant the vegetables and water them, give time to sun and Nature to do their work, and finally cook all that into a nutritious soup? Remember we talked about wanting instant results? This is what I was referring to then."

"You are right, but I can't avoid feeling frustrated and seeing all this as my failure."

"Would you be willing to try an experiment?" I asked.

"Sure. What is it?"

"Let me adopt your position, and let's see what happens."

"What do you mean?"

"Bear with me. You'll understand as soon as we get started."

I paused for a moment to create a break before moving into another mode. "Brian, I hear that you didn't make any progress during the last couple of weeks on the issues that we have been working on together. Is that so?"

"Well, yes, I haven't made any progress at all," said Brian, looking puzzled.

"I wouldn't be surprised if you are deeply discouraged. If I were in your situation, I would be discouraged, too."

"That's my case," said Brian, still looking perplexed. He didn't know where the conversation was going.

"Seeing that you are not making progress here's my suggestion: let's give up. Why beat a dead horse?"

Brian became silent for a while. He smiled playfully for a moment. "Wouldn't that be a little premature? We just got started."

"Not really," I said with a serious look on my face. "It has been a few weeks now."

Brian started to push back in earnest. "Yes, that's true, but the first few weeks, I made a lot of progress. I'm showing up at work looking sharp, and I'm working on my presentation skills. Ah, and I already lost ten pounds!"

"All that is good, but for the last two weeks, you made no progress. Considering that, I believe we should both give up. If this is not working, we shouldn't waste your time and mine."

"What about the progress I did make?"

"The progress you made was pointing in the right direction, but what should we think about your not making progress the last couple of weeks?"

"Just a respite on a process that's working well."

"Brian, I'm not sure. Convince me if you can!" I said.

"We have been working now for over two months. I knew about your previous work with Michael, my boss, and that gave you a lot of credibility in my eyes. I embraced your suggestions on a number of fronts. I have to share with you that when I look at myself in the mirror, I start seeing the image of a new me; it's starting to take shape. And I like what I see. I do not want to give that up."

I became silent for a moment, signaling that a different mode would be engaged again.

"Let's stop here, Brian. I'm not playing with you. As I said before, this was an experiment to better understand the inner forces at work in you. Sometimes there are polar aspects of self, and each sit at an extreme of a continuum, but we are only aware of one side of the polarity. The operating idea in our experiment is that if I occupy one of the poles, you have to move to the other one. I was joining the 'discouraged' part of you to give room to the 'hopeful and engaged' part of you to show up. And show up it did."

"I see. At the beginning I was a little confused, but then I sort of understood what you were doing. My own strong reaction surprised me. I do have a part of me that's discouraged and another part of me that understands that this is no time to give up and wants to persevere."

"What part is stronger in you? Which one will win?"

I was appreciative of how Brian would sometimes become silent and concentrate on a question, looking internally for the response. "Take your time," I encouraged.

"I'm not a quitter. I'm convinced that my desire to succeed at our plan is stronger. I do want to move forward with my career. Even if it's not accurate, I feel that this is my last chance to get what it takes to do that."

"Brian, it's perfectly normal to feel discouraged when we forget how we change. Continuous uninterrupted progress rarely exists in a personal transformation process. We experience ups and downs from the beginning of our lives when we learn to walk and literally have 'ups' and 'downs.' Sometimes we make progress in steps. For instance, how many pounds did you lose so far?"

"Ten about two weeks ago and none since then."

"Okay, you achieved a step. Ten pounds lost. Your body is registering that. After a while, it will be ready to lose a few more pounds. Your body is taking a breather. That's how healthy weight loss works."

"What about my working relationship with my boss and my team?"

"I'm curious. What would you tell a member of your team that came to you a bit discouraged because he made good progress so far, but is stalling on improving the way he relates to others?"

Brian became pensive for a while. He looked left and upward, imagining the situation I just described in his mind's eye. "I would say, 'Focus on what you accomplished so far, and when you are ready, take the next step.' How's that?"

"Excellent. I wouldn't be able to say it better."

"Maybe it's okay that I took a breather," said Brian.

"I think so. A breather lets you build momentum again and tackle your goals with renewed gusto. I suggest we don't push things but respectfully accept your pace. Let's call it a day and meet again in a week."

"What should I focus on next?"

I liked how he always kept a running list, asking for a forward step. "Run it by me again. What are you focusing on that you are going to keep going until we meet again?"

"Okay, here I go. Losing weight, dressing sharp, communicating well—not too many unnecessary details, no 'uhs' and 'ehs' and statements instead of questions—adopting a coaching mode with my boss instead of getting impatient and inspiring my team."

"You are awesome, Brian. Yes, you got them all. Next time we'll continue working on communication skills."

MEANING AND INSPIRATION

"I'm ready," said Brian, as soon as we sat around the conference table. "I know we are going to focus today on my communication skills, and I'm ready to practice. But I want to report that by now I've lost sixteen pounds. I also had a productive conversation with my boss as I used the same approach I use with my reports, patiently explaining my point of view, and it worked!"

"You made my day!" I exclaimed. "I'm so glad things are working. Let's keep building on that, still making sure that *you don't make progress too fast*. What did you learn from your experience of getting discouraged and now being back on track?"

"A couple of things. I was trusting that you would steer this process to non-stop progress, and now I realize that I also need to trust myself. Trust that I can recover from a setback and continue improving. Second, I learned that I need to be patient. I can see today that I will be successful, but it will take time."

"Time is on your side."

"What do you mean?"

"The more you stay on course, the less chance that you will go back to your old ways."

"I like that. What are we going to work on today?"

"In a moment, I'm going to turn on my video camera, and you're going to pretend that you are addressing your team. We inspire others when we are in touch with our own inspiration and share it with others. You are going to tell your team what motivates you to come to work. There must be more than a paycheck for you to be so dedicated to your work. By sharing what stirs your soul about your work, your motivation, you'll tap and activate your team members' passion and motivation."

Brian reflected for a moment. "You know, these thoughts are so personal. I don't know that I ever shared any of this with my team or anyone at work for that matter."

"That probably explains why you scored low on Inspirational Vision," I said. "Addressing the content of the work, what needs to be done, the 'what,' is necessary from an operational point of view. But we need to complement that with communication about the 'why,' which gives meaning to what we are doing."

I then told him an old proverb-style story. Two masons performing the same kind of work were asked what they were doing. The first mason responded, 'I'm working this piece of stone into a column.' The second mason said, 'I am building a cathedral.' Making a column was fine, but a column didn't hold deep meaning or stir the soul. But building a cathedral! That was amazing work, a structure of beauty and high inspiration that could move souls for many centuries.

"I got it," Brian said. "Give me a couple of minutes to think about it and let the video roll."

After a few minutes of recording Brian's address to his team, we stopped to watch the short video. Brian and I dedicated a moment to critique his presentation. We were going to add a few things to consider and be mindful of when presenting to a group. For instance, every time I asked Brian a question, he would walk backwards, away from me. This happened either during his response, or while he was contemplating a response. The unconscious message to the group is not positive: "Wow, I'm threatened by your question, and I retreat." Instead of that, I instructed Brian to move toward the person asking the question, even if he only took one or two steps. Also, I encouraged him to become more animated, walking back and forth, at time moving his hands, exuding confidence, "taking the space."

"With your body language, you are saying 'I'm presenting now, I have strong convictions and I'm taking the space,'" I explained, "while being stationary with your hands at your side reflects a passive attitude and sends a message of 'I'm intimidated and I'm frozen.'"

Brian practiced until he was able to keep in mind and enact all the aspects of talking to a group that we discussed so far. He also practiced modulating his voice to reflect different levels of excitement instead of a droning monotone.

PUTTING IT ALL TOGETHER

Over the next few sessions, we continued refining his presentation skills. At the beginning, the focus was more on style and process, but as Brian continued to improve, we moved into substance and content. He focused on making succinct and clear statements. He realized his love for details made him present too much data to support a point, aspects of which would be perceived by a high-level audience as minutiae. He also incorporated creating a connection between the current issues discussed and how they would affect the future of the organization, repeatedly bringing forward a visionary, strategic thinking approach to the framing of his ideas.

"Remember, when you deliver your ideas in a way that will engage and inspire people, you will know that behind your seemingly spur-of-the-moment, improvised words, you'll have hours and hours of rehearsal and preparation," I said.

"Still, many times I wonder if there's a way to speed up our process."

"You developed your past style over decades. It's not that bad if you're able to create a new style in a few months."

"I know, I know. Otherwise you would suggest we quit, right?" asked Brian.

"You got that right."

Another issue that appeared on Brian's 360° feedback was his silence in meetings involving members of the upper management of his firm or other companies with which the firm had strategic alliances. The feedback indicated that if Brian participated, his input would not only be welcomed, but increasingly encouraged.

"I don't know what to do about that. I'm mostly silent because usually I agree with what's going on," said Brian.

"Silent sounds good but being invisible is not. If you don't make your voice heard, then you become invisible to the people in the room."

"What if I just agree with what's happening?"

Time to move him out of his comfort zone. "By now, Brian, you know how I work. Let's not stay with the obvious. I always appreciate how reflective you are about your own process, and that has been the foundation of how we work together. Is there a chance that you feel intimidated when higher-ups are present?"

Like many other times, Brian fell silent and reflected for some time on my question. "I have trouble being honest with myself about this, but if I am, I have to admit that's true. I fear making a blunder. Silence is a safe harbor for me."

"Would you be willing to try an experiment?" I asked.

He smiled nervously. "Uh oh, another experiment?"

"Yes. When you are in one of these meetings, is there a way for you to keep track of time?"

"There's a clock in all our meeting rooms, and also I usually set my cell phone on the table so I can see the time."

"Excellent. This is what I want you to do. Once the meeting gets started—without interrupting anyone—you will say something at a minimum of every five minutes. More often is okay, less is unaccept-able."

"What if I agree with what's being said?" Brian asked. "I wouldn't have anything to add!"

"That's not a problem. This is not about *adding* but about *being present* in the room and counted. In that case, you will say, 'I agree with what you said and this is why.' In that way, you are also saying without words 'I'm here, I'm present, I'm a player in this group and my word counts.' What do you think?"

"And I have to do that at least every five minutes?"

"That's right."

"So far, everything you suggested has worked. I can see why you would suggest this. Reluctantly, I will do it."

"Reluctance is okay, as long as you make it happen."

As we continued working together, Brian sustained his sharp way of dressing and slowly continued losing weight. I commended him at different times for his display of discipline and commitment. By the fifth month of our engagement, Brian had lost almost thirty pounds and was far too vested in his new image to drop that effort. He received reinforcing feedback from co-workers, his friends and his family. "My wife's support has been key to my being able to sustain this effort," he told me. "After all the support I received from family and friends, I can't let them down now."

Eventually our focus shifted to future interaction with a prospective employer. Knowing that the time approached for Brian to start exploring job opportunities in the market place, we discussed updating his resume and refining his interviewing skills. "How do you feel about going into the big world out there, talking with recruiters and eventually sitting for a job interview?" I asked.

"I feel excited and a little intimidated. Working in my current job and company is familiar now, and change is always hard."

"The good news is that you don't need to change anything. You could always keep coasting and not take any risk."

"Gustavo, I know your tricks now. I could always give up my dreams, right?"

"You got that right. You could always move from a place of passion and creativity, or you could shrink because of fear. Your choice."

A few days later, I met with Michael, the CEO of the company and Brian's boss.

"Gustavo, I've wanted to talk with you for some time. I haven't been part of your work with Brian, but I have been carefully observing his transformation. How did you do it?"

"I only pointed the way. It was Brian who had to act. This was his work, and he deserves our recognition."

"This has been an amazing transformation. I heard from a colleague at another company, a fairly large organization, that they have an opening for a VP of Engineering, and I feel confident that I can refer Brian for that opportunity."

"Great. I suggest you talk with Brian and move forward on that," I said.

"I'm not ready," Brian said.

"My grandma told me—many years ago—that if she would have waited until she was ready to get married, she would still be single," I replied.

Brian overcame his apprehension and contacted Michael's colleague. He applied for the position and, after a long round of thorough interviews, got the job over all other candidates considered. The most surprised person in the process? You guessed it: Brian.

A few days later, we celebrated over dinner at a restaurant. Michael and a number of Brian's coworkers were present. The smile on his face made all the effort worthwhile.

Chapter 6 Summary
Brian: Developing Executive Presence

Brian is the consummate right-hand man for any CEO—a hard-working, results-focused executive whose motivating attitude and ability to get things done have helped drive the organization to a series of successes. However, in the eyes of his CEO, who wants to help him find a higher position in a larger company, he lacks one critical component to be a strong executive: executive presence. What is executive presence and how do we "get it"? That's the question Brian and I explored together in this chapter.

Humility and a sense of humor are needed to go through any transformational process, particularly trying to acquire executive presence. The key is to see all that needs to be changed within yourself, without judgment, to avoid damaging your self-esteem in the process. We need compassion and being able to laugh at ourselves, our quirks, at what makes us human.

I. EXECUTIVE PRESENCE: BEGINNING THE PROCESS: Working from outside appearance to inner beliefs and tendencies, and leaving no stone unturned.

1. Relationship between embarrassment and self-judgment—when together, they create lower self-confidence and self-esteem.
2. Embarrassment lets us know that there's judgment about an issue.
3. Judgment makes a person feel inadequate and prevents work on major issues that demand sharp focus.
4. Try vs. Commit: When people "try" to do something, there's a very low chance of success. When people "commit" to doing something, the success rate climbs exponentially.
5. Critical Eye: Allows you to see something that needs correction but does not imply fault.

II. ESTABLISHING AN INSPIRATIONAL VISION

1. Connect with your own visionary capacity, align it with the vision of your organization and communicate it to bring meaning to people's work.
2. Our vision is supported by our sense of presence and communication skills.
3. Once a month, dedicate a meeting to refreshing the organization vision in people's minds and aligning the team towards that vision.
4. Execution comes from a strategy. Strategy comes from a desire to fulfill a vision.
5. Link vision, strategy and execution together while inspiring team.
6. An inspirational vision gives meaning to our work.

III. OVERCOMING THE IMPRESSION OF BEING STUBBORN, DOGMATIC

1. When possessing a different point of view: employ a didactic, coaching mode. Explain reasoning behind your point of view.
2. Turn conflict into an instructive conversation, exercising patience.
3. Have articulate, confident conversations.
4. Link together the issue at hand and supporting the strategy of the organization

IV. PROCESS OF CHANGE TO EXECUTIVE PRESENCE

1. Not a matter of unwavering progress, but of sustained progress. A gentle rising with some ups and down ensures long-term results.
2. Take occasional breaks, allowing momentum to build and tackle goals with renewed gusto.
3. Trust you can recover from a setback and continue improving.
4. Practice patience. Stay on course.
5. Maintain contact with your own inspiration and share it, thus inspiring others. Your motivation is what motivates others: what stirs your soul about your work?
6. Utilize dynamic body language—take the space, exude confidence.

V. PUTTING IT ALL TOGETHER

1. Fill presentations with substance, content and animated delivery rife with body language.
2. Make succinct and clear statements.
3. Repeatedly bring forward a visionary, strategic thinking approach to the framing of ideas.
4. Seek to engage and inspire everyone in the room. Be *present* in the room— present and counted.

CHAPTER 7

Dean: The Road to a Culture of Accountability

Lessons in Skillful Confrontation

GETTING STARTED

The first thing that struck me upon meeting Dean was his office. It seemed to be a strange place to locate the director of Formulation and Manufacturing of a bio-pharmaceutical company.

Dean's workspace was located at the end of a long, white and bright hallway. The more I walked down this hallway, the more I felt as though I was entering a vacuum, so sterile and lonely the place seemed. Once his assistant showed me through his open door, I understood a little better. Two of the four walls were floor-to-ceiling-glass. The wall I was facing, behind his desk, overlooked the company's green and luscious front grounds. The other glass wall gave visual access to a complex landscape of steaming steel contraptions wrapped and interconnected through a web of different colored pipes that held various valves and measuring devices. The contrasting views through both walls were stunning.

Dean smiled warmly and shook my hand. He was a short and lean man. His blue eyes crinkled at the corners, and thick wire eyeglasses perched over his eagle nose. A white mane of hair mirrored his white smock, emphasizing my impression of the prototypical scientist. I estimated that Dean was in his late forties or early fifties and by the way he moved and carried himself, probably maintained a healthy lifestyle.

I learned from Dean that his company based most of its 3 billion dollars in sales on a proprietary genetic technology. Despite the slow performance of some of its work groups, customers had been buying for years and the company's stock had sustained its value. For a long time, Dean's prevailing thought about the execution of his department was simple and succinct: "The boat's not sinking. Why change?"

Only one problem: there was change. At the top. Thanks to the appointment of a new CEO, the wind of change was sweeping through the company. The sales group reported new steep levels of competition. The organization moved through a profound restructuring, and internal and external pressure mounted for more reliability from Dean's group.

Dean held a Ph.D. in biology and had previously worked for twelve years at a major university lab. In his current role, he was responsible for a complex operation with many moving parts. For some time, his group had been missing deadlines and commitments. He'd always thought deadline slippage was somewhat inevitable; complex work takes time, after all, and it is hard to anticipate all possible complications. Other groups dependent on Dean's team's delivery—particularly Sales and Finance—complained, but Dean didn't see much he could do about it. Commitments were broken, decisions were slow to be made, and other teams recently characterized the general pace of Dean's group as "crawling" and "utterly frustrating." But now Dean decided to seek help changing how his department worked and delivered results.

I looked across the desk. "Dean, why have you called for assistance at this particular time, instead of earlier or at some point in the future? Why now?"

"To tell you the truth," Dean said, sighing, "our new CEO didn't give me many options. I have three or four months to shape up my department, or I should acknowledge that I can't or prefer not to."

"What would happen in the case of the latter?"

Dean grimaced. "I'd be moved to a 'prestigious' position—probably Chief Scientific Officer—with no direct reports or people to manage." Bitterness tinged his voice. "I'd become just a figurehead."

"Have you given the CEO a response yet?"

He averted his eyes. "No."

Dean used the rest of our conversation to describe the urgent mandate he faced for more accountability and effectiveness across his organization. He and his 670-member group were responsible for creating complex enzymes and bio-compounds, key ingredients in the products manufactured by the company. He was aware that although his organization had a solid strategy, it was lacking in execution. The missed deadlines triggered other complications, most notably project costs soaring consistently over budget, and less than mediocre overall implementation of the company's strategic plan. Dean had the unequivocal impression that with the arrival of the new CEO, the company's internal landscape was rapidly shifting, and his reputation and position were at risk if he failed to deliver. The issue was not limited to Dean's group. At different times, his team needed input and deliverables from other groups that were also slow to deliver. This, in turn, further slowed his operation.

Our conversation jumped rapidly from one issue to the other. I wondered for a moment if this was how his mind operated. Dean was clear about the problems concerning his large group's performance, but I thought he probably didn't have a sense of the root causes or corrective measures. "I can clearly see all the ways in which our current methods aren't working, but I can't put my finger on why or what to do about it," he said, plucking the thought from my mind.

My impression of Dean was that he was probably a good—maybe even brilliant—scientist, but not a skillful group leader and manager. He even alluded to this when he said, "I had a team of *seven* at the university research lab. Nothing in my training or career prepared me to manage a group of almost seven hundred people."

"I see."

"And another thing. I cannot afford a long, protracted consulting engagement. If you're going to help us, you'll need to come in as a lightning rod and make things happen."

The way my psychologist mind works, I considered that statement to be a revealing projection. I wouldn't have imagined engaging in a 'long, protracted engagement.' After a rapid organizational assessment and design of targeted interventions, I like to see my typical effort with a company begin to yield results within sixty to ninety days.

ACCOUNTABILITY STARTS AT THE TOP

From everything Dean revealed, it was clear that the level of accountability in his group was low, an organization-wide issue. While he wanted his group to become a starting point for the organization to build a solid culture of reliable execution, it was apparent that Dean did not have a strong understanding of how he contributed to the existing culture of his group.

Some people have different reactions—not all positive—when I mention "culture"; they think that working on culture involves a drawn-out and mostly futile effort. So I have learned to avoid using the word and replace it with the essential meaning of culture: the way we work here. I have found that if we start changing 'how we work here', prevailing cultural norms will offer initial resistance and then shift accordingly, often quite rapidly. But accountability, like many other cultural traits, has to cascade from the top and be sustained over time for the cultural shift to take hold.

"Dean," I said, "to increase the level of effectiveness and accountability across the organization, the most effective method we could adopt is a three-pronged approach."

While Dean listened intently, eyes focused behind his glasses, I explained that our approach would tackle the following areas:

A. **THE LEADER:** focusing on Dean's own style of leadership and his capacity for assertive communication, healthy management of conflict, and holding people accountable.

B. **THE TEAM:** designing and implementing interventions to create clarity of roles and responsibilities and to build accountability within the group.

C. **THE LARGER ORGANIZATION:** improving the level of communication and coordination with teams in other divisions holding back Dean's group performance.

I anticipated and proposed that the primary work would be completed in 90 to 120 days, and the follow-up work would require an additional 60 days. "Dean, to accomplish this, you would need to dedicate two or three hours a week to this process. Could you commit to that?"

Dean rolled his chair back and shook his head. "Gustavo, I'm already working too many hours. I'm chronically behind. I cannot free two or three hours a week. It'd be a miracle to find one hour open every two or three weeks."

In a flash, my intuition indicated that if I pushed gently for Dean to become more available, he might accept now, only to bail out later. Lack of accountability, is often generated by a passive-aggressive approach: an inner voice saying "don't offer resistance now, just go with the flow and agree—later, you'll manage to wiggle out of your commitment."

"In that case, I will not be able to help you." I stood up abruptly and offered a farewell handshake while adding, "I wish you the best of luck. I believe that it will be impossible to accomplish what you want without your being available to steer, sponsor, and lead the effort. As much as I'm excited about tackling the issues your organization is challenged by, it'd be unethical for me to do so in a way that guarantees failure."

"Sit down, sit down!" exclaimed Dean, waving his right hand toward my chair. "Please tell me, why can't I empower you to work with my organization and make the changes necessary to improve our execution?"

I sat down on the edge of my seat, ready to bolt again. "It'd be like sending your heart for surgery while you continue your normal life. No way to make it happen. We are discussing a transformational process for your organization, and at the heart of that will stand your personal transformation as a leader."

"What if I commit to the time you require and then it's too difficult to comply? What do we do then?"

"Our written agreement will clearly spell out what we do then: by the second week of your not being available, my firm would bill you for the time spent thus far and consider the contract terminated. In that case, your company would also be charged with a cancellation fee equal to 15% of the total contract," I said.

Dean laughed. "It sounds as if you're not sure you want this consulting work!"

"Dean, maybe I should explain why I'm proposing to contract in strict terms. Your organization is a living system with its own ways of doing things and its own cultural norms. The moment we sign an agreement, I become, to some extent, part of that system. If we don't specifically agree about the rules of engagement, we are ruled by your ways of doing things—which means that the work will be performed without accountability, deadlines will probably not be met, and results will be less than mediocre. Remember Gandhi's idea that 'You must be the change you wish to see in the world'? And Einstein's concept that we can't solve problems by using the same kind of thinking we used to create them? We can't focus on changing the way you work *using* the way you work."

Dean raised one thick white eyebrow. "Which means that you are going to hold me accountable as we work on accountability?"

"That's the idea," I said.

"Hmm, as a scientist, I have to say: it makes sense. It feels as if we've already started working on this—accountability in action. I accept your terms. Now you can shake my hand, but not because you are declining to work with us."

Dean and I shook hands enthusiastically. We then discussed logistics and how to launch the process to maximize success. We agreed to look at his leadership style and launch a 360° multi-rater feedback to better understand how he was leading and managing his people.

Key people in the organization who interacted regularly with Dean would complete his 360° feedback, showing unequivocally, how Dean was impacting people around him. Since personality drives leadership style, Dean's leadership profile would show his traits and tendencies at work in multiple dimensions and contrast them with our database of more than 2,000 executives who had also completed this evaluation, providing powerful normative data.

At the end of our meeting, Dean said that he felt confident enough to go back to the CEO and commit to turning around the performance of his group. "Don't count on collecting that 15% cancellation fee!" he joked, and we laughed as I waved goodbye.

The sky formed a wide blue bowl before me as I drove back to my office. The meeting had gone well. Now it was time to focus on how I was going to approach this particular kind of engagement.

I had encountered situations like this in the past and found the framework provided by the Socio-Technical Systems (STS) approach to be very useful. Originated in the 1960s by Eric Trist and Fred Emery, the STS approach recognizes the interaction between people and the technical aspects of organizational structure and processes in the workplace. This diagram shows the main components on both the social and the technical sides of a socio-technical system. *Please see figure 1.*

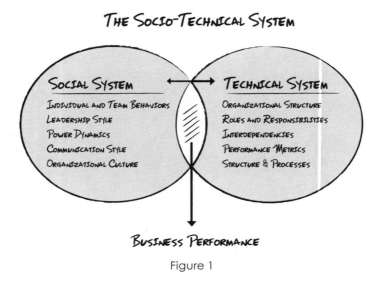

THE SOCIO-TECHNICAL SYSTEM

SOCIAL SYSTEM

INDIVIDUAL AND TEAM BEHAVIORS
LEADERSHIP STYLE
POWER DYNAMICS
COMMUNICATION STYLE
ORGANIZATIONAL CULTURE

TECHNICAL SYSTEM

ORGANIZATIONAL STRUCTURE
ROLES AND RESPONSIBILITIES
INTERDEPENDENCIES
PERFORMANCE METRICS
STRUCTURE & PROCESSES

BUSINESS PERFORMANCE

Figure 1

When working with a socio-technical system, it is useful to think about hardware and software as a metaphor for the interaction between the technical system (hardware) and the social system (software). We have to address both sides of the equation to make the system work well and achieve high organizational performance.

The challenge presented by Dean and his organization required a focus on both sides of the system:

A. **THE SOCIAL,** represented by the personal leadership and communication style of Dean and his team leaders and the unspoken accountability (or impunity) rules in place across the group.

B. **THE TECHNICAL,** represented by the current strategic plan of the group; the goals and objectives and the metrics chosen to track progress; the distribution of roles and responsibilities; and the interdependencies between individuals and teams in the group.

As I parked in front of my office and emerged into a breezy California afternoon, I reminded myself to keep a disciplined approach to my work with Dean: in the next step, I would look carefully at his leadership style.

A few days later, Dean and I met in a conference room to review his leadership profile. In keeping with the look and feel of the rest of the office building, the conference room was smartly and starkly furnished: a glass-and-chrome table seating twelve; a large white board with the echoes of unintelligible scribbles still visible; and a console table holding a tray of bottled water and fruit. Dean and I each took a bottle of water and sat beside each other at the table.

"Why don't we take a few moments and review your profile together?" I asked.

Dean nodded, and we both looked down at the papers before us.

Dean's profile indicated a low level of Assertiveness and high Conflict Avoidance traits. However, it takes the opposite traits—developing a strong presence and voice and confronting others when necessary to build accountability. Dean also had low scores on Dominance, suggesting that he was not comfortable exercising leadership over others, and on Social Confidence, insinuating that he was uncomfortable with interpersonal dealings. Dean's low scores in these capacities validated my first impression that the soft and indirect approach to deal with underperformance was rooted at the top. However, Dean scored highly on Self-Confidence, indicating that despite his discomfort towards others, he felt strongly and positively about his own capacity and abilities.

I shy away from thinking in stereotypes because I could easily and wrongly pigeonhole an individual and distort my perception of his real capability and potential. Still, in some cases—when it's glaringly obvious—it is hard for me not to see through a stereotype lens as I'm forming an impression of an individual. In Dean, I saw the Introverted Scientist stereotype to a 't'—high competency in intellectual and theoretical endeavors, and low competency in interpersonal skills.

To gain a deeper sense of how this would arise in a difficult situation, I suggested we role-play a scenario in which I would play an underperforming member of his team. He consented to my request to record our conversation, so we could review it together afterwards.

"Imagine that this is our third or maybe fourth conversation about my work being behind schedule," I said. In this scenario, Dean would be keenly aware that I was getting distracted with other, unimportant pet projects of mine that were keeping me from delivering on my commitments on time. "Imagine that you are frustrated about this. Your task is to communicate to me that frustration the best you can and somehow hold me accountable for my lack of performance."

"I don't have to imagine!" Dean said. "That's exactly what I'm experiencing with a few of my people, and particularly with my right hand, Mike. He's in charge of submitting a weekly analysis that I use to make key decisions every week and he's never on time submitting that report. It drives me crazy! I recruited most of my people—including Mike—from university labs, and they are accustomed to university pace. There, it seems they had all the time and money to research forever, and it was okay to get sidetracked in the process a hundred times. At this company, we're serving the community by focusing on improving health. We are working as part of a for-profit enterprise, and we have a responsibility to our shareholders."

Dean was getting worked up, but he was neither meeting my gaze nor immersing himself in the role-play.

"Dean," I said, "here I am. I'm one of your team members not performing—let's say I'm Mike for a moment—and you called me to have a turning point conversation. Talk to me. Tell me about your frustration and what you expect from me. Make me realize that I'd better change my way of working or I'll be facing a negative effect from not doing so."

Dean glanced at me and turned quickly away, his eyes dropping down to look at his leadership profile. Then he stuttered for a moment before pausing to collect his thoughts. Thirty seconds went by before he started speaking in a voice almost too low to hear, his words fumbling over each other. He related some facts, but he sounded tentative, indirect. When I paid attention to his tone of voice—hesitant, pleading— instead of the content, it sounded as if he was asking for a favor, something he wasn't sure he deserved or was entitled to. His demeanor—gaze averted, shoulders hunched— made him look as if he were apologizing for taking my time.

All in all, it was an ineffectual communication. As one of his underperforming team members, I did not get any sense of his deep frustration, the urgency involved, or what was clearly expected from me; I didn't understand that any negative consequence would come my way if I didn't step up and deliver.

After a few minutes, Dean said, "This is torture. I hate to do this, and it's obvious that I don't know what to say. I'd rather look into the microscope than into the eyes of a troublesome fellow worker. Please, don't play back the recording; I know that this is a dismal way of holding anyone accountable. Instead of holding your feet to the fire, I sound as if I'm inviting you to get cozy next to the fire!"

"Dean, don't get discouraged. Confronting someone—like many other tasks—requires a few stepping-stones to do it gracefully and in a dignified manner. Once you master this process, skillful confrontation will be as easy as anything else you do in your lab."

"Indulge the scientist in me for a second." Dean's glasses glinted as they caught the light, giving him an inquisitive, owlish look. "Why is it that I'm not assertive and able to confront people the way others do so easily?"

"As a psychologist, I find it very tempting to explore that question: why? The problem with pursuing the answer, though, is that the process takes us to personal history—early role models, life circumstances—and it becomes somewhat of a rabbit hole," I explained. "Interesting, but it doesn't help with rapid change. In the end, we may understand that some of your traits respond to some extent to nature, your DNA, and some respond to nurture, your role models, your primary caretakers, and so on. Instead of following that path, I'm fascinated by the power of asking *'Who do I want to be?'* and then learning how to be that person. If you want to be an assertive person with a strong sense of presence, a person who inspires and motivates others to do great work, then let's work on creating that!"

Dean nodded. "I see your point. I do want to be that kind of person. I agree that that should be the focus of our work."

"Great! The confrontation process will be an important tool that you will use whenever someone is doing his or her job in a way that doesn't work for you. There are six steps to the confrontation process, plus step zero.

"As we get started," I continued, "there are two caveats to be aware of. The first: these steps are not to be followed mechanically and chronologically—as in one, two, three—but in an organic way as the dialogue unfolds. If you talk in a formulaic way, it will come across as contrived and phony. These steps function best as a checklist in the back of your mind when preparing to confront someone. They are not to be delivered in a one-way conversation. That would be perceived as scolding instead of as a constructive conversation that generates change."

"I'm with you so far," Dean said. He had removed a ballpoint pen and small notebook from his pocket and was jotting shorthand notes to himself.

"Good," I said. "The second caveat: keep in mind that the confrontation process requires careful observation of our use of language and our choice of words. For instance, during our role-playing, you told me to try to deliver on time. This means I'd be fulfilling my commitment even if I only try unsuccessfully; after all, you asked me to try, and I did. We have to reflect and gain clarity of what we expect and what we want to create in our interactions. A short story may illustrate this well, are you interested in hearing a story?"

"Please go ahead, I love stories!"

A long time ago in a faraway monastery, I told Dean, two monks were happily living the monastic life. Life was almost perfect. But having a lot of time for themselves and little contact with the outside world, they found that a small desire could become enormous over time.

For a long time, the monks had been wanting to smoke but never dared to ask the abbot for permission. These two monks would have been happy just smoking one or two cigarettes a day, without having to hide three levels below the monastery basement in the deepest cold, humid corner to do so.

They talked about it for a few months, building momentum to talk with the abbot. Eventually, they decided to put a stake in the ground: they'd ask at the end of the year, about three months away. That would give them enough time to practice the future conversation and gather the courage to face the caring but stern abbot. They decided that they would find an elegant but clear way of asking for permission.

The three months passed, and the time came to face the abbot. Fretting about it, they flipped a coin to determine who would venture first into this unexplored territory.

The first monk went into the abbot's office while the other monk waited, pacing back and forth in the cloister. Only five minutes later, the first monk came out of the abbot's office with a radiant smile on his face. "That was easy!" he said. "The abbot gave me his permission right away, and he blessed me in such a loving way. It was a poignant moment."

The second monk felt his whole body relax. He beamed back. "And we were worrying for months about this!"

"We really didn't need to worry," said the first monk. He patted his companion on the shoulder. "Go now. It is your turn to talk to the abbot. Aren't you lucky that you know what to expect?"

The second monk went in, confident, reassured.

Forty minutes later, he came out of the abbot's office. He was sobbing, tears streaming down his cheeks.

"What happened?" asked the first monk.

The other monk couldn't talk coherently. It took quite a few minutes for his weeping to subside.

"What happened?" asked again the first monk.

"Well, I asked the abbot for permission to smoke, and he got red-faced and began screaming at me. It was really frightening. I thought he was ready to expel me from the monastery."

"How could that be?" asked the first monk, wringing his hands. "I don't understand. What did you ask, exactly? Please tell me word for word what you said to ask for permission."

"I asked if I could smoke while I pray ..." the second monk responded, wiping his wet cheeks.

"No!" the first monk cried. "You had to ask if you could *pray while you smoke*. You see, when I asked if I could pray while I smoke, the abbot hugged me and said that I could pray all the time, while washing dishes or sweeping the floor, and, of course, while smoking too. All the time!"

The second monk shook his head miserably. "I messed up. Imagine how sacrilegious I must have sounded asking to smoke while I pray."

Dean was smiling when I finished the story.

"Well, that does drive home the point," he said, "words are powerful. I will observe carefully how I use them. Now, tell me about the confrontation process."

I started with step zero, an important step. It consists of setting the stage for the conversation and asking for agreement about when, where, and how to make it happen. Step zero asks for permission. It's disrespectful and counterproductive to approach someone— probably someone against whom you've already accumulated resentment—and dump your frustrations on her lap.

It is respectful to approach the person in question and seek agreement to have the conversation you want. One should knock at someone's door before opening it.

I then gave Dean an example. "You would say something like, 'Mike, I'd like to talk with you about how we are working together. Would you be open to that?' And assuming Mike agrees, you'd say, 'Let's find a time that would work for both of us. When would be a good time for you? How about Thursday afternoon?'"

"What if Mike tells me he's extremely busy right now and doesn't agree on having this conversation anytime soon?"

"In that case, we have to make a distinction. Is Mike reporting to you? Is he someone over whom you have positional authority? From what I gathered, there are many people that need to be confronted and held accountable, people that either directly or indirectly report to you. For Mike, this conversation is not optional. You would convey unequivocally *that this needs to happen* and respectfully figure out a time that would work for both of you.

"If Mike is a peer or someone over whom you have no authority, I suggest you convey the importance of improving the way you and your departments work together," I continued. "Here you will have to rely on your persuasion and influencing skills to make this conversation happen. And if that fails, then you have to escalate the issue, but you wouldn't stop until you resolve what's slowing down your work.

"Let's imagine that you agreed on a time and place that would work for both of you, and now you are ready to talk with Mike," I said. "For this exercise, let's use what you mentioned earlier about Mike being in charge of submitting a weekly analysis that you use to make key decisions. You've been expecting to receive this analysis on Thursday mornings, but it usually shows up in your email inbox on Friday afternoon or even Monday. You talked a few times with Mike about this, and he said he would do his best to deliver the analysis on time. Mike is still not delivering in a timely fashion,

251

though, so you have decided to confront him to solve this issue. Are you with me?"

Dean nodded.

Having set the stage, I began to explain the different steps involved in a skillful confrontation.

STEP 1: BEHAVIOR
NAME THE BEHAVIOR THAT'S NOT WORKING FOR YOU

For Dean, the specific words might sound like this: "Mike, when you don't deliver the weekly analysis on Thursday morning . . ."

This step, like the others, is deceivingly simple. But time and time again, instead of naming a behavior, the person confronting someone else names attributes, qualities, character traits, or the apparent attitude of the other person. Sometimes people speak as if they are able to enter the other person's mind and read the reason for his behavior. If Dean did this, he would say, "Mike, when you are not paying attention to what we need," or " ... when you get distracted with other things . . ." In these cases, Mike would probably not relate to what he's hearing. Mike is more likely thinking, "What does he mean? I'm attentive to my obligations!" or "Distracted? He's got to be kidding! I've been thinking about this darn analysis every single day!"

"So what kind of behavior should I mention?" asked Dean.

"Think about something that's irrefutable and objective," I said. "Something that even Mike would agree with. You don't know what Mike is thinking or experiencing, but it's a fact that it is Thursday end of day and you still don't have your analysis."

STEP 2: REACTION
NAME THE REACTION OR FEELING ABOUT THE UNACCEPTABLE BEHAVIOR

Dean's reaction might be phrased as, "Mike, when you don't submit the weekly analysis on Thursday morning, I feel frustrated [aggravated, upset, irritated, bothered, troubled] . . ."

The reason for this step is that our feelings contain the energy, the fuel, for this conversation. If Dean didn't feel frustrated, then not receiving the weekly analysis on time probably wouldn't be an issue.

Also, when you explicitly describe your feeling to the person you are confronting, he doesn't have to wonder how you feel about his behavior; you are voicing it loud and clear. In Dean's case, he feels frustrated. While frustrated, he can still remain respectful, measured, and professional.

"That's a strong statement!" said Dean. "Would I run the risk of Mike getting flustered or intimidated?"

"Keep in mind that you are not 'acting out' your reaction," I said. "You are 'expressing' your reaction. Acting out your reaction might entail pounding your desk or raising your voice. In that case, what you feel informs what you do, instead of what you say. On the other hand, when you express your reaction, you are communicating how you feel while remaining respectful and displaying a professional attitude. Telling Mike that you are frustrated gives him a clear indication that the stakes are high—that this is important to you and not something to be taken lightly."

"That makes sense." Dean scribbled another note in his notepad.

STEP 3: RATIONALE
STATE WHY THIS IS AN ISSUE

Here's where the person understands your motivation, and the reason for your reaction. Without this step, the other person may be genuinely asking himself: "What's the big deal?"

Dean's words in this situation might be: "Mike, when you don't submit the weekly analysis on Thursday morning, *I feel deeply frustrated ... because your analysis is a key component to make a timely decision about our inventory level.*"

"Why this step?" asked Dean. "Mike's supposed to know this."

"This step reinforces that there are solid reasons, something important to you and the organization, driving your reaction. By mentioning the rationale for what you need, it is clear that the requirement is not capricious; it is not just because 'I say so'. It's actually something that you need to do your job."

"Understood. I'm ready for the next step."

STEP 4: DIALOGUE
GIVE THE OTHER PERSON A CHANCE TO RESPOND

This is the place in the confrontational process where you give the other person a chance to explain his situation and point of view. With this step, you want to ensure that this conversation is a dialogue and not solely your monologue. This step is your chance to hear from the other person. Be ready to listen attentively. Why, in Mike's case, was he unable to perform on time? What's really going on?

"You're a scientist," I said to Dean. "You have a cultivated sense of curiosity and interest, and you should apply it to this step. Almost everybody wants to do a good job at work and deliver results; people need to see themselves as effective and respected."

"I don't mind hearing what Mike has to say," Dean said, "but this could be opening a door to lame excuses."

"Still, you must give Mike a chance to voice an explanation, his point of view, or maybe his concerns. You might find something unexpected." I paused to take a much-needed sip of water and develop an example. "For instance, Mike might say that he has been performing this task for almost two years, and he's bored and in need of renewal at work. You may have to redesign his job or suggest a job rotation to keep an appropriate level of engagement and offer enough intellectual stimulation. Or maybe, you find out that Mike hasn't been receiving the data he needs to perform his analysis on time, in which case, he wouldn't be at fault.

"If Mike expresses his desire to perform the job the way it's required and there are no obstacles in front of him," I said, "then you could move forward with the next step in the process."

Of course, it's also possible that the person you're confronting doesn't have an explanation. This step is in no way intended to embarrass or persecute the individual. It is intended to ensure that the individual has a chance to explore the possible reasons for his behavior and to voice his point of view.

So far, we'd covered the first four steps of this communication process. If Dean were to stop here, no progress has been achieved. He would have explained what Mike wasn't doing, how he felt about it, and why. Mike may have apologized, but not made any effort to change his behavior—*because he hasn't been guided down that path yet*. And Dean still needs that analysis every Thursday morning.

Stopping here would only amount to Dean venting his feelings, but drawing no closer to solving the problem. That's why one or both of the final two steps are necessary.

STEP 5: REQUEST/AGREEMENT
MAKE YOUR REQUEST AND SEEK AGREEMENT

This step has two distinct parts. The first is to request a very clear, specific behavior from the person you're confronting. I have seen people stumble on this step and ask for an attitude. For example, Dean might say, "Mike, I want you to stay focused on preparing this weekly analysis." This may ensure Mike's attention, but it is NOT the behavior Dean needs. "Mike, I want you to make this a priority and stay attentive to making it happen," sounds better, but Dean would still be asking for commitment about an attitude, not a be-havior. Mike could come back and say that this was a priority for him and he was very attentive, BUT … it didn't happen anyway!

The second action within this step is obtaining the other person's agreement and commitment to comply with your request. Ask the other person to reflect upon his or her decision before committing to what you require.

For Dean, the two parts of this step might look something like this: "Mike, when you don't submit the weekly analysis on Thursday morning, I feel frustrated *because* your analysis is a key component to make a decision about our inventory level. *What I need, Mike, is for you to deliver that analysis on Thursdays before noon. Please think carefully about this. Could you commit to that?*"

"This is a circumstance that requires you to be literal and clear," I said to Dean.

"Now, Mike may need some time to make sure that he will get what he requires to complete this task on time, and that's acceptable. What's not acceptable is a non-committal response like, 'I'll try' or 'I'll do my best'. There's a big gap between 'I'll try' and 'I commit to doing it'. I am sure everybody is *trying* today at your group," I said, "though very few are *committed* to delivering on time and as agreed. As Yoda said in Star Wars: "There is no try. There is only 'do.' ""

As I said this, Dean nodded in agreement. "The goal is to get Mike's realistic agreement and commitment to deliver his analysis in a timely manner. Once you and Mike agree and symbolically shake hands on this issue, the rules of engagement are clear and set."

"That all sounds good," said Dean, looking pensive, "but what if, after this conversation, Mike *still* doesn't deliver the analysis on time?"

"You will find that often—if you follow the previous five steps thoroughly and crisply—the issue is resolved: next week comes and the analysis is sitting on your desk on time. It's a happy resolution that only needs recognition to be reinforced. But," I added, "there will be times when, even if you have gone through this confrontation process to the letter, things are not working out. It's the agreed time, and Mike is back to his old ways; the analysis is nowhere to be seen. This is why it's important to include a sixth step. This final step is probably the most difficult and thorny to navigate."

Dean winced a little, perhaps recalling his ineffectual communication during our role-playing exercise. I smiled and said, "Bear with me."

STEP 6: CONSEQUENCES
EXPLORING POSSIBLE REPERCUSSIONS

One of the most powerful ways in which we change is through experiencing the consequences of our behavior. Both positive and negative consequences shape our learning and future behavior.

"Many people get confused about this step of the confrontation process," I told Dean. "Some hear the word 'consequences' and immediately interpret it as punishment or firing the person. I often hear, 'You don't understand. We can't let John go. He is a key person to the team, and we need his expertise.'"

"That's exactly the case with Mike! He has specialized knowledge of our biochemical processes, and I would be in trouble if I had to replace him."

"In that case, there should be nothing in your words that even remotely implies that you would let him go. The real point here is that on the previous step, you reached clear agreement with the other person on a certain future behavior, and how we relate to our agreements always has consequences—negative *and* positive. Positive consequences should be explored as well. When we keep our agreements, we instill trust in other people. We are seen as reliable, and people know what to expect from us. Keeping our agreements also supports our effectiveness, and it may get a fatter bonus! There's a lot of value in exploring positive consequences, and I suggest you make them part of the process.

"On the other hand," I continued, "when we don't keep our agreements, there are always some negative consequences. The obvious ones are that people don't see us as trustworthy and dependable, and instead of receiving appreciation, we stand to be rejected or become redundant. In a team environment, it fosters a low level of accountability and low morale."

I told Dean that in some situations, he may not know or be clear about the negative consequences that could follow lack of delivery on commitments. That's why this step—looking at consequences—is an exploration that takes place in the context of a dialogue. It is not about threatening, warning, intimidating, or instilling fear. For it to work, it must be a coaching moment where you genuinely explore with the other person what the consequences of non-compliance may be, thus allowing the other person a deeper understanding of the real cost of failing to fulfill his commitments.

"Through this conversation, you and the other person may realize that the work assignment is not a good fit; the person is not fulfilling his potential, and you are not receiving what you need to do your job effectively. Maybe, both of you deepen the understanding of how the lack of follow-through is hurting the morale of the group. Powerful insights often arise out of conversations like this, the simplest of which is the realization that your request is important enough to justify looking for someone else to do the job if a lack of compliance continues."

It is not unusual for the confronting person to be uncertain about the potential consequences. Sometimes, that person, like Dean, can only think about two options: a) living with the problem because the person is key to the organization's success or b) the level of frustration is too high, and they have to let this person go. This polarized thinking is not productive; we feel hostage and resentful of the situation because the other person holds knowledge that our company needs, or we fail to create the learning moment that motivates the other person to change.

Reflection about consequences requires serious soul searching. Sometimes, the aggravation caused by the situation is too deep to continue working with someone unreliable. Or, as I heard once, the accountability in the group "was tanking because someone else was getting away with murder."

"Even if you are not absolutely clear about consequences," I said to Dean, "it's advisable not to delay a crucial conversation to confront someone who is not keeping their word. Just putting the issue on the table is a healthy practice and lets the other person know that you are exploring possible consequences to their behavior."

"What should I expect from making these kinds of conversations more common around here?"

Through the window behind Dean, I could see that the afternoon was transforming into evening, the sky shaded in plum. Dean's attention was holding, so I continued. "This skillful confrontation process creates a transparent work environment," I said. "There's a clear and common understanding of what's going on and what may happen. If I'm the person who is not delivering on my commitments, I know exactly what it is that I'm doing (or not doing) that's not working for you, and how you feel about it; I am clear about why this issue is important to you and the organization, and I know unmistakably what the consequences will be if I don't deliver on my commitments."

"So there are no surprises," Dean said, nodding.

"Exactly."

I have heard many times from people who have been terminated or laid off that 'they never saw it coming'. Some were surprised, shocked, or utterly stunned by the news of a major change or their termination. The majority of these folks probably would have behaved differently if only they'd had known about consequences.

"There are also ways to use this confrontation process in reverse," I said.

Dean cocked his head slightly. "What do you mean?"

"Well, there are people who are reluctant to confront us, and therefore, become so indirect that we don't know what they are trying to tell us. For example," I said, smiling, "my friend Peter, a hand surgeon, told me a few times, 'Gustavo, you are so busy!'"

I explained to Dean that the first few times my friend mentioned it, I agreed. Yes, I was busy, and my calendar was filled with commitments. I guessed that Peter saw me running between meetings with clients, conferences, and classes. But after hearing him saying a few times, "Gustavo, you are so busy!" I suspected that he was trying to tell me something else. So one morning, over the phone, I explained this confrontation process to him and asked him if he was willing to go through the process with me. As he accepted the challenge, we went through the different steps.

I said, "So, Peter, what's my specific behavior that's not working for you?"

"Well, as I said before, you are extremely busy," he replied.

I clarified and insisted, "Let's call that a temporary attribute, a quality—my being very busy. What is my specific behavior that's not working for you?"

"I invited you a couple of times to have breakfast or lunch together," he sounded tentative, "but you weren't able to join me because of other commitments."

"Thank you, Peter. That's very specific. How did you feel when I did that?"

Peter thought for a moment. "I felt rejected, as if I wasn't important enough to spend some time with, just to catch up."

I probed further. "Why is this important to you? Why do you feel so strongly about this?"

Again, he thought about his response. "You know, I believe that friendship is like tending a garden; it needs care. A garden needs water, sun, and good soil. Friendship needs time and openness to share and participate in each other's lives."

"Thank you, Peter. I totally agree with you. What specific behavior do you need from me?" I asked. "What is your request?"

Even over the phone, I could tell that Peter was smiling. "What I need from you is that you become more available, not always busy, busy, busy . . ."

"Peter, that could be again interpreted as an attribute, not something specific you request I do," I said. "I could promise to be more available but nothing different may happen. Think for a moment about this. What is your specific request of me?"

After a few seconds of silence, Peter said, "My specific request is that we meet for lunch in the next couple of weeks."

"Great!" I looked at my calendar. "How about Thursday next week?"

"Perfect!"

"I'll be there, wherever we agree to meet for lunch, and I'll be on time," I said, "but to complete our exercise, what would be the consequence of me canceling our appointment? Maybe you would be understanding if I do it once, but what if I cancel twice?"

He was reflective now. "I would interpret your canceling twice as a lack of interest in our friendship, and I would move you from my short list of close friends to my long list of acquaintances."

Now I was the one smiling. "Thank you for bearing with me, Peter. You did great! I'm crystal clear now about what you want, my commitment, and what the consequences will be if I let you down. I value our friendship, so I'm going to make darn sure I show up and have a great time with you."

Dean was smiling, too, as I related the story. "So, did you make it for lunch?"

"I did," I said. "We had a good time. Peter got what he wanted, and I kept a good, caring friend."

At this point, it was nearing six o'clock, a good time to end this productive session. I suggested that Dean take some time to think about the process we'd covered and reflect on how he would use it—not just with Mike, but with everybody. Dean nodded and ran a hand through his white mane. Then we parted ways, with another meeting set for the next week.

At this point, I started asking myself whether Dean would be able to use the confrontation process effectively. Just acquiring a new tool—an intellectual endeavor—does not change the internal dynamics of an individual's emotional world. To become the assertive person he wanted to be, Dean needed to gain a higher level of awareness of the inner forces at play, and make new, informed choices.

During our next meeting, I mentioned to Dean that at the very core of who we are, in that primordial inner space, there are only two forces at work: fear and passion. Fear is such a big word. Sometimes we may feel hard-pressed to admit we are afraid, so we may call it by other, more socially acceptable names; we say we are worried, uneasy, concerned, and so on, but these are all expressions of fear. Passion has many faces: courage, enthusiasm, excitement, and inspiration. Even greed is a face of passion—passion for wealth—as we know the markets are moved by fear and greed.

I discussed these concepts with Dean and how, in subtle ways, lack of assertiveness is an expression of fear.

Dean grasped the concept right away. "In a way, what you are saying is and is not new to me. I can relate to fear having a role in my lack of assertiveness and tentative communication. If I have to confront someone, I fear I'll alienate the other person and damage the relationship, or I'm afraid of being seen as a hard-nosed leader, a tyrant. Or I'm anxious about being misunderstood and losing some of my key colleagues. Some of them are scientists that hold special knowledge; how would I replace them? I could keep going on and on, and I see how these are all expressions of fear."

"I'm glad you're able to see this so openly," I said. "Sometimes it's hard to admit we experience fear."

"Well, I'm motivated. I'm sick and tired of not addressing our problems in a way that would bring pride to how we contribute to our colleagues, and to our company. I want to be an effective leader of my group, and I'm smart enough to see that fear has been permeating how I relate to people. How do I make my fear disappear?"

"Great question!" I exclaimed. "The bad news is that fear never completely goes away. And that serves a purpose because an adequate amount of fear makes us cautious and careful. The good news is that we can contain fear, have an awareness that it's there, inside us, alive and crying for attention. But we give the steering wheel of our behavior to passion, to that energy we feel when we get in touch with our purpose and our desire to serve others."

Dean was listening attentively, so I continued, "When fear is at the steering wheel, it dominates and informs our actions, and makes it difficult or impossible to feel and act assertively when facing conflict. All our energy goes to managing our frustration while avoiding the conflict as much as possible. Only when we tackle the difficult situation with courage and an appropriate tool, such as the confrontation process, can we find resolution and move on."

"You mentioned containing fear," Dean said, removing his glasses and wiping them with a soft cloth. "Could you elaborate on that?"

"Sometimes, consciously or unconsciously, we are waiting for fear to go away before we act courageously. That doesn't work," I said. "We can remain afraid for a very long time. So, while waiting for fear to go away, we learn to live in a constant state of unhappiness and frustration.

"Let fear remain a good advisor. Fear of making a mistake might make you think carefully about appropriate responses to work situations. If fear was nonexistent, you may act hastily. What works is to feel the fear, understand where it is coming from, and make a space inside yourself for it. That's what we call containment. Then, summon courage and passion for what you want to accomplish and how you want to show up in the world and *let that inform what you say and do.*"

"As you're talking, I'm realizing how much fear is a component of how I think and work," Dean pointed out. "The CEO asks to meet with me and I fear the worst. The COO sends me an email, and before I open it, I'm fretting that something went wrong with our deliverables. It never ends."

"I'm glad you're tired of that game. It's a good time in your life to consider how you want to live and work and to become deeply intentional about how you show up every day."

"How can I remember this?"

"How do you remind yourself of things that are important to you?"

"I write them down on my calendar."

"Great! Write this down on your calendar and use the 'repeat' function to see this item every day: **'Feel the fear and do it anyway!'** Instead of inscribing it on your shield like in old times, inscribe it on your PDA."

We both laughed.

After agreeing on a time to meet the following week, we shook hands. "I'm afraid you'll think I'm dense," Dean said, "but I will courageously continue to tell you the truth, and I will keep asking questions."

"That's all we need. This will work!"

Over the next few weeks, Dean and I agreed that he would conduct a series of increasingly difficult conversations. I suggested that one way of seeing assertiveness and courage was to imagine these two personal qualities as a set of muscles. If they were underutilized for a long time, they would be feeble today. But through exercise and careful training, they would become powerful.

Of course, training doesn't begin with hundred-pound weights. It's more sensible to start where we feel comfortable. Maybe it's twenty-pound weights, or even ten or five; our personal experience between comfort and discomfort, determines the starting point. Then we build from there.

I gave Dean an assignment: make a list of all pending conversations he needed to hold with key people who weren't delivering on their commitments. Most of these folks were in his group, but some worked in other groups and functions. Next, I told him to intuitively determine the degree of difficulty of the pending conversations, and to measure them in pounds (to keep our weight training analogy going). He wrote down twelve people he needed to confront, and the degree of difficulty ranged from twenty to 150 pounds.

Over the next few meetings, Dean rehearsed his conversations with me through role-playing. Then he got started, one by one, and in increasing order of 'weight'. It was not easy at the beginning— Dean reported bringing an extra clean shirt to work because he sweated profusely during these meetings. But with each conversation, he fine-tuned and calibrated his tone, words and demeanor. Slowly, he started experiencing, to use his words, "a growing sense of relief and liberation." By the sixth or seventh conversation, he was leading the meetings with a fair degree of competency and ease. By the tenth difficult conversation, Dean told me, smiling: "I'm a pro now. You have someone not performing? Give them to me!"

It was a moment of triumph, and I suggested he figure out how to celebrate his new competency. We still had a lot of work ahead. We needed to move into working with his top team and expanding this work across his group.

To further propel the desired change for accountability and better execution within the group, Dean, my partner Stacy McCarthy and I designed and implemented an off-site strategic planning meeting with the twelve top managers in his group. We created three different working sessions with each team in Dean's division. In these sessions, I would introduce to the teams a Responsibility Assignment Matrix, an Interdependency Matrix, and the Skillful Confrontation training Dean had been practicing.

Off-site meetings are a good practice because they remove people from their everyday environments and distractions. Ringing telephones, incoming e-mail, and spontaneous meetings, are all briefly left behind, allowing people to focus intensely on the work we set out to do.

Our objectives were ambitious:

A. Develop crisp organizational goals for the next six and twelve months.
B. Redesign the group with a focus on maximizing execution capability.
C. Create a timeline, critical path, and milestones for each major organizational goal.
D. Develop metrics and a tracking process for each goal.

In addition to strategic planning, some of our most meaningful work would include helping the group develop trust to give one another feedback in real time. That was the focus of our first activity.

We met in one of the hotel's large conference rooms. A wide window along the back wall framed the ocean beyond the green grounds. The group seemed both excited and curious about the work ahead.

"If you think about it," I told the group, "we usually develop what Chris Argyris has called 'left column/right column.' The right column is what someone *says,* but the left column is what that person is actually *thinking.* And they may differ greatly"

I pressed Play on the remote control to the large, wall-mounted flat-screen television. Immediately, Woody Allen and Diane Keaton joined our session. In the ensuing scene from *Annie Hall,* Annie and Alvy walk out to the balcony. They're enjoying a glass of wine, and Alvy says, "I love Japanese engraving. Maybe I could show you some at my place . . ." On the bottom of the screen, however, are subtitles displaying what Alvy is thinking (versus saying), and what he's *thinking* is that he'd like to get much closer to Annie.

The group laughed gamely at the scene. I could tell by their knowing smiles that they instantly understood the concept of left column/

right column. Most likely, they recognized something from their everyday interactions.

Smiling, I pressed Stop at the end of the scene.

"The goal for this offsite," I said, "is for you to leave without the need for these two divergent currents between what you say and what you think. Instead, I hope there will be one central column—no subtitles!" I added to a few chuckles. "That's what I call speaking your mind and providing real-time, on-the-spot feedback."

I continued explaining that "immediate feedback," can only be established with trust. That's what makes a team really thrive, because the team members' energy is no longer deterred by power play, politics, or any kind of interpersonal game. Instead, they are free to focus and take action on the real issues.

"So," I said to the group, "it's up to you. You could be authentic, show up and get things done or pretend agreement and leave frustrated."

I looked at the group of people sitting around the table: an even mix of men and women that ranged in age from mid-thirties to mid-fifties. Many of them nodded, a few looked skeptical.

"Let's do this," Dean encouraged his team. His determined, willing smile made me think we were off to a good start.

Our work was intense. By Friday afternoon, people were displaying commitment to change how they worked to generate better results from their efforts. They reported that by joining together to create a plan to reach their goals, they were achieving a level of alignment that they hadn't experienced before. With some gentle coaxing, they were also able to practice healthy management of conflict; they worked to debate and agree upon their differences in opinion on how to achieve the goals.

We designed a number of interventions during the offsite, each intended to support the group's transformational process and the creation of a culture of accountability. One of the most powerful was to publish the results of each team's performance on the company's intranet, using the newly created metrics. From experience, I anticipated Dean's group would eagerly await the posting of the weekly team metrics and that the winning team would celebrate and tease the other teams. The healthy competition was meant to promote transparency and solid efforts across the group.

All the work was captured in real-time, and everybody walked out of our final meeting with a binder under his or her arm outlining their goals—and everything they committed to in order to achieve them.

Despite the positivity teams often feel at the end of offsite sessions, I have found time and again that ambitious organizational goals get diluted as they transition from layers of management to the individual. Eventually, it's the sum and integration of the work performed by a large number of *individuals* that determines whether an organization will reach its goals or not. But it's not uncommon for an individual to feel murky about the specific scope of his own work, the tools needed, and the processes that should be followed to reach the objectives. To prevent this lack of clarity, each manager at the offsite committed to establishing and clarifying the individual goals and objectives for his team members. In this way, every person on every team would know exactly how his work contributed to the team's goals and ultimately to the group's execution of its strategy.

Shortly after the offsite, I scheduled meetings with each of the eight teams in Dean's division. The goal was for them to undertake three key interventions during the next forty-five days:

RESPONSIBILITY ASSIGNMENT MATRIX (RAM)

The objective of a RAM session—also known as a RASCI session—is to clarify each team member's roles and responsibilities for every relevant task or deliverable constituting the charter of the team.

The name RASCI is an acronym derived from the five key responsibilities assigned to team members:

A. **RESPONSIBLE:** Those responsible and accountable for the performance of a task or deliverable. Ideally, there should be only one person with this assignment.

B. **ASSISTS:** Those who participate in the completion of the task.

C. **SUPPORT:** Those who need to provide some kind of support towards the completion of the task or deliverable.

D. **CONSULTED:** Those whose opinions will be sought (two-way communication).

E. **INFORMED:** Those who must be kept updated on progress (one-way communication).

I like to compare the results of this activity to what happens at a pit stop in a car race. When the racecar roars into the pit stop for service, the tires get changed, fuel gets added, and many other vital adjustments performed—all in a matter of seconds. And every second counts; nearly as many races are won and lost in pit row as they are on the track. To accomplish that, every person in the team must know his or her exact responsibility and how to coordinate actions with the other team members. The RASCI allows that level of clarity and coordination.

Here's an example *(please see Figure 2)* of a typical RASCI matrix:

Task or Deliverable	Peter	Carol	Jim	Ian	Jorge	Kevin	Linda	Stuart
Task #1	R	A	A	C	S	A	S	I
Task #2	A	A	R	I	C	C	S	C
Deliverable #1	C	C	R	N/A	S	I	A	A
Deliverable #2	I	N/A	C	A	R	S	A	A

R = RESPONSIBLE   A = ASSIST   S = SUPPORT   C = CONSULTED   I = INFORMED

Figure 2

The typical length of a RASCI session varies from two or three hours to a full day, depending on the size of the team and the complexity of its tasks and deliverables. During this meeting, for each task or deliverable, the group will confirm or assign one of the possible roles to an individual or group of individuals. It's not unusual to discover how much ambiguity has existed regarding the different roles and responsibilities; one team member might discover, to his surprise, that he was never seen as someone to consult, but rather, to only inform.

The metrics across all teams after the RASCI session showed a marked increase in productivity and degree of satisfaction about how people were approaching work and getting things done. Dean mentioned that someone summarized really well the new situation at work, the person stated: "I now know exactly what I'm responsible for and whom to go to when I need to coordinate my work with other teammates."

The second intervention was:

THE INTERDEPENDENCY MATRIX

Knowingly or not, most people at work perform their jobs within a matrix of interdependencies. Here's an example of different types of interdependencies as they run through a continuum from "No Relationship" to fully "Interdependent". *(see Figure 3)*

SCALE

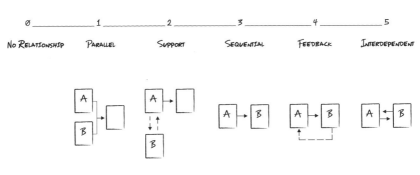

Figure 3

I've found that short sessions geared to understand the flow of work between individuals, and then between teams, help people understand how to eliminate negative situations that hinder work progress and, conversely, accelerate how work is done and results achieved.

Here's an example of an Interdependency Matrix outlining the type of interdependency between each pair of team members. *(see Figure 4)*

	John	Peter	Carol	Gerard	Linda	Jim	Sam	Jorge	Kevin	Stuart	Jenny
John											
Peter	2										
Carol	3	4									
Gerard	2	1	5								
Linda	3	4	2	5							
Jim	2	5	3	1	0						
Sam	4	2	5	2	3	0					
Jorge	2	3	3	1	4	0	5				
Kevin	4	4	3	3	4	1	0	3			
Stuart	2	3	0	2	0	2	2	0	2		
Jenny	3	4	2	2	4	3	4	3	5	3	

0 = NO RELATIONSHIP   3 = SEQUENTIAL

1 = PARALLEL   4 = FEEDBACK

2 = SUPPORT   5 = INTERDEPENDENT

Figure 4

In this example, Peter and John have a "support" type of inter-dependency, in which Peter's work allows John to complete his deliverables. Meanwhile, Carol and Peter have a "feedback" kind of interdependency, requiring an information loop that periodically recalibrates the flow of work.

During the course of the six weeks following the offsite, I held sessions with every team in Dean's group to meticulously map the flow of work and clarify internal interdependencies. I also held a session with other teams to uncover dependencies across teams and discuss the best ways to manage work accordingly. This focus on the "white space" between teams greatly increased the inter-team coordination; many metrics experienced a positive jump, reducing the time needed to get work done and increasing the quality of the work outcome.

Meanwhile, the third intervention, already familiar to Dean and the subject of the first half of this chapter, was focused on building accountability across the group:

SKILLFUL CONFRONTATION

I introduced the confrontation process to all sixty managers within Dean's group through experiential workshops. I delivered each three-hour workshop to a group of twenty managers, allowing for small training circles in which participants had a chance to practice with one another. Dean showed up at the beginning of these practical sessions to emphasize his full support and sponsorship of this initiative. He mentioned that he expected no more "business as usual" but a renewed commitment by everybody—starting with himself—to arrive at clear agreements, deliver on promises, and hold self and others accountable. Meanwhile, the managers who participated in these sessions committed to coaching and practicing Skillful Confrontation with their team members.

Finally, to focus on improving communication and coordination between Dean's teams and those in other parts of the organization, we launched a similar approach to the work done across Dean's group. It was easy for Dean to convince his delighted CEO of the importance of sponsoring the coordination effort across divisions and groups. The CEO showed up at different meetings, always unexpectedly, to send a clear message to the organization: he was committed to making the positive changes stick. Instead of being content at remaining on the top floor, focused only on strategy, investors, and finances, he demonstrated how he would do everything in his power to highlight the importance of execution.

Six months passed since I began to work with Dean and his division. Our focus turned to tracking the progress of the different teams and the group as a whole. As Dean plainly stated in our first meeting, he wanted his group to model a new level of accountability across the organization; to do that, we needed to maintain momentum. Dean and I worked together to create a "dashboard," which would indicate the status and progress on the goals and objectives of every team in the group.

The dashboard was color-coded to identify three status types: green, for the areas that were operating according to plan; yellow, for those slightly behind; and red, for any serious delays in execution. Every other week, a key group of managers in Dean's group would review the updated dashboard. The main purpose was to find ways of turning all areas green.

"What's remarkable," said Dean in one of our meetings, "is that the whole process, in its success, has created an unexpected problem."

"And what's that?" I asked.

Dean glanced through the glass side-wall at the gleaming pipes and valves with a thoughtful expression on his face.

"Some of my managers are reporting that there are a number of people who said they can work like this for a short period of time, but that they can't sustain the pace."

"What's your point of view on that?"

"The organization is humming with activity," Dean said, "and all metrics and results are now published. My best guess is that some individuals in the group had become accustomed to working light while hiding in the dark. Now that there's total transparency, they may not like it; there's too much pressure to perform. What do you suggest?"

"The sensible thing to do is not jump to conclusions," I said. "We ought to perform a quick audit of the workload of the individuals who are reporting an unsustainable pace."

After a moment, Dean nodded. "You're right. I'll personally work with my managers on some of these cases. Do you have any simple advice about this?"

Consejos vendo, para mi no tengo, I thought. *I sell advice, for me I have none.* I was about to give Dean advice that I had a hard time incorporating into my own work.

"While teaching me to drive when I was a teenager," I responded, "my father told me that our car may be designed to reach a maximum speed of 140 miles an hour, but that if I drove the car for a prolonged period of time at that speed, the acceleration of wear and tear would be exponential."

"Maximum speed isn't sustainable," Dean said.

"Exactly. And that's true for people, too. We can run very fast for a sprint but have to slow down for a marathon. Again, I suggest you review duties and responsibilities case by case."

"That's what I'll do."

Eventually, Dean's group reviewed thirteen reports of overly high workloads and unsustainable pace. After thorough examination, eleven required some adjustment to more realistic goals. The other two cases were people who preferred a slower pace and weren't a good fit for the new way the group was approaching and getting work done, and found other opportunities within the company.

After three months of tracking progress, Dean and I met to reflect on our nine months working together, take stock, and establish closure. In the first ten minutes of this meeting, Dean told me that the group was performing well, deadlines were being met, and productivity had increased across teams by an average of almost 30%. Dean had received positive comments from the CEO and was glowing with satisfaction, having led an impressive turnaround for his group.

"The CEO said that my group is setting the bar on delivering results for the rest of the organization," Dean said, beaming. "But even better, I have to tell you, Gustavo: I have a new level of confidence in interacting with people, both inside and outside my group."

I smiled. "So I've noticed."

Dean's newfound social comfort was clear in the way he now met my eyes throughout a conversation, rather than taking any opportunity to look away. He spoke clearly and with greater authority, no longer sounding as though he were asking for undeserved favors. I'd observed the change in him for some time, and it pleased me to know that he felt it, too.

"I'm a late bloomer," said Dean, smiling. "I'm almost fifty years old, and I've just learned how to talk to people who are not carrying their weight. But now I know how to hold them accountable in an effective, professional way."

"That's very rewarding to hear."

"I wish I'd had these skills when my three boys were growing up," Dean added with a chuckle.

"It's never too late."

Dean looked me squarely in the eye and nodded. "If there's one thing I've learned through this engagement, it's that. Thank you!"

Chapter 7 Summary
Dean: The Road to a Culture of Accountability

One of the most difficult but necessary skills to master in business is skillful confrontation. The further we rise through the management, leadership and executive ranks, the more we need this vital skill. This chapter focuses on my work with Dean, the Director of Formulation and Manufacturing at a bio-pharmaceutical company, the overseer of a 670-member department who came to me dead-set in his work routine and resistant to the change sweeping top-down through the company. He would have no choice—except to change his approach. That would involve confronting his charges, and peers, in a way that instilled greater confidence and reliability in themselves and the department as a whole.

I. INCREASING EFFECTIVENESS AND ACCOUNTABILITY: The goal was to create reliable execution within Dean's department. It required a three-pronged approach:
1. Focus on leadership style
2. Create clarity of roles and responsibilities for team, build accountability within group
3. Improve communication with other divisions

II. ACCOUNTABILITY IN ACTION: Dean needed to develop strong assertiveness and the ability to confront others when necessary. He lacked both. We undertook the following approaches:
1. 360-degree feedback, coming from those who work with Dean
2. A Socio-Technical System (STS) approach, focusing on interaction between the department's people and technical processes in the workplace.
   a. The Social: leadership and communication style of Dean and his team leaders; unspoken accountability rules in place; and prevailing culture of the organization.
   b. The Technical: current strategic plan of the group; goals, objectives and metrics chosen to track progress; distribution of roles and responsibilities; interdependencies between individuals and teams.

III. 6 STEPS TO SKILLFUL CONFRONTATION: Like other tasks, skillful confrontation requires a few stages to work gracefully and in a dignified manner:
1. Step 0: Getting permission and agreement on where, when and how to make this conversation happen
2. Step 1: Behavior—Identify and name the unacceptable behavior
3. Step 2: Reaction—Share your reaction or feeling about the unacceptable behavior
4. Step 3: Rational—State why this is an issue
5. Step 4: Dialogue—Give the other person a chance to respond
6. Step 5: Request—Make your request and seek agreement
7. Step 6: Consequences—Explore possible repercussions

IV. EFFECTIVELY USING SKILLFUL CONFRONTATION TO DEVELOP ASSERTIVENESS AND EXERCISE COURAGE

1. Gain higher level of awareness of most basic, primordial inner forces at play: fear and passion
2. Examine their validity
3. Make new, informed choices
4. Contain fear: "Feel the fear and do it anyway!"
5. Drive what you say and do with courage and passion for what you want to accomplish
6. Make a list of pending conversations with people not delivering on commitments
7. Intuitively determine degree of difficulty of conversations
8. Conduct these conversations in an increasing level of difficulty

V. STRATEGICALLY PLANNING THE CHANGE: We created three different working sessions with each team in Dean's division. Our objectives:

1. Develop crisp organizational goals for the next twelve and twenty-four months.
2. Redesign the group with a focus on maximizing execution capability.
3. Create a timeline, critical path, and milestones for each major organizational goal.
4. Develop metrics and a tracking process for each goal.
5. Real-time feedback, which pairs well with Skillful Confrontation.

VI. KEY INTERVENTIONS TO ACHIEVE STRATEGY

1. RAM (Responsibility Assignment Matrix): to clarify each team member's roles and responsibilities for every relevant task or deliverable constituting the charter of the team. Also known as RASCI session (Responsible-Assists-Support-Consulted-Informed).
2. Interdependency Matrix: To recognize all interdependencies of individuals, groups, and departments when performing a work task. This approach helps us to understand how to eliminate negative situations that hinder work progress, accelerate work pace, and achieve greater results. It also increases inter-team organization.
3. Skillful Confrontation to ensure accountability.

VII. MEASURING THE STRATEGIC/BEHAVIORAL SHIFT: Creating a dashboard to allow tracking of status and progress on the goals and objectives of every team in the group and the group as a whole. Reviewed bi-weekly, it is coded into three status types:

1. Green (areas operating according to plan);
2. Yellow (those slightly behind);
3. Red (serious delays in execution).

The purpose, which Dean and his department fulfilled: To keep all areas green.

Mary Anne: Stepping Into the Future

*Combining Diligence and Strategy to Make Winning
Decisions*

MARY ANNE was spending quiet time at home with her family on a
Saturday morning. She promised to take her three children to see a
new movie that afternoon. Getting them to agree on the same show
proved challenging, due to their ages: they were 11, 9 and 3 years old.
For once, they all said they'd love to see the new 3-D movie; she
appreciated when everyone shared an activity together. Her husband,
Gary, planned to join them for dinner after the movie.

THE INVITATION

Mary Anne went to the den and opened her laptop to buy tickets
online. She noticed a few new emails had come in and decided to
check them out before buying the tickets, figuring the emails were
nothing more than weekend spam.

Which they were—except for an email from Carl. He was the
ex-CEO of a large media company based in Silicon Valley, and currently a senior partner at a prestigious venture capital firm. Furthermore, he was an influential board member for several well-known

companies. Mary Anne knew of Carl and had seen him present at a couple of technology conferences, but had never spoken with him directly.

The tone of the email caught Mary Anne's eye: Carl was apologizing for reaching out to her "out of the blue." He mentioned that a couple of colleagues in the field referred him—including someone with whom Mary Anne had worked at her previous job. As she read, her eyes opened widely a second time: He wanted to arrange a meeting to get to know her and discuss a business opportunity.

Mary Anne was intrigued and excited, though certainly not in a job-hunting frame of mind. As the Chief Operating Officer (COO) of a small digital media company, she felt satisfied with her position, her current role, and her team. Her position mandated that she work closely and be well aligned with her CEO. She had served in her current position for two years, and was starting to see tangible payoff for the extraordinary efforts and energy that she poured into the company. She planned to stay with her company, regardless of how tempting the offer from any other organization. Still, she was flattered to be the target of a "fishing expedition" for her services.

Carl's email didn't annoy her. To the contrary, she felt pleased and proud that, apparently, her colleagues had spoken highly about the quality of her work and that she may be considered for an interesting post. She also knew that, no matter what, she needed to see through the completion of the multiple initiatives at her current job, and the company was close to launching a big new effort that would require all her attention.

Nonetheless, she also knew that Carl was someone good to have on your side. His influence reached far and deep in Silicon Valley. Even if she knew she was going to decline any offer, it wouldn't hurt to have a business relationship with someone so well known. Powerful allies are invaluable networking assets, and having Carl as an advocate could serve her well in many boardrooms.

Mary Anne consulted her calendar and responded to Carl's email.

After thanking him for thinking about her, she offered a couple of possible meeting times. To her utter surprise, Carl responded right away, inviting her to lunch on one of the dates she offered. Not what she expected, especially on a Saturday morning. She quickly accepted and finally bought the movie tickets. *Not the time to be thinking about work,* she thought.

MEETING CARL

A few days later, Carl and Mary Anne met at the front door of Left Bank, a restaurant in Menlo Park. Mary Anne arrived on time. Carl was already there, engrossed in a cell phone conversation. When he saw her approach, he quickly ended the call and warmly shook her hand, a pleasing smile on his weathered, tanned face. Mary Anne estimated Carl to be somewhere in his early to mid-seventies. Actually, he'd just celebrated his eightieth birthday, not easy to guess considering his ramrod straight posture, trim and fit physique, and strong, youthful energy.

A moment later, they were seated. "Mary Anne, you came towards me so decidedly that I knew it had to be you. Let's look at the menu and get the ordering out of the way," said Carl.

An hour passed; it felt like minutes. *How classy,* Mary Anne thought, *we have been sharing lunch for some time now, and he hasn't mentioned work.* Carl asked her about her family, interests and latest travels. He shared enthusiastically about his recent birthday party; he felt so proud to be eighty and still active on so many fronts.

Neither of them ordered dessert, but both got tea. At that time, Carl started to talk about the reason for their meeting. "I'm a member of the board of AlphaMedia," said Carl, "as you may know, a major player in the digital media market."

"Of course, I know AlphaMedia. It's the eight hundred pound gorilla in our field. I can't say we compete against them. I should probably say that we aspire to compete with them. I've heard Tim, their CEO, as a keynote speaker at a couple of conferences some time ago."

"Ah, you saw Tim. Although still not made public, I need to share with you confidentially that Tim will be resigning to take care of his health."

Concern stretched across Mary Anne's face. "I'm sorry to hear that; my best wishes to him. It's always sad to hear that an illness disrupts the life of someone you care for."

Carl nodded. "I'm very sad about the whole thing. He will be missed. He had a terrific run; he built a great team, grew the company and created great opportunities for the future. The current situation has been very hard for him and for everybody around him. In any case, the other members of the board of directors and myself are actively looking to fill that position. After a thorough analysis we concluded that there are no viable internal candidates, which brings me to the reason I reached out to you."

"How can I help?" she asked, as she felt her heart racing.

"Mary Anne, you made it to our final short list of candidates for the position of CEO of AlphaMedia."

"But, but I'm not looking for a new job!" she blurted. She wasn't sure if she should be upset finding out about it for the first time now, over lunch, or feel flattered about being considered as a candidate for the position.

"I know. I have been following the progress made by your company. Through the industry articles, I learned that many of the innovations introduced by your company have been your ideas. I know that you are not looking for a job, and that you are successful where you are. Still, imagine how many more resources you'd have at AlphaMedia, how much you could get accomplished, and how much you could influence the field."

"I don't know what to say."

"There's nothing you need to say now. I want to warmly suggest that you think about the possibilities and entertain the idea of being our new CEO. If you decide that you want to explore the idea, then there's a two-way road to navigate."

Mary Anne felt puzzled. "What do you mean?"

"Well, we would be interviewing you, but you would also be interviewing us and determining if you could do great work with us while having fun and certainly being financially well rewarded. We will also be interviewing two other candidates, so we still have to walk that road."

Mary Anne sat in silence, absorbing Carl's words. Finally, she said, "Again, I wasn't prepared for this. I don't believe that I have it in me to leave my team at this time. We are in the midst of a number of key initiatives, and I'd feel that I'd be letting them down. That's not a good feeling. On the other hand, it'd be foolish not consider the opportunity you are presenting to me. How much time do I have to respond?"

"No matter what, Tim will have to leave in four weeks and ideally we prefer not to have a temporary CEO. I apologize for the short time frame but—as you can imagine—this wasn't planned. That means that we need to move fast. Could you get back to me by Monday next week? At least that will give you a few days to reflect and imagine what would be possible as the CEO of AlphaMedia."

"You are charming and a great salesman, Carl."

He smiled. "I have many years of practice! But seriously now, it'd really be a coup to get you. Please think about all this. If you decide to move forward, we will start scheduling some interviews with key stakeholders."

"I will seriously think about this, consult with my family and get back to you by Monday. Thank you for thinking about me and for the opportunity."

Carl extended his hand. "That's all I needed to hear. I hope we get lucky, and thank you for meeting with me on such short notice."

SEEKING HELP

Mary Anne left the meeting feeling both exhilarated and anxious. It was not her nature to "play hooky" at work, but she decided not to return to the office that afternoon. She was experiencing too many feelings at once—*how would my team feel if I leave? How would I feel if I don't take this position? Would I let my family down? Would I let myself down? Imagine, CEO of AlphaMedia ... But who would pick up the pieces at work if I leave my company? How would I feel if I miss this opportunity?* The questions left her confused; she needed time to reorient herself.

Instead of jumping back into her car, she started walking down the street to give herself some time to think. She always liked thinking while walking. *Wow,* she thought, *to be at the helm of AlphaMedia! If only my father could see me.* Sadly, he'd passed away a few years before. He always encouraged Mary Anne to reach for the stars: "And if that doesn't work, at least you'll get the moon," he used to say.

Her mind continued to spin. *How should I think about this? Where should I start? I know how to think about my company, how to operationalise our strategy, how to think problems through with my team. But I never really spent time thinking about my career. Some people have clear goals for their careers. Mine just happened. I worked hard and positions kept being offered to me. It doesn't seem to be a career strategy at all ... but it worked! I'm forty-three years old now. What should I do? Where do you go when you have to make this type of decision? I could go to Gary (her husband); he's always been supportive. But I can almost hear his voice saying, "It's your career and you have to decide." And he would be right, it is my career and I have to decide. And how do you make a decision like this? I would feel disloyal to my team if I just packed up and left.* "Oh, by the way guys, I forgot to tell you that I'm leaving. I got a better opportunity at AlphaMedia and you can call me 'gone.' So long and good luck." *Darn, I don't see myself doing that. It doesn't feel right. And what about Ian (her company's CEO)? He placed a lot of trust in me naming me COO. I owe him. Yes, I owe him and the right thing to do is to feel flattered and do nothing. I can't leave my work in the middle of the race. That's it. I'm clear now.*

Mary Anne looked up and found herself walking on the Stanford campus, her alma mater. Had she gone there as a coincidence? Was she unconsciously looking for something she found there? Inspiration? Her dreams from long time ago?

"Elegir es renunciar" (to choose is to renounce/give up). I heard those words and its translation at a leadership class at Stanford not long ago. That's how life works. If I have to choose between A and B, and I choose A, I'm giving up B. What am I giving up here? The CEO of AlphaMedia. Am I ready to renounce to that? Is it possible that I'm wrong, feeling that it'd be disloyal to my company? Maybe it's a woman's trait to think about loyalty above career? What would my Dad say? I only hear questions in my mind, not answers. And I don't even know if I'm asking myself the right questions. Thinking by myself worked before. But it's hard when the thinking is about myself. And when I don't know the right question? Whom should I ask? An objective person. How could I be myself in turmoil and objective at the same time? I probably can't. What do I know about mulling over an idea? If I don't have the answer, then I need to look for an expert. Where could I find an expert?

By sheer coincidence (or was it?), she found herself in front of the Meyer Forum—the room where she attended the leadership workshop a few weeks ago. That was the moment when Mary Anne realized her unconscious mind had a plan of its own. The professor teaching the class mentioned that he was also an executive coach.

I will reach out to him and seek a consultation. At that moment, she felt a profound serenity. She knew what to do next. With a spring to her step, she walked back to her car and drove home.

Within a few hours, I was reading Mary Anne's email. I remembered her as a warm, intelligent woman, one of the most participative students in the workshop. There was such urgency in her words, asking me to meet with her as soon as possible, that I decided to reschedule a couple of other engagements so I could see her the next day.

A DECISION-MAKING PROCESS

We met at the faculty club at Stanford. "I never thought I'd be seeing you again so soon," she said. "Thank you for meeting with me on such short notice."

"Your email certainly made it sound urgent."

"It is." She leaned forward. "I owe a response Monday on a difficult issue. Needless to say, what I'll relate to you has to be kept confidential."

Not wasting any time, Mary Anne shared the situation at Alpha-Media, the offer she received from Carl, her desire to be loyal to her colleagues at work, how tempting the opportunity was, and how much she didn't have a clue about how to move forward.

"How can I help?" I asked.

"My husband and a couple of dear friends I confided in said basically the same thing: 'Only you could know what's the right decision,' and I was grateful for their not saying, 'What an opportunity! You have to take it.' But to be honest, 'only you could know' didn't bring me closer to clarity. I need someone objective to look at the situation with me and help me make a sound decision. So here I am, seeking your professional help."

I nodded. "Let's say that we do engage in a coaching process. How would you define success?"

Mary Anne grew silent for a moment. "Success would mean that a year from now, I'd look back at my decision and feel sure that it was a good one."

"So you are concerned about experiencing regrets. What may cause you to feel that way?"

"I remember from your class how important it is not to think in black and white. If I decide to accept the position I'm offered, I know that it will come with big responsibilities. I don't want to be naïve and ignore the fact there will be big challenges and that I will be in the spotlight. A lot. Regrets will mean that I'll be missing the beauty of working in a small company, where I know probably more than half of the employees by first name and don't have to deal with politics, Wall Street analysts and the like. Conversely, if I choose to stay where I am today, a year from now I might feel that I had the opportunity of my life presented to me and turned it down."

"That's quite clear. There's a very simple process that we may try right here and now. Would you be willing to try an experiment?"

"Sure."

"Okay then." I pulled my computer from my briefcase. "Let's get started."

I opened a new spreadsheet and divided it into two parts. "We have two excluding options." On the top left side of the screen, I wrote, "staying with my company;" on the top right side, I wrote, "moving to AlphaMedia." Then I created two columns under each heading, with the plus sign on the left and the minus symbol on the right. It looked like this: *(See Figure 1)*

STAYING WITH MY COMPANY		MOVING TO ALPHAMEDIA	
+	-	+	-

Figure 1

"This exercise works well when you lay out your options by following your gut response, your intuition, and not thinking and analyzing. So please, in any order, I want you to name—as they come into your mind—positive and negative aspects of both decisions."

Mary Anne studied the chart for a minute. "Well, if I stay in my current position, a positive thing would be that I'm familiar with everything and everybody." She paused, she looked anxious, perhaps wondering if she was already kicking into analytical mode.

"Good start," I said, "keep mentioning positive and negative aspects of both scenarios."

Over the next few minutes, Mary Anne proceeded to give me the pros and cons; I started filling the four columns. I guided her to keep the same number of items in each column, to keep a sense of balance between options. We ended up with the following: *(See Figure 2)*

STAYING WITH MY COMPANY   MOVING TO ALPHAMEDIA

+	-	+	-
Things are familiar	Slow advancement. My career slows down	I can learn a lot from the experience	I don't know the people there
I bring current company's plan to fruition	No room to go up - I like our CEO and don't want to replace him	More resources, great intellectual property, a lot to accomplish	I will be a foreign object in a new system will face resistance
I hold a lot of knowledge useful to the company	Missing resources, money, people, a sense of scarcity	Expand my influence in our field and create opportunities for others	The buck will stop with me -- a huge responsibility!
I like my team	Uncertainty about the company's future	Better compensation	More time at work less with family

Figure 2

"This was more difficult than I expected." Mary Anne caught her breath. "What now?"

"You did great! Now, let's move to the next step. Again, I want your gut reaction. I will mention each of these pros and cons, and I want you to rate, as a percentage, how important is each to you. For example, 'Things are familiar.' If that's of utmost importance, it could be anywhere between say 90% and 100%, and so on. By the way, how would you rate 'Things are familiar'?"

"I'd say not really very important, say 40%"

After a few minutes of work, this is how the chart looked: *(See Figure 3)*

STAYING WITH MY COMPANY   MOVING TO ALPHAMEDIA

+	%	-	%	+	%	-	%
Things are familiar	40	Slow advancement My career slows down	70	I can learn a lot from the experience	90	I don't know the people there	30
I bring company's plan to fruition	70	No room to go up - I like our CEO and don't want to replace him	60	More resources, great intellectual property, a lot to accomplish	85	I will be a foreign object in a new system will face resistance	40
I hold a lot of knowledge useful to the company	60	Missing resources, money, people, a sense of scarcity	80	Expand my influence in our field and create opportunities for others	90	The buck will stop with me — a huge responsibility!	60
I like my team	95	Uncertainty about the company's future	50	Better compensation	85	More time at work less with family	100
Total	265	Total	260	Total	350	Total	230

Figure 3

"Good work, Mary Anne. Here are the results. What do you think?"

She studied the chart for a while. "This was an interesting exercise. I relate to each single number on this chart ... and I'm still surprised about the final result! What I see is that I don't have a strong bias regarding pros and cons in my current situation; it looks very balanced. But I'm more positive than negative about moving to AlphaMedia."

"What other insight may be available when you look at the chart?"

"I noticed that the total of positives for 'Moving to AlphaMedia' is higher than the total for 'Staying with my company.' What should I conclude from this?"

"Nothing yet; we are not done. This is an important decision that will affect you over quite some time. Let's bring in the time element. Imagine it's a year later as we review the same aspects. How do you feel about 'Things are familiar? What number would you assign to it?'"

Taking that approach, Mary Anne and I played the chart forward by one year. Her numbers and results looked radically different: *(See Figure 4)*

STAYING WITH MY COMPANY — MOVING TO ALPHAMEDIA
ONE YEAR LATER

+	%	-	%	+	%	-	%
THINGS ARE FAMILIAR	10	SLOW ADVANCEMENT MY CAREER SLOWS DOWN	90	I CAN LEARN A LOT FROM THE EXPERIENCE	90	I DON'T KNOW THE PEOPLE THERE	0
I BRING COMPANY'S PLAN TO FRUITION	70	NO ROOM TO GO UP - I LIKE OUR CEO AND DON'T WANT TO REPLACE HIM	80	MORE RESOURCES, GREAT INTELLECTUAL PROPERTY, A LOT TO ACCOMPLISH	85	I WILL BE A FOREIGN OBJECT IN A NEW SYSTEM WILL FACE RESISTANCE	10
I HOLD A LOT OF KNOWLEDGE USEFUL TO THE COMPANY	40	MISSING RESOURCES, MONEY, PEOPLE, A SENSE OF SCARCITY	90	EXPAND MY INFLUENCE IN OUR FIELD AND CREATE OPPORTUNITIES FOR OTHERS	90	THE BUCK WILL STOP WITH ME — A HUGE RESPONSIBILITY!	60
I LIKE MY TEAM	95	UNCERTAINTY ABOUT THE COMPANY'S FUTURE	80	BETTER COMPENSATION	85	MORE TIME AT WORK LESS WITH FAMILY	100
TOTAL	215	TOTAL	340	TOTAL	350	TOTAL	170

Figure 4

Mary Anne stared at the chart for a while. Her eyes seemed to express surprise, even a little bewilderment. She seemed to need some time to reflect. "This is remarkable. I'm having the same experience as before. I relate to each single number; after all, they come from me. But I'm surprised about the final result."

"What comes up for you looking at this chart?"

"With time, there's more negative than positive in my staying in

290

the position I have today. Also, with time, there's more positive to my making the move, and the negatives have shrunk."

She'd hit the center of a difficult area even for the most visionary, forward-thinking executives when presented with career-changing opportunities: Projecting into *their own* futures.

"Yes, this highlights something very significant about facing change," I said. "First, that many of our concerns related to the 'unknown' are temporary and will greatly diminish or vanish over time as you become familiar with your new environment. So, instead of focusing exclusively on current conditions, a sound decision is made when you are able to project yourself into the future. Second, when considering a big decision like this one, we may focus almost obsessively on one or two elements, instead of looking over the whole picture. We lose perspective."

Mary Anne looked pensive. "That happened to me. I was almost exclusively thinking about not being disloyal to my current company but there's a lot more to making this decision. I was thinking small, as if I'm irreplaceable."

"I did notice that you are concerned about the time you spend with your family deteriorating, and that's a genuine concern. We should work on the way you shape how you work, so you do not lose balance between work and family life. In this new position, you may have a very hectic first three months, but after that, things should go back to normal—what *you* define as a sustainable pace."

Mary Anne looked like an entirely different person than the excited but conflicted woman with whom I started this meeting. "Gustavo, I've been fretting about this decision, but now there's no doubt in my mind that despite all my fears and reservations, I should accept this opportunity and see if I can get the CEO job."

"That seems to be the case. I'm glad this worked out. Still, I suggest you ponder a bit more the pros and cons, revisit this chart later and then firm up your position. Please feel free to call again on me, and good luck!"

MOVING FORWARD

I perceived Mary Anne as such a smart, capable person that I thought she'd have a very good chance of landing the CEO job, even if she competed for it against other solid, experienced candidates—which I assumed would be the case, given the rich pool of talent in Silicon Valley. However, I didn't expect to hear from her so soon. She sent me an email the next morning asking if I could coach her through the transition process.

"Here we are again," said Mary Anne during our next meeting. "How do I get ready for the upcoming process?"

"Well, there are at least three fronts to take care of," I responded. "The first is your family and yourself. The second relates to the company where you are working today, and the third your potential new employer. How are you reacting to this process so far, and how's your family responding to it?"

"My family has been very supportive. Me? I have moments when I feel I could be a good CEO for AlphaMedia, and other moments when I think I'm crazy for even considering that."

"Good. That's excellent."

She looked at me like I'd just landed from another planet. "How could that be good?"

"It sounds balanced and realistic. Both extremes would be a negative. To be completely sure about the great work you could perform as a CEO would be manic; you probably have a steep learning curve in front of you. Conversely, harboring only doubts about yourself would be depressing and debilitating. At this point of the game, falling somewhere in between these extremes is just right."

"What about dealing with my current company? Should I disclose what's happening? I feel torn about that. Either way is difficult."

"I have a strong opinion about this. I believe that transparency— within the boundaries of confidentiality—supports our personal integrity. You cannot disclose what's happening at AlphaMedia and their CEO because the information was given to you in confidence.

On the other hand, by being transparent, you may share that you are being considered for an 'extraordinary opportunity' that you're willing to explore."

She rubbed her forehead. "Wouldn't that make my colleagues at work feel insecure about my situation?"

"It might, and with good reason. Your situation is in a transitional place right now. Disclosing this will give you a sense of integrity and honesty. If you don't get the job, at least your colleagues would know that you are a viable candidate for a bigger game. That would certainly not hurt your reputation. If you do get the job, that will not take them by surprise, because you shared with them what was going on."

"I guess you're right. It sounds like such a difficult conversation to have."

"Mary Anne, what you are doing and what's ahead of you requires a high level of courage. Remember, courage is not the absence of fear. It's the capacity to contain fear and still do what you have to do."

She smiled. "Thank you for reminding me. I want to be transparent, and I know that's what will make me feel good about myself and what I do."

As I expected from someone of her caliber, Mary Anne's level-headedness and her thoughtful way of working through issues met again to create levity in this tough situation.

"What about AlphaMedia?" she asked. "How could I prepare myself for the upcoming interviews?"

"First, gather all the information needed to familiarize yourself as much as possible with the company. Being a public company, you will find a lot of data available. Secondly, as part of our work, I will interview you a few times, asking difficult and sometimes unexpected questions. Don't forget the secret to success of the master of improvisation: rigorous rehearsal. Finally, start thinking about the following: What's the future of your field? What would you do if you were the CEO of the company? How could you create competitive advantage for the firm? I will create a list of questions that will stimulate your visionary thinking."

"It sounds as if you have done this before," said Mary Anne.

"I have," I said, and we shook hands enthusiastically.

Over the next couple of weeks, Mary Anne and I met a few times, even as she was conducting a series of meetings with the AlphaMedia board, the current CEO and some key members of his management team. She continued learning about the company, submitting to interviews by me and stretching her visionary capacity to imagine what was possible for the organization.

Holding the required conversations with her CEO and colleagues at her current job proved to be difficult. "I dread talking with them about the fact that I'm exploring another opportunity and my potential departure," said Mary Anne during one of our meetings. "Those conversations will create a lot of uncertainty around me, and I don't feel good about that."

"Mary Anne, there is a lot of uncertainty around you. If you have those conversations and get to become the CEO of AlphaMedia, you will leave behind a group of colleagues that saw your integrity in action and will respect you for it. Without those conversations, you will have a group of people that felt deceived by your handling your transition completely behind the scenes. What would you choose? Also, AlphaMedia has a tight timeline. By your full disclosure, you will be open to discuss an accelerated but workable transition instead of leaving abruptly and leaving things in disarray. Bring forward the 'ingredient' we discussed, and these conversations will be possible."

"I know, I know. I need to gather the courage to do this, and I will. I realize that at times it's impossible to display integrity without being courageous."

Mary Anne did gather her courage. She opened dialogue with her colleagues about her possible transition to a post that she didn't seek but was presented to her. Even as they worried about the possibility of her leaving, her co-workers were intrigued about Mary

Anne's opportunity and reluctantly became grateful about her candor and openness.

MAKING THE TRANSITION

Not long afterward, Mary Anne shared the news: to my delight, she'd been formally offered the position of CEO at AlphaMedia. "No time to celebrate," she said, "there's so much to do. You mentioned that this is a transitional period. I want to continue the coaching process until my transition ends and the situation becomes stable. I have never been a CEO before and I want to minimize blunders and mistakes. I'm supposed to be at AlphaMedia in two weeks. Let's discuss the next steps."

I imagined how excited the people at AlphaMedia must feel to be receiving a CEO like this—committed and thoughtful about preparing herself to do the best possible job. "Regarding your existing job, I suggest you carefully plan your departure to end with a feeling of completion," I said. "No 'unfinished business' left behind. Help to plan your succession, provide guidance to the person replacing you, and take time to celebrate the time you spent there and the friendships you forged along the way."

"I'm so glad you're pointing me in that direction," Mary Anne said. "All my thinking has been directed to tasks I need to do and my new responsibility."

With that piece in place, we discussed other aspects of the transition. "About your new responsibility, to keep things simple, I see ahead three steps you should lay on top of each other in an ongoing process. The ongoing process will be your ability to gain a deeper understanding of the inner workings and capabilities of the company. I suggest that you make no big decisions until you have completed at least three quarters or more of this process. You are entering a new and complex system, and it'd be foolish to change anything before you know enough about the organization. There will always be something new to learn, but at some point, you should exercise leadership and steer the ship.

"So, first and above all, strive to understand AlphaMedia from the inside out. The three steps layered on top of that are: a) making sure that you have the right people on board; b) then revisiting with them the company's vision and 'refreshing' the strategy to realize it; and c) shifting the main focus to the execution of that strategy. *(See Figure 5)*

Figure 5

We then discussed the first step—People. "This can be aided by an executive management assessment, a process that my firm is often requested to perform by companies in a transitional situation."

"What would that entail?" Mary Anne asked. "How long will that take? I have such a high sense of urgency."

"We'll move things along as fast as we can, but we can't skip this step." I spoke slowly and clearly, to underscore the deliberate nature of this step. "Each member of the management team will complete their leadership profile and go through a 360° feedback process. Then, interviews will be conducted with them and their team members. The management assessment should not take more than three weeks. During and after that—with the assessment report in your hands—you'll interview each member of the team in depth to better understand how they fit into your company, and their level of alignment and commitment. At the end of this process, the people side of the equation should be clear."

"I have to change my perspective," said Mary Anne "I realize that I was prepared to work with the existing team and wasn't thinking about introducing any changes."

I considered her comment for a moment. "That may be the case. But you need to know who is on your team and give yourself the latitude of reshaping the team according to a number of variables, but mostly to ensure solid working relationships that make success possible. Meanwhile, start the process of looking under the hood to thoroughly understand how your new company works, its strengths and weak points. You will find all sorts of guides throughout the company to help you with this while getting to know them. Once you know the lay of the land and the final composition of your team, you'll be ready to meet with them for two or three days to revisit the vision and refresh the strategy of the company. Finally, the focus will shift to execution."

Mary Anne smiled and shook her head. "You make it sound so simple."

"It is simple when you get to see it from thirty thousand feet high. Of course, as you fly down, there are myriad details, but it's useful to keep the big picture perspective about what you're doing."

As she digested my remarks, I thought of a powerful tool to assist her in her transition to CEO—a transition that is unlike any other job in a company. Not only does the person face the daunting task of learning a new culture, meeting new faces and settling into a new environment, but she must also truly hit the ground running, namely, setting and driving the company's strategic plan and vision.

This led to the tool I had in mind. "We will also start developing different strategy maps that will prove useful for your work," I said.

"Strategy maps?"

"It's easier to navigate complex territory when you have a map. For instance, a constituencies map. This will plot out the geography of groups and people you need to pay attention to and strategize about, such as investors, bankers, Wall Street analysts, vendors, key customers and so on. If you want to lead strategically, you need strategy maps."

Mary Anne's lips pursed together as she nodded. "I can see that maps may be useful for my work. How would I use them?"

"You will use them in a variety of ways, but keep in mind that—different from geography maps—the territory here will change over time. Strategy maps are to be understood as periodically needing update. You could use the constituencies map to:

A. Determine your goals and objectives with each group or individual

B. Create a roadmap and a timeline to accomplish them

C. Outline the resources you may need to support you in this process

D. Decide on the timing of periodic contact points and communication with each group or individual—which you will transfer to your calendar

"Each map will allow you to develop and flex your strategic thinking to the maximum."

"What other kind of maps do you have in mind?"

"A basic set of strategy maps will include—among others—the following:

A. Your job, and the different areas of focus as the CEO

B. Your team, outlining their strengths and weaknesses, and their potential internal successors

C. Your competition and their strengths and weaknesses

D. Your customers and market forces at work

"We'll probably develop a couple more, but that should give you a good idea of what we're going to do."

"I guess I have my work cut out for me. This is exciting," concluded Mary Anne.

A few weeks later, she and I reviewed the results of the executive management team assessment. We discussed each person's strengths and weaknesses, along with her impressions from the series of one-on-one interviews she conducted with each team member.

"I'm concerned," she said. "From the nine people on my team, I feel confident about working with six of them. These six are really capable people, and they have a lot to contribute. Regarding the other three, Tom doesn't have the depth and breadth of knowledge I expected. Carol has very different ideas from mine about where the company should be steered, and Jim has a leadership style that is incompatible with me; he's all about command and control. What do you suggest?"

"Well, you have three different situations. I suggest three different approaches." Earlier, we had talked about how one of the roles of the CEO is to act as a coach. I reminded her of that. "For Jim, I suggest you determine if he's coachable and if he is, to engage him through a coaching process. Jim has an old-fashioned style and has never worked in a distributed leadership work environment. He holds a lot of organizational knowledge, so if he's open to your coaching, he will be a valuable member of your team."

"I may need some advice on how to tackle that, but I'm willing to try. What about Carol?"

"You mentioned that Carol has different ideas from yours about the company's strategy. I encourage you to see that as a plus and something that is worth supporting. She could stimulate healthy discussion about the current strategy and the future of the company. You need someone like her to keep everybody thinking, and not fall into complacency or 'group think.'"

"I haven't seen it that way. Wouldn't that be disruptive for the team?"

"Only if open discussion and conflictive ideas are seen as a problem by *you*. I encourage you to stimulate heated discussions that end with commitment from everyone in the room to aligned action. If you model that for your team, you'll always have the best final product coming out of the team.

"Finally, the situation with Tom is different. As head of R&D he's in a key position. You mentioned him not having the depth and breadth of knowledge you need. That will not change quickly. You may need a different person in that position."

She considered my remark for a moment. "I've thought about keeping Tom, but in a different position, and hiring someone to replace him that could bring the thought leadership and experience needed in our R&D department."

I liked the way she already seemed to be thinking two steps ahead—another trait of a proactive CEO. "If Tom is amenable to that, I'm always in favor of keeping valuable people and organizational knowledge. Mary Anne, you accomplished a lot in a short period of time. Do you feel ready to move to the next step?"

"Every day I feel more comfortable with my level of familiarity with how the company operates and the relationship with my team. I want to schedule our first strategic planning session soon. What's a good way to get us thinking about strategy and the future?"

"I think it will be useful for you and your team to go through the following exercise. Each person will project his or her imagination ten years into the future and imagine that the company has achieved extraordinary success. Not only on one front, say financially, but in a number of relevant dimensions, like the relationship with delighted and loyal customers, spearheading innovation, creating a supportive culture for the employees, developing new products and services, creating value for shareholders and the community, and so on. Then each individual will write in present tense, as if he's witnessing all this, a thorough description of that successful company ten years from now. Have each of your team members do this on their own.

"Once they're done, everybody will bring his or her 'homework' to the offsite meeting. The activity at the offsite will consist of sharing and merging all of these possible visions of the future into a coherent gestalt that will work as a magnet, pulling the team towards this worthy aspiration. Once that's accomplished, the next step is to transform that common vision of the future into a set of goals and objectives that—if achieved—will make the vision a reality."

I took a quick break to let Mary Anne assimilate the idea. The increasingly deep look in her eyes told me that she was already seeing all this in her mind's eye. No surprise there, as I was learning about this most impressive client. "OK, the next activity for the team will be to break down each goal and objective into an actionable plan that will outline milestones and targets along the way. The process will include creating a roadmap and a timeline that shows what should be accomplished by when. The next step will be to assign resources—people and funds—to make all this possible.

"Finally, the team will design a process to cascade down the goals and objectives across the organization and a dashboard to continually track the execution of the master plan." I smiled and leaned back in my chair. "There you have it."

"A roadmap to create a roadmap," she said. "It makes me feel reassured to have clarity about how to imagine our future."

As I write this chapter about my work with Mary Anne, I read often in the news about her company. AlphaMedia is quickly becoming one of the most admired companies in its field, and the company stocks have been steadily climbing. Recently, a major business magazine featured Mary Anne on its cover—a testament to her hard work and her capacity for visioning her company forward.

You wouldn't learn how successful Mary Anne and her company became by listening to her. She is still the humble, warm person I met at that class I taught at Stanford. "I still have so much to learn!" she told me in our last meeting.

"While you feel that way, you will continue to get better and better. Don't lose your 'beginner's mind,'" I responded.

"I promise not to," said Mary Anne. "I owe my success to my team, and the people of our company that made all this possible. I owe them to keep learning!" I saw her eyes shining with the enthusiasm I always admired in her.

Chapter 8 Summary
Mary Anne: Stepping into the Future

Mary Anne, a highly successful Chief Operating Officer of a medium size company who was very happy in her job, was approached with a can't-miss offer: to become the CEO of the biggest company in her industry. While flattered with the fact that she was the target of such a "fishing expedition," her initial reaction was not to take on the position—especially with a vitally important initiative coming up in her company, one toward which she'd been working for months. The representative for the recruiting company gave her a short time to decide—during which she could interview key stakeholders as they interviewed her, to see if the two were a good fit. Nothing says "we want YOU" more than this approach ... and it left Mary Anne perplexed as to the right decision to make.

I. A DECISION-MAKING PROCESS: The decision-making process relies on a crucial bit of self-awareness: our own definition of success.

1. Chart of Excluding Options: List the plusses and minuses of staying with the current company versus moving to the new company. Fill out with gut responses, intuition, no analyzing.
2. Assigning Percentages to Chart: How important is each pro and con to you? Rate between 10% and 100%.
3. Project Pros and Cons One Year into the Future: This is a major problem with even the most visionary, forward-thinking executives when presented with career-changing opportunities. Things evolve with time, look over the whole picture and over time. Gain perspective.

II. MOVING FORWARD

1. Three major concerns: family, the company currently employing you, and the potential new employer.
2. Exercising courage—the containment of fear, and moving forward.
3. Maintaining transparency and integrity through a job transition.
4. Gather all the information needed to familiarize yourself as much as possible with the new company.
5. For great improvisation, practice rigorous rehearsal!
6. Peer into the future: What's the future of your field? What would you do as CEO? How would you create competitive advantage?

III. MAKING THE TRANSITION

1. Leave current position with a feeling of completion. Help to plan succession, provide guidance to the replacement, and celebrate the time spent there and the friendships forged along the way.
2. Understand the new company from the inside out.
3. Make sure to have the right people on board.

4. Co-create company vision and strategy with new team.
5. Shift focus to the execution of the strategy.

IV. STRATEGY MAPS: Navigate complex territory with strategy maps. Each map will allow you to develop and flex your strategic thinking to the maximum. Update periodically.

1. Constituencies Map
   a. Determine goals and objectives with each group or individual
   b. Create a roadmap and a timeline to accomplish them
   c. Outline needed resources to support you in this process
   d. Decide on the timing of periodic contact points and communication with each group or individual
2. Other Types of Strategy Maps
   a. Strategic areas of focus for the CEO position
   b. Strengths and weaknesses of team, and their potential internal successors
   c. Competition strengths and weaknesses
   d. Customers and market forces at work

V. ACTIVATING THE NEW TEAM, LAUNCHING THE NEW VISION

1. Each person projects his or her imagination ten years into the future and imagines that the company has achieved extraordinary success in relevant dimensions: financial, customer relations, innovation, supportive culture for employees, new products and services, shareholder value.
2. Each person writes "eyewitness" description of the successful company ten years into the future.
3. Hold offsite meeting to share and merge possible visions of the future into a coherent gestalt that will work as a magnet, pulling people towards this worthy aspiration.
4. From this vision derive the set of goals and objectives that will make the vision a reality.
5. Break down each goal and objective into an actionable plan—milestones and targets.
6. Create a roadmap and timeline to show what should be accomplished, and when.
7. Assign resources to make it possible.
8. Design a process to cascade goals and objectives across the organization, and revisit periodically to update the plan.

CONCLUSION

I slept and dreamt that life was joy.
I woke up and saw that life was serving.
I acted and found that service was joy.
—Rabindranath Tagore

MAN looked up towards heaven and asked: "What is the meaning of life?" and the response came back right away. It started with these words: "Once upon a time ... ," implying that the meaning of life would be found in the unfolding story.

My deepest learning—when the mind and the heart listened at the same time—came from stories. While writing this book, I hoped that you, dear reader, might also find applicable, practical learning through some of the stories of challenge, struggle and triumph that my coaching clients experienced.

I also hoped that throughout the stories, the principles embedded in the process of change and personal transformation would emerge and become accessible to you.

The lifetime cycles of personal development highlight again and again that learning is not an "event" but a process, a series of iterations that constantly refine us in the crucible of exercising leadership at work and personal life. We act the best we can and eventually receive feedback, which we use to leverage our strengths and mitigate our weaknesses by improving our level of competency. Then we return into the world and act again. In the iteration of these cycles, we draw closer and closer to mastery and greatness.

The role of the coach seems to be at its greatest value when we assist the individual in correctly interpreting the feedback, and then providing the tools and processes that accelerate learning and increase our client's competence.

I found the method that Benjamin Franklin described in his short but poignant autobiography to be deeply inspirational. Franklin developed a list of thirteen virtues (today we would call them "competencies") that, if refined, would drive him towards mastery. He'd focus intently for one week on enacting the first virtue. The next week, without losing sight of the first, he would bring the focus to the second virtue. He'd continue on this path until moving through all thirteen virtues included in his list.

Why did he choose thirteen? Because there are thirteen weeks in a quarter! After completing a cycle, Franklin would restart the process for another thirteen weeks, again and again, four times a year, always moving a little closer to mastery.

Given that the only instrument we have to navigate through life is our self, Franklin's process seems to be an amazing example of continuous improvement. He constantly worked on himself towards the ultimate goal of serving others. Along the way, he achieved mastery—or nearly so—in these thirteen virtues.

I hope you have found inspiration in these stories and are intrigued about how others are experiencing you and your leadership. Remember, as we act in the world, we regularly develop blind spots. Sometimes, we grow unaware of what we need to do differently to improve ourselves at leading others, our team and our organization. In the same way that we constantly adjust the steering wheel to drive straight on roads of all lengths and contours, we can only calibrate our leadership through what we hear from those around us.

If you're interested in getting your 360° feedback from your colleagues and co-workers, please email us at *info@skylineg.com*. We'll gladly assist you on your journey of personal transformation towards becoming a great leader!

ABOUT THE AUTHOR

DR. RABIN is Founder and Managing Partner of Skyline Group—a leadership development and organizational consulting firm—headquartered in Silicon Valley, California. His practice area focus is on individual leadership development, with an emphasis on coaching executives to improve their overall effectiveness, their capacity for strategic thinking and their focus on execution. His work has focused also on identifying and developing organizations' talent pool, culture transformation and renewing employee engagement. Dr. Rabin is a licensed psychologist with over 20 years of experience in partnering with clients to improve leadership and organizational performance. He actively trains and supervises consultants active in the field of executive development and leadership. Gustavo teaches at Stanford University and leads personal and professional development workshops at Esalen Institute. His clients include major corporations in a range of industries: high-tech, bio-tech, professional services, financial, educational institutions, and not for profit. Current and recent projects have included Google, Yahoo!, Linkedin, Intel, The Gap, Blue Shield, AMD, Barclay's Global Investors, Wilson, Sonsini, Goodrich and Rosati, UC Berkeley, and Stanford University.